ZEN AND WESTERN THOUGHT

In the past few decades Zen has become widely disseminated in the west. Zen is, however, often misunderstood as a form of anti-intellectualism, or an encouragement of animal-like spontaneity without thought of good and evil. But, in fact, Zen embraces a profound philosophy. It is a philosophy based on a 'non-thinking' which is beyond both 'thinking' and 'not thinking', grounded upon 'Self-Awakening', arising from wisdom and compassion. Zen expresses and lives this philosophy, however, in a non-philosophical, vivid and direct way. In this book, Masao Abe, the leading exponent of Zen and Japanese Buddhism for the West since the death of D. T. Suzuki, clarifies this philosophy through an encounter with the Western intellectual tradition. He compares the standpoint of Zen with those of Aristotle, Spinoza, Kant, Hegel, Nietzsche, Whitehead and the Christian tradition, including Paul Tillich. In particular Professor Abe shows that the basic difference between the Western and Buddhist ways of thinking lies in the understanding of 'Negativity'.

Firmly rooted in his personal Zen experience, Masao Abe opens up a new spiritual horizon for the hoped-for unified world through the confrontation between Zen and Western thought. It is a challenge to Western ways of thinking and will stimulate creative dialogue with Western philosophers, theologians, and psychologists. It will also help Western Zen practitioners to locate their Zen practice in their own Western intellectual context.

Masao Abe has been Professor of Japanese Philosophy at the Department of Philosophy of the University of Hawaii since 1983. A graduate of Kyoto University in Japan, he studied and practised Buddhism, especially Zen, with Shin'ichi Hisamatsu, while also studying Western Philosophy. As a Research Fellow of the Rockefeller Foundation, he studied Christian Theology at Union Theological Seminary and Columbia University, 1955–57. In Japan he was Professor of Philosophy at Nara University of Education from 1952 to 1980. Since 1965 he was served as Visiting Professor of Buddhism and Japanese Philosophy at Columbia University, the University of Chicago, Carleton College, Princeton University and other universities in the USA. In 1980 he moved from Japan to Claremont, California, to join the faculty of the Department of Religion at the Claremont Graduate School.

Since the death of D. T. Suzuki, Professor Abe has been the leading exponent of Zen in the West. As a member of the Kyoto School of Philosophy, he is also deeply involved in the comparative study of Buddhism and Western thought and in Buddhist–Christian dialogue. His numerous articles have been published in a variety of journals, including *International Philosophical Quarterly, Philosophy East and West, Numen, The Eastern Buddhist* and *Japanese Religions*. This, his first book in English, is a collection of his important essays on Zen in its relation to Western thought.

William R. LaFleur, the editor, is Associate Professor of Oriental Languages at the University of California, Los Angeles.

ZEN AND WESTERN THOUGHT

by

Masao Abe

Edited by
William R. LaFleur

Foreword by
John Hick

UNIVERSITY OF HAWAII PRESS
HONOLULU

First published 1985 by
THE MACMILLAN PRESS LTD
London and Basingstoke
Companies and representatives
throughout the world

Published in North America by
University of Hawaii Press

Printed in Hong Kong

Library of Congress Cataloging in Publication Data
Abe, Masao, 1915–
Zen and Western thought.
Includes index.
1. Zen Buddhism—Doctrines—Addresses, essays,
lectures.   2. Philosophy, Comparative—Addresses, essays,
lectures.   3. Buddhism and philosophy—Addresses, essays,
lectures.   I. LaFleur, William R.   II. Title.
BQ9268.7.A34   1985   294.3'372   83–24153
ISBN 0–8248–0952–1

To the memory of Shin'ichi Hisamatsu Sensei

Contents

Foreword

Zen Buddhism is often thought of in the West as a kind of anti-philosophy, a matter of living in the present moment of experience without any intellectual framework or presuppositions. Zen does indeed lead to a new quality of consciousness in which the world is experienced directly and not through a grid of culturally created concepts. But behind the Zen practice of meditation there lies a profound and subtle philosophy developed over many centuries and stemming ultimately from the spiritual insights of the Buddha two and a half thousand years ago. This book makes that philosophy available to the West by presenting it in dialogue with some of the major traditions of Western thought.

Zen philosophy presents a radical alternative to various presupposed doctrines of Western thought which seem (in the words of T. E. Hulme) 'not doctrines, but inevitable categories of the human mind ... [People] do not see them but other things through them'. The fundamental alternative to a set of Western assumptions is not another set of Western assumptions but the genuinely different presuppositions of much Eastern thought. Such an alternative occurs in one of its most powerful and thoroughgoing forms within Buddhism, and specifically in the philosophy of Zen. The West can only be enriched, if at the same time puzzled and provoked, by awareness of this fundamentally different possibility.

The author of this book, Masao Abe, has been the leading philosophical exponent of Zen to the West since the death of D. T. Suzuki. Abe belongs to the vigorous Kyoto School and is a successor of its greater figures, Nishida, Hisamatsu and Nishitani. It has been a characteristic of this school of Zen thought to be interested in the wider intellectual world and in particular to foster Buddhist-Christian interactions. Abe's book is accordingly a major contribution both to East–West dialogue and to the developing encounter between Buddhism and Christianity.

Department of Religion   JOHN HICK
Claremont Graduate School
Claremont, California

Editor's Introduction

Although written twenty-five years ago, the following statement by the noted historian Lynn White, Jr seems just as valid and worthy of attention today:

> Prophecy is rash, but it may well be that the publication of D. T. Suzuki's first *Essays in Zen Buddhism* in 1927 will seem in future generations as great an intellectual event as William of Moerbeke's Latin translations of Aristotle in the thirteenth century or Marsiglio Ficino's of Plato in the fifteenth. But in Suzuki's case the shell of the Occident has been broken through. More than we dream, we are now governed by the new canon of the globe.[1]

What Suzuki had tried to do at the time was to present Buddhism as something other than a relatively arcane tradition of ancient Asian texts; throughout his long career of lecturing and writing he demanded that his audiences consider it as a fully contemporary and valid alternative to the intellectual and religious traditions of our Western experience.

It was possible for Suzuki (1870–1966) to do this precisely because when he had been a young man – that is, around the turn of the century – the intellectual life of Japan had been vigorously engaged in the study of the Western philosophical and religious tradition. But this process of intelligent absorption was at the same time one of sensitive comparison; just then many of the best thinkers of Japan, while mastering the terminology and endemic problems of Western thought, contrasted these with the approach, direction, and bases of their own Mahayana tradition. Although Suzuki was not trained as a professional philosopher, he had been and always remained fairly close to these discussions going on in Japan and, as a result, he was unusually able to engage his Western audiences with the promise that, through an understanding of Zen, they might grasp the 'difference' offered to the West by Buddhism as a whole.

The thing worthy of note here, however, is that, although Suzuki was a uniquely skilled and eminent communicator, he was neither the beginning nor the end of the religious and intellectual interaction between Buddhism and Western thought. Concurrent with his own career something usually referred to as the 'Kyoto School' of philosophy came into being and played an important role in the intellectual life of Japan. The founder of this school was a personal friend and lifelong acquaintance of Suzuki, Kitarō Nishida (1870 –1945). Although still largely unknown in the West, the Kyoto School has undoubtedly been the most vigorous group of indigenous philosophical thinkers in Japan. This is in part because of the stature of Nishida, a nonpareil among philosophers in modern Japan. But it continued on with thinkers such as Hajime Tanabe, Shin'ichi Hisamatsu, and Keiji Nishitani.[2] Each of these men was completely familiar with the problematics and vocabularies of Western philosophy and at the same time concerned to articulate what might be considered valid but alternative thought-structures informed by traditional Buddhist ideas.

It is precisely within this tradition that Masao Abe has done his work. In his student days at Kyoto University he was deeply influenced by Nishida who, although retired at the time, still dominated the intellectual landscape. Tanabe, Hisamatsu, and Nishitani were all teachers of Abe and the cast of his mind was clearly formed by them. Unlike these important figures of the Kyoto School, however, Abe has spent much of his life – a good part of the past three decades, in fact – in the West. Thus there is in him something also of another of his teachers, namely D. T. Suzuki. If Abe shares the Kyoto School's interest in defining with care the difference and creative synthesis between Western thought and the Mahayana tradition, he also has been very much concerned to teach and communicate these things in ways that are intelligible and meaningful to students and scholars working in Western settings.[3]

It was my good fortune to be involved in the study of Japanese thought and literature at the University of Chicago when Professor Abe was there in 1969 to give the Charles Gooding lectures in Zen Buddhism. It was he who first introduced me to the writings of the major thinkers of the Kyoto School and successfully whetted my appetite for the broader range of philosophical and religious questions which lie, I suspect, at the basis of what is most interesting and most important about the ongoing interchange between ourselves and the Japanese, one which over the past few decades has moved away from the stage of fear and hostility and into one of a much more fruitful and positive interchange.

Nevertheless, for the most part we remain profoundly ignorant of modern Japanese thought. In sharp contrast to the intense intellectual energies which the Japanese have now for more than a century devoted to the study and mastery of our traditions, our attention to theirs has been meager and sporadic. We have, wrongly I think, often assumed with a kind of cultural hauteur that Japanese thinking has merely been undergoing a process of westernization, one which will eventually transform it into an exact carbon-copy of current thinking in our own academies. Such false assumptions have led us to overlook the fact that the Japanese engagement with Western thought has been one in which sustained attempts have been made to refine and modulate the process of absorption – precisely so that there might be a deeper understanding and retention of those things considered most valuable within the pre-modern Buddhist and Japanese traditions. If we in the West have at times painfully discovered that there are real costs incurred when we naïvely assume postures of superiority in business and technical matters, we might wisely ask ourselves whether we are being any less benighted in the less tangible areas of philosophy and religion when we assume that we in the West have everything to say worth saying.

The reader of these collected essays by Masao Abe will very quickly discover that they show a mind deeply steeped in the traditional problems and vocabularies of Western thought. Abe, however, also demonstrates the hard-mindedness of the Kyoto School's insistence that philosophy ought to be *truly* comparative; while it should be totally engaged with the deepest problems of our existence in this world, it may not be permitted to take a facile route to the dissolution of religious and philosophical dissimilarity. That is, it may not be allowed to erase the significant differences between, for example, the Buddhist and Christian traditions through the postulation of some sort of simple and single monad at the apex of all things. This is not to foreclose the possibility of creative unity; it is merely to insist that it be dynamic and able to give place to diversity as well. In my opinion, therefore, these essays by Masao Abe comprise not merely a sustained presentation of a Mahayana Buddhist's outlook on perenniel philosophical questions but also a rigorous defence of *philosophy itself* as an intrinsically and necessarily comparative enterprise. As such these essays defend, I think, something not only Eastern but also something once thought by us to be a special concern of Western thinkers.

Although trained primarily as a philosopher at Kyoto University, Abe's intellectual interaction with Western thinkers over the past few decades has tended to be most lively and creative when it has been with those engaged in the academic study of religion and with those theologians who represent the Christian and Jewish traditions. One reason for this is certainly the fact that Abe himself is committed to the religious practice of Zen and in this sense is not merely a speculative thinker or one personally uninvolved with religion. The reader of these essays will quickly discover that their author is deeply concerned with the most fundamental issues of man's existence and eager to explore ways in which the confrontation with basically religious questions might open up new ways of thinking about our common humanity and give us some direction through those problems which collectively make our human predicament both distinctively 'modern' and frighteningly precarious.

But, in addition, to me one of the more interesting reasons for Abe's creative interaction with theologians and religionists has to do with the fact that in the middle decades of our century the representative disciplines of philosophy and theology in the Western academic setting appear to have virtually exchanged and traded off to one another their customary postures with respect to the careful scrutiny of 'alien' or non-Western traditions. For many centuries, of course, it was the philosopher who was the more curious about non-indigenous traditions, whereas the theologian would have been interested in such traditions only for the sake of finding an opportunity to engage in apologetics – that is, in order to point out the 'errors' of the other tradition and in this way preserve the domestic and established patterns of thought and belief. In the past it had almost always been the theologian who had been conservative on this matter and the philosopher who showed genuine intellectual curiosity about things still unknown or culturally unfamiliar. While theologians kept the faith intact, philosophers such as Schopenhauer showed curiosity about the philosophies originating east of Europe.

But in recent decades these traditional postures have now come to be virtually reversed. In many ways professional philosophy in the West has become a culturally insular discipline, engaged in a repeated reviewing of the classic treatises of Western philosophy and arriving at merely newer formulations of old problems that were indigenous to the Western way of posing the questions of knowledge and the like. At the same time these philosophers have quite stubbornly refused to become seriously engaged with problems and formulations that have arisen outside the ambit of the West. To see philosophy as so many 'footnotes to Plato' is to be aware, of course, of the existence of continuity within our own tradition but it is at the same time a way of being profoundly *ignorant* of things outside the Western tradition. To that extent philosophy has become, I think, a new scholasticism, a discipline which feeds itself only on itself. So extreme did this become that, even although the Western academy was concerned with Western philosophy alone, there have been whole decades during which those doing Anglo-American style philosophy had almost no ground for common discourse with those philosophers of the continent who posed all the traditional problems slightly differently.

It is now fairly clear that this extreme insularity and fragmentation has been, at least in part, due to a certain anxiety among philosophers about the relevance and viability of their own discipline. They have swerved widely, therefore, between one assumption that they were on the verge of disclosing the certain 'foundations' of knowledge – the ongoing hope since Descartes – and its virtual opposite, namely, the expressed fear that professional philosophy may never be able to demonstrate its own necessary place within the academy. My own suspicion is that professional philosophy's indifference to non-western thinking during the past few decades has been partially caused by the lurking fear that any such interest was a diversion from the real work needing to be done, namely, the securing of philosophy's own place within the academy. At least – for whatever reasons – there has been a cultural introversion on the part of Western philosophy so that among philosophers there has been no time, no desire, or latitude of mind to deal with thought having its origins in such exotic and still – to them at least – philosophically 'unproven' places as India, China, and Japan.[4]

During these same decades things were noticably different in the various divinity schools and departments of religious studies in most American universities – especially, of course, during the sixties and seventies. It was in these parts of the academic world that thinkers from Asia and Africa were able to find persons ready and willing to talk with them and compare approaches to fundamental human questions. From my own experience as well I know that it was in that corner of the university devoted to the study of religion that some of the most bright and inquisitive young minds appeared, insisting that their education be universal in the best sense, that it help them see more than a convoluted corner of Western experience. In surveying aspects of the modern history of teaching philosophy, Richard Rorty has noted that at times things such as culture criticism were 'hardly visible to philosophers, though little else was visible to the best students they were teaching.'[5] My impression is that the same could be said for student interest in non-Western thought; it had a magnetic hold on some of the brightest students in our schools even though their professors of philosophy had consigned it to a place beneath their own gaze. Again and again I saw such students enter readily and seriously into an exchange of ideas with Professor Abe during those years. Somehow he seemed to touch on issues that seemed fundamental to our existence as human beings and was not reluctant to discuss them.

It is *these* questions – having to do with life and death, being and non-being, religion and morality, the nature of time, the concepts of God and of Emptiness, and so forth – that the serious student found Professor Abe willing to address. It is these same questions that the serious reader will find him addressing in this book of essays. Masao Abe has been a peripatetic thinker and has sharpened his own thoughts about such things through his many interchanges with students and colleagues on three continents. The result in this book is the emergence of a point of view which not only seeks to articulate what it means to be a Buddhist philosopher in our era but also throws uncommon light on some of the neglected assumptions and presuppositions in our own Western tradition. The heuristic value of these essays cannot be overestimated; they have much to say not only about Buddhist alternatives to Western positions but also provide a bold disclosure of why it is that much of Western thought, even while consistent with its own original assumptions, appears from the Buddhist perspective to be philosophically askew. Earlier readers of Professor Abe's 'Non-Being and *Mu*' – included here – have, for instance, found it to be an unusually penetrating and provocative piece, something that provides an aperture through which much of Western thought can be seen in a new light. It detects, some have said, a certain blindspot in Western ontology that stretches from Plato to Whitehead.

But these essays are part of an even more ambitious intention. They are not conceived with the purpose of merely articulating the conceptual and religious boundary-line between something called 'the West' and something else called 'the East'. Such an act of demarcation – or that, for instance, between Buddhism and Christianity – is interesting but to Professor Abe less than satisfying in any final analysis. To note the separations is, from his point of view, to do only half of the necessary religious and philosophical work. Equally important – and in our time a matter of consummate urgency as well – is the discovery on our part and in our own time of our common humanity. Readers of this book will discover that its author is totally engaged in an effort to raise us out of certain kinds of intellectual and religious slumber, a state in which we are presently more benighted than enlightened. The final chapters of this book press upon us the urgency of discovering the *religious* reasons and means for taking our own destiny in our own hands as human beings and as a single world. I find them compelling; all readers will, I am sure, find them at least provocative and engaging.

During the three decades of his creative dialogue with Westerners Masao Abe also turned his home – whether in his own Kyoto, or in Chicago, Princeton, or California – into something of an arena for the most engaging kinds of conversation. I have visited him in his 'home' in these various places and I invariably found there a small group of people talking animatedly with him about philosophy and religion. His concern to do this was always without discrimination; it included notable philosophers as well as curious undergraduates. He has always been eager to carry on this kind of inter-religious and inter-philosophical dialogue not only with his professional peers but also with the next generation which will themselves take it up and continue it in new ways in the years to come.

There is something true about the old supposition that philosophy is most truly itself when it is peripatetic; it is then and only then that it can be really universal and really comparative at the same time. A certain price, however, is paid for such a peripatetic way of life and till now it has been paid by Professor Abe inasmuch as his essays in English have been scattered over three continents. His natural generosity prompted him to give his writings freely to friends, colleagues, and editors in Europe, America, and Japan. While this has meant a certain fortunate dispersion of his ideas and deepest convictions, it has also made it difficult for the interested student to locate the entire corpus and see it as it really should be seen, namely, a consistently developed and rich point of view. Moreover, it has tended to eclipse the really wide range of things with which he has dealt. Since a mere glance at the table of contents will immediately suggest to the reader the extent of this book's concerns, I refrain from repeating it here. I am, however, grateful to the various editors of those publications who have permitted these essays to be amended and given to the public in the form of this book. I am, of course, most grateful to Professor Abe himself for providing the basic structure of the book and for generously discussing it with me on a number of occasions. I trust that it adequately represents his most important concerns.

I am grateful to the editors of the various journals in which these essays have earlier appeared for granting their permission to republish them here. In some cases the titles have been slightly changed to fit the format of this book and the content too has been altered accordingly. Specifically, I would like to thank the editors of the *Theologische Zeitschrift* (33) for Chapter 1; of *The Eastern Buddhist* (New Series) for Chapter 2 (4:1), Chapter 3 (2:1), Chapter 6 (6:2), Chapter 8 (1:1 [there entitled 'Christianity and the Encounter of World Religion']), Chapter 12 (11:2), and Chapter 16 (8:1); and *The International Philosophical Quarterly* (10:4) for Chapter 4. Chapter 5 first appeared in *Religious Studies* (11) and is used with the permission of Cambridge University Press and Chapter 7 is reprinted from *Philosophy East and West* (25:4) with the permission of the University of Hawaii Press. Chapter 9 appeared in *Japanese Religions* (8:3) as did Chapter 13 (2); Chapter 10 is reprinted from *The Ecumenical Review* (25:2), Chapter 11 from *Numen* (13:3), and Chapter 14 from the *Proceedings of the First International Conference of Scientists and Religious Leaders* (1978). Chapter 15 has not previously appeared in print.

1   Lynn White, Jr., 'The Changing Canons of our Culture,' in Lynn White, Jr., ed., *Frontiers of Knowledge in the Study of Man*. New York: Harper and Brothers, 1956, pp. 304–305.

2   Concerning the Kyoto School the most extensive study in a Western language to date is Fritz Buri, *Der Buddha-Christus als der Herr des wahren Selbst: Die Religionsphilosophie der Kyoto-Schule und das Christentum* (Bern and Stuttgart: Paul Haupt, 1982). The most recent publication in English by a major thinker of that school is Keiji Nishitani, *Religion and Nothingness* (Berkeley, Los Angeles, and London: The University of California Press, 1983.) *The Buddha Eye: An Anthology of The Kyoto School*, edited by Frederick Frank and published by The Crossroad Publishing

Company, New York, 1982 should also be consulted for a variety of writings by members of this school and some antecedent thinkers.

3   Fritz Buri devotes a chapter to a synopsis and analysis of Abe's work in *op. cit.* pp. 323–379 and takes special note of Abe's crucial role in the developing dialogue between Christianity and Buddhism.

4   An important exception is Herbert Fingarette, *Confucius – The Secular as Sacred.* New York: Harper Torchbook, 1972.

5   Richard Rorty, 'Professionalized Philosophy and Transcendentalist Culture,' *The Georgia Review* 30, p. 766.

The University of California at Los Angeles   WILLIAM R. LAFLEUR

Author's Introduction

The selection of essays constituting this book were written at one time or another during the past eighteen years. The focus is on Zen, Buddhism, and the comparative study of Buddhism and Western thought. The essays were selected primarily to present my understanding of Zen, especially its philosophical and religious significance in its encounter with Western thought. Some address themes with which I was asked to deal, while others elucidate subjects I myself wanted to explore. Several were directed to Japanese readers and hence were originally written in Japanese. Others were directed to a Western audience and were written in English. The selection includes addresses which were originally delivered orally and are hence somewhat informal in comparison to the more academic articles. Accordingly, the book was not written systematically with a consistent intention. Heeding the advice of the editor, Professor William R. LaFleur, I have tried to select and compile the essays in such a way as to make the work as systematic as possible. The result is the book now before you.

The fundamental ideas which ground these essays are, I believe, consistent throughout. They may be summarized as follows.

Firstly, although Zen is often misunderstood to be an anti-intellectualism, a cheap intuitionism, or an encouragement to animal-like spontaneity without consideration of good and evil, it embraces, in fact, a profound philosophy. It is a philosophy based on a 'non-thinking' which is beyond both thinking and not thinking, grounded upon 'Self-Awakening', and arising from wisdom and compassion. And while in pratice, Zen expresses and lives this philosophy in a non-philosophical, vivid, and direct way, the philosophical basis is never lacking. I try to clarify this point, especially in Part I, 'Zen and Its Elucidation'.

Secondly, the ultimate in Zen (and in Buddhism) is neither 'Being' nor 'Ought', but rather 'absolute Nothingness' or 'Emptiness', which is dynamically identical with 'wondrous Being' or

'Fullness'. As the unobjectifiable, Emptiness indicates one's true Self, the suchness and interdependency of all things. It is the root-source of liberation and creativity. A twofold negation, that is, the negation of being and non-being, life and death, good and evil, transcendence and immanence, is crucial to the true Buddhist position. This is discussed in comparison with various forms of Western thought, particularly in Part II, 'Zen, Buddhism, and Western Thought'. In an essay entitled 'Non-Being and *Mu*: the Metaphysical Nature of Negativity in the East and the West', I try to clarify the structural difference between the Western and Buddhist ways of thinking.

Thirdly, Buddhism is a radical realism and a compassionate way of life. The desire to reach the 'other shore' of nirvana by overcoming 'this shore' of samsara for the sake of wisdom is still other-worldly and selfish. In order to overcome attachment to the 'other shore' of nirvana, one must return to 'this shore' (samsara), and in compassion identify with others to save them from the suffering of transmigration. This is the genuine meaning of Buddhist life. Thus both wisdom and compassion are the two essential aspects of the realization of Emptiness. I adhere to this idea consistently throughout the book, but discuss it directly in Part III, 'Three problems of Buddhism', as well as in the essays entitled 'True Person and Compassion' in Part I and 'Tillich from a Buddhist Point of View' in Part II.

Fourthly, to cope with the human predicament we face in this global age, a new cosmology, not a new humanism, is needed. It is urgently necessary to clarify authentic religiosity within human existence, not only in order to overcome the anti-religious ideologies prevailing in our societies, but also in order to establish a spiritual foundation for the hoped-for unified world. To meet this need, I wish to advance a 'personalistic cosmology' (which is inseparable from a 'cosmo-personalism'), or a 'self-awakened cosmology,' which is beyond objective cosmology and anthropocentrism. I believe that on the basis of this new cosmology, a Buddhist teleology can be established which, on the realization of Emptiness or Suchness, provides meaning, purpose, and direction for human society and history. This issue is discussed, though only in an embryonic fashion, particularly in Part IV, 'Religion in the Present and the Future', and in an essay entitled 'Dōgen on Buddha Nature'.

With these four basic ideas in mind, my purpose in making this selection of essays can be said to be twofold:

1 I wish to clarify what I consider the authentic spirit of Buddhism in general and of Zen in particular. Such clarification is necessary in order to avoid entanglement in the doctrinal complexity and stereotyped practice of the traditional forms of Buddhism (and Zen) and to firmly establish this core in our rapidly changing, turbulent, contemporary world.

2 Beyond this interest as a Buddhist, I am more profoundly concerned with providing a spiritual foundation for future humanity in a global age. To provide this foundation, a comparative and dialogical study of Buddhism and Western thought, Christianity included, is absolutely necessary. I try to elucidate the philosophical and religious significance of Buddhism and Zen primarily for the purpose of articulating what they may contribute to the establishment of the new spiritual horizon which future humanity requires.

Whether, or how far, I have succeeded in this twofold purpose, is of course for the reader to judge. Also, I am well aware that at some points important issues are merely mentioned, with no solutions given.

My indebtedness and gratitude to many people, both in Japan and the United States, for help in writing and compiling these essays, are too great to be fully and properly expressed in words. My first and principal acknowledgement must go to Professor William R. LaFleur, who about five years ago urged me to publish a collection of my essays in book form and who has been working carefully as the editor right up to the present. Because of my hesitation in publishing a mere collection of essays rather than a systematic work, I would not have decided to publish this book had it not been for his sincere and eager persuasion. I am also grateful to Professor John Hick, the General Editor of Macmillan's Library of Philosophy and Religion, who has kindly accepted this book as a part of the Library.

I want to take this occasion to express my gratitude to the people who made efforts in translating those of my essays which were originally in Japanese: to Professor David A. Dilworth ('Zen and Western Thought' and 'Zen and Nietzsche'), to Ms Kimiko Hirota ('Religion Challenged by Modern Thought') and to Professor V. H. Viglielmo ('Sovereignty Rests with Mankind'). Also, my debt to the following friends and colleagues is enormous because in the various stages of my writing, both in Japan and the United States, they kindly and carefully polished my English and made valuable suggestions: Professors Thomas J. J. Altizer, Morris J. Augustine, Gary A. Bollinger, John R. Carter, William A. Christian, John B. Cobb, Jr, Winston Davis, Richard J. DeMartino, Winston L. King, Samuel I. Shapiro, Norman A. Waddell, and Mr Wayne S. Yokoyama and Christopher A. Ives. Professor Gishin Tokiwa helped me confirm the appropriateness of some technical terms. The final and sole responsibility for the presentation in this book, however, is mine.

I also extend my special and heartfelt gratitude to Mr Steve Antinoff who, in the later stages of the manuscript, read all essays with great care, suggested revisions, and helped me develop the clarity and comprehensibility of my discussion so that Western readers might more easily grasp my arguments. The result was a thorough revision of all of the original essays, including the addition of many new sentences and paragraphs in various parts of the manuscript. This is especially the case in the essays: 'Zen Is Not a Philosophy, but . . .', 'Dōgen on Buddha Nature', 'Zen and Western Thought' and 'The Idea of Purity in Mahayana Buddhism'. Without his thoughtful help and suggestions the book would have contained many more imperfections.

A further expression of thanks is due to Mr Leslie D. Alldritt for reading the proofs and to my wife, Ikuko Abe for preparing the index. Ms Charlotte Tarr and Ms Earlyne Biering typed the manuscripts quickly and competently, for which I am most grateful.

Finally, the greatest debt without doubt is to my three teachers: Drs Daisetz T. Suzuki, Shin'ichi Hisamatsu, and Keiji Nishitani. Without the Dharma rain they poured upon me, a rain which nourished me for many years, even this humble bunch of flowers could not have been gathered.

Claremont, California 1983   MASAO ABE

Part I
Zen and Its Elucidation

1 Zen Is not a Philosophy, but . . .

Religion is difficult to understand with sufficient depth and subtlety. Zen is no exception. In one sense, Zen may be said to be one of the most difficult religions to understand, for there is no formulated Zen doctrine or theological system by which one may intellectually approach it. Accordingly, it is not surprising to find various superficial understandings or misunderstandings of Zen among Westerners interested in Zen, whose cultural and religious traditions are entirely different from those in which Zen has developed.

I

In Zen we often encounter such ordinary statements as: 'Willows are green, flowers are red', and 'Fire is hot, water is cold.' When he returned from China, Dōgen, who is credited with founding Japanese Sōtō Zen, said: 'I return to my homeland empty-handed. What I learned in China is only that the eyes are horizontal, the nose vertical.' Observations as these are so self-evident and ordinary that to place emphasis on them may seem puzzling.

But Zen also includes such paradoxical sayings as, 'A bridge flows, whereas water does not flow', 'The blue mountains are constantly walking, the stone woman gives birth to a child at night', and 'When Lee drinks the wine, Chang gets drunk.' Indeed, Zen is full of such sayings, which are extremely illogical and unreasonable in contrast to the self-evident statements mentioned above. Thus, both self-evident and illogical modes of expression are used in Zen. Hence it is often said that 'Zen is something enigmatic, beyond intellectual analysis.' Zen is thus taken to be a form of anti-intellectualism or a cheap intuitionism, especially when satori in Zen is explained as a flash-like intuition.

Again, Zen often says, 'When you are hungry, eat; when you are

3

tired, sleep.' Thus Zen is misunderstood as something amoral, something which you simply let flow from your desires or instincts, just like an animal, without thinking of good and evil. At best, Zen is labelled 'oriental mysticism'. But to answer the question 'What is Zen?' with such a label, is nearly devoid of meaning.

It is clear that Zen is not a philosophy. It is beyond words and intellect and is not, as in the case of philosophy, a study of the processes governing thought and conduct, nor a theory of principles or laws that regulate people and the universe. For the realization of Zen, *practice is absolutely necessary*. Nevertheless, Zen is neither a mere anti-intellectualism nor a cheap intuitionism nor is it an encouragement to animal-like spontaneity. Rather, it embraces a profound philosophy. Although intellectual understanding cannot be a substitute for Zen's awakening, practice without a proper and legitimate form of intellectual understanding is often misleading. An intellectual understanding without practice is certainly powerless, but practice without learning is apt to be blind. Therefore, I would like to clarify as much as possible the philosophy which Zen embraces.

The following discourse given by the Chinese Zen master Ch'ing-yüan Wei-hsin (Ja: Seigen Ishin) of the T'ang dynasty provides a key by which we may approach Zen philosophy. His discourse reads as follows:

Thirty years ago, before I began the study of Zen, I said, 'Mountains are mountains, waters are waters.'

After I got an insight into the truth of Zen through the instruction of a good master, I said, 'Mountains are not mountains, waters are not waters.'

But now, having attained the abode of final rest [that is, Awakening], I say, 'Mountains are really mountains, waters are really waters.'

And then he asks, 'Do you think these three understandings are the same or different?'[1] This question is crucial to his whole discourse.

The first stage of understanding described here insists: 'Mountains are mountains, waters are waters.' That was the master's understanding before he studied or practised Zen. But after he studied Zen for some years and came to an insight, he understood that 'Mountains are not mountains, waters are not waters.' This is the second stage. When he came to satori, however, he clearly realized that 'Mountains are really mountains, waters are really waters.' This is the third and final stage. At the first stage of understanding, Wei-hsin is differentiating mountains from waters, and waters from mountains. 'Mountains are not waters, but mountains, waters are not mountains, but waters.' Thus he discriminates the one from the other. And in so doing, he affirms mountains as mountains and waters as waters. Here, then, we have differentiation as well as affirmation. However, when he comes to the second stage, 'Mountains are not mountains, waters are not waters'; there is neither differentiation nor affirmation, but only negation. Finally, when he reaches the third and final stage, 'Mountains are really mountains, waters are really waters', we again have differentiation as well as affirmation.

II

Many important issues are involved in this discourse. In the first understanding, Wei-hsin differentiates and affirms mountains and waters as two different entities. At the same time, he objectifies mountains as mountains, waters as waters, thereby coming to have a clear understanding of both. In addition to differentiation and affirmation, then, there is also objectification.

If he were asked, 'Who is it that differentiates mountains from waters?' he would of course answer, 'It is I. I differentiate mountains from waters, and I affirm mountains as mountains, waters as waters.' Hence, in the first stage, mountains are understood as mountains in that they are objectified by him or by us, and not understood as mountains *in themselves*. Mountains are over there and we are standing here, looking at them from our own vantage point. 'Mountains are mountains' only insofar as they are objectively looked at from our subjective point of view and are not grasped in themselves. They are grasped from the outside, not from within. There is a duality of *subject* and *object* in this understanding. And in differentiating mountains, waters, and all the other things which constitute our world, we also differentiate *ourselves* from *others*. Thus we say, 'I am I, and you are you: I am not you, but I; you are not I, but you.' Behind the understanding in which mountains are discriminated from waters lies the understanding in which self is discriminated from other. In short, the distinction between mountains, waters, and any other phenomena in the objective world, and the distinction between self and other are inseparably connected. Herein, the 'I' is the basis of discrimination, placing itself as the centre of everything.

Let us call this type of I an 'ego-self'. By differentiating itself from some other self, the ego-self understands itself in comparison with that other self. The ego-self thus stands in contradistinction to all other selves. It is therefore unavoidable that the ego-self puts the question to itself, 'Who am I?' This is a natural and inevitable question for the ego-self because it objectifies everything including itself. But with regard to this question we must ask, 'Who is asking, "who am I"?' The ego-self may answer, 'I am asking, "who am I?"' But in this answer there are two 'I's: an 'I' which is asking and an 'I' which is inquired into. Are these two I's the same or different? They must be the same, and yet they are also different from one another because the 'I' which is asking is the subject of the asking, while the 'I' which is asked about is the object of the asking. The self is divided in two. In other words, here 'I' am asking about 'myself', and 'myself' is in this case not the subject but the object of my own asking. This 'myself' is not the true 'I' because it is already objectified and an objectified self can never be a living, truly Subjective[2] Self. The living, acting, and Subjective Self is the 'I' which is *now* asking – that is the true Self.

But how can we grasp this 'I'? How can we realize our true Self? To do so, we may raise the question, 'Who is asking, "who is asking, *who am I*"?' Now another 'I' appears as a new subject and converts the entire situation into the object of still another question. That is, the 'I' which was the subject of the previous question is now objectified, transformed into the object of a new question. This means that 'I' as the genuine Subject, as the true Self, must always stand 'behind', ever eluding our grasp. We thus remain forever estranged from our true Self, anxiety-ridden, and unable to come to rest.

Self-estrangement and anxiety are *not* something *accidental* to the ego-self, but are inherent to its structure. To be human is to be a problem to oneself, regardless of one's culture, class, sex, nationality, or the era in which one lives. To be human means to be an ego-self; to be an ego-self means to be cut off from both one's self and one's world; and to be cut off from one's self and one's world means to be in constant anxiety. This is the human predicament. The ego-self, split at the root into subject and object, is forever dangling over a bottomless abyss, unable to gain any footing. Of course there are those who deny the existence of this basic anxiety. But even those who deny it are not free from it. Though flight from or repression of this anxiety is common, the futility of such a 'path' cannot but be recognized upon rigorous self-scrutiny. Examining one's life, one cannot fail to stumble upon either the fear of death which threatens to hurl us into a chasm of meaninglessness, or the mind-assailing guilt which often arises as a condemnation of the impurity of our acts. This fear and guilt rupture any semblance of tranquility we may have gained through our endeavour to escape or repress the fundamental anxiety in which we abide. Therefore, the basic anxiety and self-estrangement inherent in human existence can never be overcome unless we first overcome the ego-self and awaken to our true Self.

But the true Self continually recedes, step by step, as we repeatedly ask about ourselves. This process is endless – it is an infinite regress. And yet, while increasingly compelled to engage in this endless process of grasping, we are also forced to realize that that which can be grasped is never anything more than an objectified, dead self.

This is the reason why, referring to the realization of the true Self, Nan-ch'üan (Ja: Nansen) says: 'If you try to direct yourself toward it, you go away from it.' Lin-chi (Ja: Rinzai) also says: 'If you seek him, he retreats farther and farther away; if you don't seek him, then he's right there before your eyes, his wondrous voice resounding in your ears.' The endless regression implied in the 'objectification approach' indicates the futility and inevitable collapse of this approach.

Thus the true Self as a genuine Subject cannot be attained through this type of approach, no matter how rigorously we pursue it. Faced with infinite regression, therefore, we cannot help but realize that the true Self is unattained. No matter how many times we may repeatedly ask ourselves, our true Self always stands 'behind'; it can never be found in 'front' of us. The true Self is not something attainable, but that which is unattainable. When this is *existentially* realized with our whole being, the ego-self crumbles. That is, the existential realization of the unattainability of the true Self culminates in a deadlock, the breaking through of which results in the collapse of the ego-self, wherein we come to the realization of no-self or no-ego-self. And when the ego-self disappears, then the 'objective' world disappears as well. This means that the subject–

object duality which underlies the first stage of understanding is now eliminated. The result is that mountains are not mountains, waters are not waters. Now the differentiation of mountains and waters based on objectification is overcome. In other words, the veil which we projected onto mountains and waters from our subjective vantage point is torn away. At the same time, the differentiation between self and other is also overcome in the realization of no-self. With this realization of no-self we come to the second stage.

III

In this second stage there is a negation of the first stage of understanding and we realize that there is no differentiation, no objectification, no affirmation, no duality of subject and object. Here it must be said that everything is empty. This negative realization is important and necessary[3] in order for ultimate Reality to be disclosed, but to remain solely within the confines of this negative realization would be nihilistic. Furthermore, although in this second stage, differentiation of mountains and waters, self and other is overcome, another form of differentiation is still implied. That is a higher level of differentiation, namely, a *differentiation* between differentiation as in the first stage and no differentiation as in the second stage. 'No differentiation' as a mere negation of differentiation is still involved in a distinction because it stands against and is opposed to 'differentiation'. This higher level of differentiation which is hidden behind 'no differentiation' must be overcome in order to realize the genuine non-differentiated sameness of ultimate Reality. We must negate even 'no differentiation', 'no objectification', and go beyond the second stage. The negative view must be negated. Emptiness must empty itself. Thus we come to the third stage.

At this point it must be noted that the second stage has a twofold aspect:

1   The second stage represents a kind of conclusion or solution of the problem involved in the first. It is reached only through the realization of the *endlessness* of the regression implied in the 'objectification approach' of the ego-self, and through the realization of the *unattainability* of the true Self. As this realization of the endlessness of the regression and of the unattainability of the true Self must be a *total* and *existential*, rather than a partial and conceptual

one, the anxiety and restlessness of the ego-self are in one sense overcome. When both the futility and necessity of its inquiry push the ego-self to an extreme situation in which the 'objectification approach' can no longer be sustained, the subject–object structure of the ego-self collapses through the painful disclosures of the unattainability of the true Self. In this regard, we must point out that in order for the ego-self in the first stage to actualize no-self in the second stage, it is not sufficient that the ego-self, while still *enroute* or engaged in the process of trying to solve its dilemma in terms of the 'objectification approach', merely *feel* or *intellectually intuit* the unattainability of the true Self. Were this the case, the ego-self, thus realizing the true Self to be unattainable, would be in even more desperate straits, since its sole aim and hope had been the attainment of its true Self. And such desperation is a sign that the ego-self is still not free from attachment. On the contrary, it is necessary that, by overcoming even this extreme form of desperation, the ego-self push itself further, *come to a deadlock*, and *collapse* through the *total* realization of endlessness and unattainability with its whole body and mind. To realize that the true Self is really unattainable is to realize that the true Self is empty and nonexistent. This means that there is no continuous path from the first stage to the second, but rather a discontinuity which can be overcome only by a leap in which the ego-self is radically and completely broken through. Realization of no-self thus entails a kind of emancipation from the ego-self and liberation from the anxiety inherent in the ego-structure. Hence, the genuine realization that the 'true Self is unattainable' is not a source of desperation, but is freedom from restlessness, because in this realization it no longer matters that true Self cannot be attained. The self and its related world are grasped in the light of detachment. This is why in the second stage Wei-hsin said, 'I got an insight into the truth of Zen.' In this insight, there is peace of mind and tranquility.

2   However, as mentioned above, even in its 'no differentiation', the second stage implies a hidden form of differentiation – that is, the differentiation between 'differentiation' and 'no differentiation', ego-self and no-self – and is thereby not completely free from distinction. Hence one is apt to objectify and become attached to no-self as something to be distinguished from ego-self. There remains an implicit, negative form of attachment latent in the 'detachment' realized in the second stage. Such attachment to no-self results in an indifference to, and a nihilistic view of, both self

and world. There is no positive ground for one's life and activity. In this sense the second stage cannot be said to be free from a hidden form of anxiety. Even 'tranquility' is not completely free from an implicit restlessness. Thus it is therefore necessary to overcome the second stage and to break through to the third stage. In order to awaken to the true Self, even no-self and its hidden form of attachment and anxiety must be negated. This negation as well must be *total* and *existential*, rather than partial and conceptual. Again, as there is no continuous path from the second stage to the third, a leap is necessary in order to reach this final stage.

When we come to the third stage, there is an entirely new form of differentiation. It is a 'differentiation' which is realized through the negation of 'no differentiation'. Here we may say, 'Mountains are *really* mountains, no more no less; waters are *really* waters, no more no less.' Mountains and waters disclose themselves in their totality and particularity, and no longer as objects from our subjective vantage point.

There was negation at the second stage, and yet there must be another negation at the third stage. Logically speaking, we thus have the negation of negation. But what is the negation of negation? As a total negation of total negation, it is in fact an affirmation. And yet it is not a mere affirmation, that is, an affirmation in the relative sense, but rather an affirmation in the absolute sense. It is a great and absolute affirmation. Now, in the third and final stage, mountains are affirmed *really* as mountains, and waters are affirmed *really* as waters in their Reality. Emptiness empties itself, becoming non-emptiness, that is, true Fullness. Herein, all forms of anxiety and all forms of attachment, open and hidden, explicit and implicit, are completely overcome.

With this great affirmation of mountains and waters, we have a realization of the true Self. The true Self is realized only through the total negation of no-self, which is in turn the total negation of the ego-self. Again, the total negation of total negation is necessary to attain the true Self as the great affirmation. One can objectify not only *something positive* but also *something negative*. One can conceptualize 'no-self' as well as 'ego-self'. To overcome all possible objectification and conceptualization in order to attain ultimate Reality and awaken to the true Self, the double negation of the 'objectification approach' is necessary. Accordingly, the following must be noted in order to clarify the realization of the true Self:

As the result of the endless regression inherent in the 'objectification approach', we come to realize that the true Self is unattainable; herein occurs the leap from the ego-self to no-self. Although a realization of no-self, a realization that the true Self is unattainable, is necessary and important, it is still negative and nihilistic, entailing a dualistic view of no-self as something in contradistinction to the ego-self. Only when even no-self is existentially overcome does the true Self awaken to itself. This movement from the realization (A) *that the true Self is unattainable*, to the realization (B) *that the unattainable itself is the true Self* is a crucial turning point.

IV

We may elucidate this point through the metaphor of a wall. The ego-self (the first stage), which holds that 'the true Self is attainable', is rooted in a mode of consciousness which may be likened to an opaque wall that blocks the view of the ego-self, thereby precluding any view of Reality. In contrast to this, in realization (A), which holds that 'the true Self is unattainable', the no-self (the second stage) is rooted in a mode of consciousness which may be compared to a transparent wall through which Reality can be clearly seen without obstruction. The transition from the first stage to the second stage entails the removal of all colour and light-rejecting properties from the opaque wall. The wall in the second stage is thus completely transparent. As the colour and light-rejecting properties which in the first stage rendered impossible even a glimpse of reality are completely eradicated with the break-through to the second stage, Reality is now clearly visible to the no-self through the transparent wall.

Consequently with the realization of no-self, the 'I' is likely to confuse the transparency of the wall with its disappearance, for the wall, while merely transparent, appears to no longer exist. Thus the 'I', in 'seeing' Reality, deludedly comes to believe it is identical with Reality, without any gap whatsoever between the 'I' and Reality. No doubt there is an extremely significant difference between seeing Reality through a transparent wall and not being afforded any glimpse of it at all. Nevertheless, so long as the wall exists, the 'I' remains cut off from Reality. In both the first and second stages, therefore, the basic mode of being of the self and its ever-present 'objectification approach', are as yet unchanged, even though the manner of objectification has changed from positive to negative, as represented by the transition from an opaque wall to a transparent wall.

The essential task of the self, however, is not the removal of the colour and light-rejecting properties from an opaque wall, thereby making it transparent and allowing Reality to be seen, but rather breaking through the wall itself, whether opaque or transparent, in order to *thoroughly* overcome the distinction between 'seer' and 'the seen', the realm of 'I' and the realm of 'Reality'. This breaking through of the wall itself is a breakthrough to realization (B), wherein one realizes that *the unattainable itself is the true Self*, which is the third stage.

By breaking through the wall, both the ego-self (the self blocked by the opaque wall) and the no-self (the self blocked by the transparent wall) are overcome, and the non-differentiated sameness – which is at once the clearest differentiation – of ultimate Reality is disclosed. Herein, the 'unattainable' or 'emptiness' is no longer seen 'over there', even through a transparent wall, but is *directly* realized as the *ground* of the true Self. This constitutes not merely a change from a positive mode of objectification to a negative one, but a far more radical and fundamental change of the basic mode of being of the self.

We can illustrate the transition from realization (A) (the true Self is unattainable) to realization (B) (the unattainable itself is the true Self) by means of a logical analysis as well the wall metaphor. If we take these two realizations as logical 'propositions', realization (A) and realization (B) can both be seen to consist of a subject and predicate, connected by the copula 'is'. However, the subject and the predicate of the proposition expressed in realization (A) are completely reversed in realization (B). Realization (A) is expressed through a proposition concerning the 'true Self' in which the 'unattainable' is grasped as a predicate attribute of the 'true Self'. Since the predicate (i.e., the 'unattainable') is negative, the proposition expressing realization (A) is a negative one. This proposition may be restated: 'I as the true Self am empty, or nonexistent.' On the other hand, realization (B) is expressed through a proposition concerning the 'unattainable' in which the 'true Self' is grasped as a predicate attribute of the 'unattainable'. Although in this proposition something negative (i.e., the 'unattainable') is taken as a subject, since the predicate (i.e., the 'true Self') is positive, both in the logical and axiological sense, the proposition expressing realization (B) is a positive one. This proposition may be restated: 'Emptiness itself is "I" as the true Self.'

This logical analysis of realizations (A) and (B) may be useful in helping to understand the existential meaning of the leap from realization (A) to realization (B).

In realization (A), that is, the realization in the second stage, the true Self is realized as something negative (the '*unattainable*' or '*emptiness*'), and is thus in one sense free from objectification and conceptualization, because here the true Self is understood as non-existent. Nevertheless, in that understanding, the true Self is still somewhat conceptualized and objectified because, even with the collapse of the ego-self and the realization of no-self, the 'true Self' still remains outside as *something* 'unattainable' or as *something* empty, and is thus not completely free from *somethingness*. The true Self is still objectively conceived (though in negative rather than positive terms), in that it is *objectified* or *substantialized* as a subject of the negative proposition, 'the true Self is unattainable'. At the same time, in realization (A) the 'unattainable' is also conceived objectively from the outside and as such it is not yet totally and existentially realized as the truly 'unattainable'. It is grasped merely as an attribute of the true Self.

In brief, even though a negative predicate (the 'unattainable') is attributed to the true Self, insofar as the true Self is grasped in terms of attribute as a predicate it must be said to be conceptualized. Thus there is a gap between realization (A) and 'I' as the true Self. The realized and the realizer are still dualistically separated.

When, however, we come to realization (B), that is, the realization that *the unattainable itself is the true Self*, neither the 'true Self' nor the 'unattainable' are conceived objectively in even the slightest degree, because in this realization the 'unattainable' itself is realized as 'I' – as the true Self. In other words, in realization (B), it is not that 'I am empty', but rather that 'Emptiness is I.' Through overcoming the negative view 'I am empty', emptiness is Subjectively and existentially realized as 'I' – as the true Self. Hence there is no gap between realization (B) and 'I'. The realized is the realizer, and the realizer is the realized. Realization (B) is expressed through a proposition concerning the 'unattainable' in which the 'true Self' is grasped in terms of attribute as a predicate. Here, the 'unattainable' is not grasped as this kind of attribute of the true Self, therefore it is not *something* unattainable, but rather *the* '*unattainable*' *itself*; it is realized as the active Subject. On the other hand, the true Self as a predicate is completely free from substantialization and objectification, and is existentially realized in its reality because it is not grasped in terms of some attribute of itself and is free from *somethingness*. It is truly non-objectively awakened to itself as the true Self.

Accordingly, in realization (B) wherein it is realized that *the unattainable itself is the true Self*, all possible conceptualization and objectification, *positive* and *negative*, are completely overcome. Emptiness, which in the second stage is still somewhat conceptualized, is now completely emptied; the pure activity of Emptiness forever *emptying* itself is realized as the true Self. Herein, there is a radical and fundamental *turning over* of the basic mode of being of the self. This turning over does not consist in a mere change from a positive (albeit problematic) understanding of the self as in the first stage, to a negative understanding of the self as in the second stage. For in both stages one and two, the self is given a central position, even though in the second stage the self is grasped in negative terms as unattainable, or empty. Rather, this turning over entails a transformation in which the 'unattainable' or 'emptiness' is grasped as the true centre, replacing self as the central concern. The true Self is awakened to with the 'unattainable' or 'emptiness' – which extends boundlessly throughout the universe – as its basis and root-source.

With this awakening to the true Self, ultimate Reality is disclosed in its entirety. Here, self-estrangment and anxiety are fundamentally overcome because the 'unattainable' is no longer realized as something negative or nihilistic; rather it is realized positively as the 'true Self'. In realization (B), the realizer and the realized are not two, but one. 'Your original face prior to the birth of your father and mother', and the 'True person without rank', in Lin-chi's sense, are nothing other than this 'unattainable' true Self.

When Shên-kuang, who later became the Second Patriarch Hui-k'o, asked Bodhidharma to pacify his mind, the latter said, 'Bring forth your mind and I shall pacify it for you!'

To this Shên-kuang replied (perhaps some time later), 'Although I have sought for it, I find it unattainable.'

Then Bodhidharma said, 'There! I have pacified it for you.'

In this well-known story, Bodhidharma would not have accepted Shên-kuang's reply, 'I find it unattainable', if Shên-kuang had meant by these words realization (A), that his mind is unattainable. It is only because he is expressing realization (B), proclaiming the unattainable itself is his mind, that Bodhidharma gave him his sanction.

V

Now let us return to the question Wei-hsin raised at the end of his discourse, that is, 'Do you think these three understandings are the same or different?' The third stage is apparently similar to the first stage, because both express affirmation and differentiation of mountains and waters. In fact, however, they essentially differ, for the first stage speaks merely of an uncritical affirmation antecedent to the negation realized in the second stage, while the third stage speaks of a great affirmation consequent to and transcendent over the negation realized in the second stage. It is clear that the second stage is different from the first and third. Thus each stage differs from the other two. Are they, however, merely different from each other? This must be carefully examined.

The first stage can include neither the second nor third; nor can the second stage embrace the third. On the other hand, the third and final stage includes both the first and second stages. This means that the second stage cannot be comprehended on the basis of the first stage, or the third stage on the basis of the first and the second. There is no continuity, no ascending bridge to a higher stage from a lower stage. As discussed above, there is a complete discontinuity or disjunction between each stage. A great leap is necessary to reach the higher stages. Overcoming discontinuity here indicates negation or emptying in a total way. The second stage is reached by a negation or emptying of the first stage. The third stage is reached by a negation or emptying of the second stage. In short, the third stage is realized only through the total negation of total negation, i.e., through a great negation or double negation of the first and the second stages. And as mentioned above, great negation is simply a great affirmation. They are dynamically identical. Accordingly, the third stage is not a *static end* to be reached progressively from the lower stages, but the *dynamic whole* which includes both great negation and great affirmation, a dynamic whole in which you and I are embraced and which excludes nothing.

Consequently, to the question raised by Wei-hsin as to whether these three understandings are the same or different, we may answer: 'They are different and yet not different; they are the same and yet different at once.'

Herein the following three points must be noted:

(1) Although the above explanation concerning the relation between the three stages is rather logical, we are not dealing, of

course, with a merely logical problem, but rather with a burning existential one. 'Negation' as the means through which 'discontinuity' between the lower and higher stages is overcome is not merely a logical negation, but an 'abnegation', 'self-denial' or 'renunciation' in the *ultimate* existential sense.

In other words, the negation of the first stage (ego-self) through which the second stage (no-self) is realized must be a total, existential self-negation of the ego-self. It must not be an outward negation of something external by the ego-self, not even the ego-self's renunciation of itself as object, but rather entails the negation and collapse of the ego-self – including any would be subject-renouncer of that self, through the realization of the endless regression involved in the 'objectification approach' and the unattainability of the true Self. This entails the death of the ego-self. Likewise, the negation of the second stage (no-self) through which the third stage (true Self) is realized must be a total, existential self-negation of the no-self in which, through the total realization of its own hidden anxiety and implicit attachment, the no-self is broken through. Thus, the 'great negation' as the negation of negation must be taken in a most radical and existential sense, that is, as the total self-negation of the no-self which is in turn realized only through the total self-negation of the ego-self. This radical double negation constitutes a complete return to the most fundamental ground of the 'self', a ground more original than the 'original' state of the ego-self. The original true Self is awakened to through this radical return. Hence the 'great negation' as the negation of negation is at once a 'great affirmation'. 'Great negation' in this sense refers to the 'Great Death' which is the breaking through of both ego-self and no-self, both life and death. Without this 'Great Death', 'Great Life' as the resurrection cannot take place.

(2) The realization in the third stage, that 'Mountains are really mountains, waters are really waters,' seems to be a sheer objective realization about mountains and waters. But it is not that herein the self is talking about mountains and waters objectively. On the contrary, the true Self is talking about itself. Furthermore, this does not mean that the true Self is talking about mountains and waters as *symbols* of its Self, but rather that the true Self is talking about mountains and waters as *its own Reality*. In this statement 'Mountains are really mountains, waters are really waters', the true Self is talking simultaneously about itself and about mountains and waters realized as its own Reality. This is because in the third stage,

the subject-object duality is completely overcome and the subject as it is, is object; the object as it is, is subject.

This overcoming of the subject–object duality is possible only through the realization in the second stage that 'Mountains are not mountains, waters are not waters', the realization which is inseparably connected with the realization that 'I am not I, you are not you.' Accordingly, however similar they may appear, Zen and natural mysticism or pantheism should not be confused. For the latter lacks a clear realization of the *negation* of subject and object.

(3) Although we have used the term 'stage' in analysing Wei-hsin's discourse, the term is inadequate or even misleading as an aid to understanding the real meaning of his utterance. For the 'third stage' is, as mentioned above, not a static end to be reached progressively from the lower stages, but the dynamic whole which includes the lower stages, both affirmative and negative. It is more than the third and final stage. It is the standpoint from which the notion of process and even the notion of 'stage', as well as their implication of temporal sequence, are overcome. 'Mountains are really mountains, waters are really waters', is realized in a thoroughly non-conceptual way in the *absolute present* which is beyond and yet embraces past, present, and future. The dynamic whole which includes all three stages is realized precisely in this absolute present. From this point of view, an approach based on the idea of 'stage' is illusory, as is the notion of temporality linked with the idea of 'stage'.

In Zen the total reality of mountains and waters (and with them everything and everyone in the universe) is actualized through the double negation of the temporal sequence implied in the idea of 'stage'. It is through the negation of non-temporality implied in the 'second stage' as well as through the negation of the temporality implied in the 'first stage' that the absolute present is completely disclosed.

Accordingly, the realization of everything being really just as it is, the realization which takes place in the absolute present, is not merely the final stage or the end of an objective approach in time, but, being beyond time, is the ground or original basis on which the objective approach can be properly established and from which temporal sequence can legitimately begin. The 'three stages' in time, which were illusory in that they lacked the ground of the absolute present, are revived as something real here in this realization. The absolute present is also the ground or basis on which everything and everyone are realized as they are, without losing their individuality, and yet without opposing and impeding one another.

Thus in the Zen Awakening attained by Wei-hsin, on the one hand, mountains are really mountains in themselves, waters are really waters in themselves – that is, everything in the world is real in itself; and yet, on the other hand, there is no hindrance between any one thing and any other thing – everything is equal, interchangeable, and interfusing. Thus we may say: 'Mountains are waters, waters are mountains.' It is here in this Awakening in which the great negation is a great affirmation that Zen says, 'A bridge flows, whereas water does not flow', or 'When Lee drinks the wine, Chang gets drunk.' It is here again in the Awakening that Zen says: 'When you are hungry, eat; when you are tired, sleep.' This is not an instinctual, animal-like activity as may be seen in the 'first stage'. Instead, eating and sleeping are sustained by the realization of bottomless nothingness. When you are hungry, there is nothing behind being hungry. You are just hungry, no more no less. When you eat, there is nothing beyond eating. Eating is the absolute action at that moment. When you sleep, again there is nothing behind sleeping – no dreams, no nightmares, just sleeping; sleeping is completely realized at that moment.

Again in this Awakening we may say: 'I am not I, therefore I am you; precisely for this reason I am really I. You are not you, therefore you are me; precisely for this reason you are really you.' There is no hindrance between us and yet everyone has complete individuality. This is possible because the true Self is no-self. As there is nothing behind us, each one of us is thoroughly just as he or she is, and yet each one of us is interfusing with every other without obstruction. Hence, 'when Lee drinks the wine, Chang gets drunk.' 'A bridge flows, whereas water does not flow.' This is not an enigma, but an expression of the interfusing aspect of Zen, which is inseparably connected with the aspect of the independence and individuality of each person, animal, plant, and thing – as expressed in the formulations: 'Willows are green, flowers are red', and 'The eyes are horizontal, the nose vertical.'

VI

This is the philosophy realized within Zen. Some may feel it is not so different from Hegel's philosophy. There is certainly a great similarity between Hegel's philosophy and the philosophy implied by Zen – especially in terms of the negation of negation being a great and absolute affirmation. We should not overlook their essential difference, however. In emphasizing 'negation' as a vital notion in his account of the dialectic, Hegel grasps everything dialectically through the negation of negation. Hegel's dialectical process is understood as the self-development of the absolute Spirit (*absoluter Geist*) as the ultimate Reality. For instance, in his Philosophy of History, the meaning of history is understood as the actualization of the absolute Spirit in time through the careers of a number of world-historical individuals such as Caesar and Napoleon. For Hegel, since the essence of spirit is freedom, the actual history of mankind is interpreted as the development of human freedom in the progressive unfolding of the absolute Spirit. Although Hegel claims that all that happens in history happens through the will and selfish passion of individual human beings, he refers to the 'trick of reason' (*List der Vernunft*) which, using this will and passion as its instruments, arrives at results of which even the individual historical agents were not clearly cognizant. Although his interpretation of the role of the individual in history is quite dialectical, the notion of the 'trick of reason' indicates that the individual is not fully grasped as an individual. In order for the individual to be truly grasped as an individual, it must be paradoxically identical with the absolute. For if the individual and the absolute are understood to be even slightly separated from one another, the individuality of the former cannot be thoroughly maintained against the absolute character of the latter. Conversely, the absolute character of the latter cannot be fully realized if the absolute is somewhat separated from the individual. Admittedly, the individual and the absolute are in one sense essentially different from one another. However, for the individual to be truly an individual, it must be identical – paradoxically – with the absolute, while at the same time retaining its integrity as an individual. On the other hand, for the absolute to be really absolute, it must be identical – again, paradoxically – with the individual, while retaining its absolute character. This paradoxical identity of the individual and the absolute cannot be fully understood objectively, but only non-objectively and existentially.

The individual may be paradoxically identical with the absolute only when the absolute is grasped as non-substantial – only when there is nothing substantial whatsoever as 'absolute' behind or beyond the individual. In Hegel, the individual is not fully grasped as an individual because for Hegel the absolute is not *absolute Nothingness*, but *absolute Spirit*, which is in the final analysis something substantial. It may not be accurate to say that Hegel's notion of the absolute Spirit is simply something substantial, for it is an extremely dialectical notion which is actualized only through the negation of negation. Inasmuch as this is the case, it cannot be said to be substantial. And yet, in the light of Zen's realization of absolute Nothingness or Emptiness, the substantial nature of Hegel's notion of the absolute Spirit becomes clear. Furthermore, when his notion of a 'trick of reason' is taken into account, one cannot but think that there is something behind the individual, and that the individual is to some extent manipulated by that something – that is, by the absolute Spirit.

On the other hand, in Zen the absolute is grasped as '*Mu*' or absolute Nothingness which is completely nonsubstantial, thus the individual is paradoxically identical with the absolute, and as such is thoroughly realized as an individual. There is nothing whatsoever behind or beyond the individual. The individual is not manipulated or ruled by anything whatsoever – not by absolute Spirit and not by God. In Zen's realization of absolute Nothingness, an individual is determined by absolutely no-thing. To be determined by absolutely no-thing means the individual is determined by nothing other than itself in its particularity – it has complete self-determination without any transcendent determinant. This fact is equally true for every individual. Hence, *through* and going beyond the negative realization that 'Mountains are not mountains, waters are not waters' (the second stage), there is a positive realization both that 'Mountains are really mountains, waters are really waters' (each thing's absolute particularity) and that 'Mountains are waters, waters are mountains' (each thing's interfusing interchangability). More precisely speaking, through the negation realized in the second stage, there is a positive realization in Zen's satori both of each thing's absolute particularity and of each thing's interchangability. Particularity and interchangability are realized as simply two aspects of one and the same dynamic Reality, which, being a dynamic whole, is entirely unobjectifiable and non-substantial.

While extremely dialectical, Hegel's notion of absolute Spirit, in comparison with Zen's notion of absolute Nothingness, is not completely free from 'somethingness'. As a result, in Hegel, the negation of negation is not realized as the total self-negation of total self-negation, but is realized within the framework of the self-development of the absolute Spirit, however dialectical the process of self-development may be. In Zen, however, there is no such framework. Everything is empty. It is realized in boundless openness. Emptiness is Reality. Here, the dialectical nature of the 'negation *of* negation' – the total self-negation of total self-negation – is fully realized. The 'negation of negation' (true Emptiness) is at once the affirmation of affirmation (true Fullness of wondrous Beings). True Emptiness and true Fullness are dialectically one in a non-conceptual, existential way. Between them there is no gap whatsoever; not even a single hair can be inserted. This is precisely Reality realized in the absolute present as a dynamic whole in which the relation between individual existences in space, and their myriad developments in time, are properly grasped.

The aforementioned difference between Hegel and Zen is not unrelated to the difference in their understanding of philosophy and religion. In Hegel, philosophy stands for absolute knowledge (*absolutes Wissen*) to which religion, not yet free from representation (*Vorstellung*) in its form of faith (*Glaube*) in God, must be subordinate. This priority in rank of philosophy over religion is understood in Hegel in terms of the process of the self-development of absolute Spirit. In opposition to this, Zen, which is based on the realization of absolute Nothingness, is neither philosophy nor religion in the Hegelian sense. In Zen, religion is not subordinate to philosophy as seen in Hegel, or is philosophy subordinate to religion as in the case of Christianity. In the dynamic realization of the statement 'Mountains are really mountains, waters are really waters', wisdom and compassion, philosophy and religious solution of the human predicament are equally implied. This is the reason why Zen is neither absolute knowledge nor salvation by God, but Self-Awakening. In the Self-Awakening of Zen, each individual existence – whether person, animal, plant or thing – manifests itself in its particularity as expressed in the formulation, 'Willows are green, flowers are red', and yet each is interpenetrating harmoniously as expressed in the formulation, 'When Lee drinks the wine, Chang gets drunk.' This is not an end but the *ground* on which our being and activity must be properly based.

VII

In Zen it is said, 'The Buddha preached forty-nine years and yet his "broad tongue" never moved once.' It is also said, 'The instant you speak about it, you miss the mark.' In Zen there is nothing to explain by means of words or theory, nothing to be learned as a holy doctrine. The essence of Zen is, in fact, 'unspeakable'. Thus, to a question raised by a monk, 'What is the cardinal meaning of the Buddha Dharma?' Lin-chi (Rinzai) immediately responded with a shout, '_Katsu!_' But since Zen is concerned with the _truly_ unspeakable, it rejects not only speech, but mere silence as well. Consequently, in his discourse, Tê-shan (Ja: Tokusan) used to swing his big stick, saying, 'Though you can speak, thirty blows! Though you cannot speak, thirty blows!' And Shou-shan (Ja: Shuzan) once held up his _shippē_ (a short bamboo stick) to an assembly of his disciples and declared: 'If you call this a _shippē_, you conflict with the truth; if you don't call it a _shippē_, you run counter to the truth. What, then, will you call it? Speak! Speak!' Zen always expresses the 'unspeakable' Reality which is beyond affirmation and negation, speech and silence, in a direct and straightforward way, and presses us to present our understanding of this Reality through the injunction 'Speak! Speak!'

But Zen does not point to the 'unspeakable' solely by means of cutting off all the possibilities (speech or silence, affirmation or negation) which are available to the student, as in the aforementioned cases of Têh-shan and Shou-shan. Lin-chi's '_Katsu!_,' for example, while on the one hand an absolute negation which cuts off every conceivable response of the questioner, is at once a radical affirmation of the 'unspeakable'. This affirmation of the 'unspeakable' is quite crucial in Zen and is also expressed in a direct and straightforward way, as illustrated by the following account:

> Shih-kung (Ja: Sekkyo) asked one of his accomplished monks, "Can you take hold of empty space?"
>
> "Yes, sir," he replied.
>
> "Show me how you do it."
>
> The monk stretched out his arm and clutched at empty space.
>
> Shih-kung said: "Is that the way? But after all you have not got anything."
>
> "What then," asked the monk, "is your way?"
>
> The master straightway took hold of the monk's nose and gave it a hard pull, which made the latter exclaim: "Oh, oh, how hard you pull at my nose! Your are hurting me terribly!"
>
> "That is the way to have a good hold of empty space," said the master.[4]

All these examples clearly show that Zen always aims at grasping the living Reality of life which can not be entirely captured only by intellectual analysis. This, however, as mentioned above, must not be taken as mere anti-intellectualism. Although Zen transcends human intellect, it does not exclude it. A so-called Zen 'realization' or *satori* which degenerates or disappears when grasped and expressed intellectually or philosophically must be said to have been inauthentic from the outset. Authentic Zen realization or *satori*, even should it undergo rigorous intellectual analysis and philosophical reflection, will never be destroyed; on the contrary, analysis will serve to clarify that realization and confirm it more definitively in oneself, further enabling one to convey the depth of that realization to others, even through the medium of words.

There is a four-line formulation which expresses the basic character of Zen:

Not relying on words or letters,
An independent self-transmitting apart from the doctrinal teaching,
Directly pointing to one's mind,
Awakening to one's original Nature, thereby actualizing his Buddhahood.

'Not relying on words or letters', however, does not, as is often misunderstood even by Zen practitioners, indicate a mere exclusion of words or letters, but rather signifies the necessity of not clinging to them. Insofar as one is not attached to words and letters, one can use them freely even in the realm of Zen. This is the reason why, in spite of the emphasis on 'Not relying on words or letters', Zen has produced an abundance of Zen literature and a profound speculative thinker of the caliber of Dōgen.

It is said in Zen, 'Those who have not attained Awakening should penetrate into the meaning of Reality, while those who have already attained it should practice giving verbal expression to that Reality.' It is also said, 'It is easier to attain enlightenment than it is to speak of it freely and without attachment.' Zen is a double-edged sword, killing words and thoughts, yet at the same time, giving them life. Although beyond human intellect and philosophy, Zen is their root and source.

When Yüeh shan (Ja: Yakusan) was sitting in meditation, a monk asked, "What are you thinking while sitting immovably?"

The master said, "I am thinking of the very matter of not-thinking."

To this the monk asked, "How do you think of the matter of not-thinking?"

The master replied, "*Non*-thinking!"

Zen does not establish itself on the basis of either thinking or not-thinking, but rather *non*-thinking, which is beyond both thinking and not-thinking. When not-thinking is taken as the basis of Zen, anti-intellectualism becomes rampant. When thinking is taken as the basis, Zen loses its authentic ground and degenerates into mere conceptualism and abstract verbiage. Genuine Zen, however, takes *non*-thinking as its ultimate ground, and thus can express itself without hindrance through both thinking and not-thinking, as the situation requires. Lin-chi's shout, Tê-shan's blow, Nan-ch'üan's (Ja: Nansen) killing of the cat, Chü-chih's (Ja: Gutei) raising of one finger, all contain that philosophy of *non*-thinking. It is this philosophy which Zen will have to make full use of if it is not to stay within a monastery, but to deal effectively with the many agonizing problems plaguing the contemporary world. Zen is not an anti-intellectualism nor a cheap intuitionism nor an animal-like activity, but includes a most profound philosophy, although Zen itself is not a philosophy.

2 Dōgen on Buddha-Nature

I

Dōgen (1200–53) is one of the most outstanding and distinctive figures in the history of Japanese Buddhism. He is unique in at least the following three senses.

First, rejecting all existing forms of Buddhism in Japan as inauthentic, he attempted to introduce and establish what he believed to be the genuine Buddhism, based on his own realization which he attained in Sung China under the guidance of the Zen Master Ju-ching (Ja: Nyojō, 1163–1228). He called it 'the Buddha Dharma directly transmitted from the Buddha and patriarchs'. He emphasized *zazen* (seated meditation) as being 'the right entrance to the Buddha Dharma' in the tradition of the Zen schools in China since Bodhidharma, originating from Śākyamuni Buddha. Yet he strictly refused to speak of a 'Zen sect', to say nothing of a 'Sōtō sect', which he was later credited with founding. For Dōgen was concerned solely with the 'right Dharma' as such, and regarded *zazen* as its 'right entrance'. 'Who has used the name "Zen sect"? No buddha or patriarch spoke of a "Zen sect". You should realize it is a devil that speaks of "Zen sect". Those who pronounce a devil's appellation must be confederates of the devil, not children of the Buddha.'[1] He called himself 'the Dharma transmitter Shamon[2] Dōgen, who went to China'; and he did so with the strong conviction that he had attained the authentic Dharma that is directly transmitted from buddha to buddha, and that he should transplant it on Japanese soil. Thus he rejected the idea of *mappo*[3] i.e., the last or final (and degenerate) Dharma, an idea with wide acceptance in the Japanese Buddhism of his day. It may not be too much to say of Dōgen that just as Bodhidharma transmitted the Buddha Dharma to China, he intended to transmit it to Japan.

Secondly, though Dōgen came to a realization of the right Dharma under the guidance of a Chinese Zen master whom he continued to revere throughout his life, the understanding of the

25

right Dharma is unique to Dōgen. By virtue of religious awakening and penetrating insight, Dōgen grasped the Buddha Dharma in its deepest and most authentic sense. In so doing, he dared to reinterpret the words of former patriarchs, and even the sutras themselves. As a result, his idea of the right Dharma represents one of the purest forms of Mahayana Buddhism, in which the Dharma that was realized in the Buddha's enlightenment reveals itself most profoundly. All of this, it is noteworthy, is rooted in Dōgen's own existential realization, which he attained through long and intense seeking. Based on this idea of the right Dharma, he not only rejected, as stated above, all existing forms of Buddhism in Japan, but also severely criticized certain forms of Indian and Chinese Buddhism, though, it is true, he generally considered Buddhism in these two countries as more authentic than that in Japan.

The third reason Dōgen is unique in the history of Japanese Buddhism, is because of his speculative and philosophical nature. He was a strict practitioner of *zazen*, and someone who emphasized *shikantaza*, i.e., just sitting. His whole life was spent in rigorous discipline as a monk. He encouraged his disciples to do the same. Yet he was endowed with keen linguistic sensibility and a philosophical mind. His main work, entitled *Shōbōgenzō*,[4] 'A Treasury of the Right Dharma Eye', perhaps unsurpassable in its philosophical speculation, is a monumental document in Japanese intellectual history. In Dōgen, we find a rare combination of religious insight and philosophical ability. In this respect, he may be well compared with Thomas Aquinas, born 25 years later.

He wrote his main work, *Shōbōgenzō*, in Japanese, in spite of the fact that leading Japanese Buddhists until then had usually written their major works in Chinese. Dōgen made penetrating analyses and tried to express the world of the Buddha Dharma in his mother tongue by mixing Chinese Buddhist and colloquial terms freely in his composition. The difficult and unique style of his Japanese writing is derived from the fact that, in expressing his own awakening, he never used conventional terminology, but employed a vivid, personal style grounded in his Subjective realization. Even when he used traditional Buddhist phrases, passages, etc., he interpreted them in unusual ways in order to express the truth as he understood it. In Dōgen, the search for and realization of the Buddha Dharma and the speculation on and expression of that search and realization are uniquely combined.

I shall now discuss Dōgen's idea of the Buddha-nature, which may be regarded as a characteristic example of his realization.

II

In the opening of the 'Buddha-nature' fascicle of *Shōbōgenzō*, Dōgen quotes the following passage from the Nirvana Sutra:

一切衆生悉有仏性　如來常住無有變易

(*Issai no shujō wa kotogotoku busshō o yūsu: Nyorai wa jōjūnishite henyaku arukoto nashi*), 'All sentient beings without exception have the Buddha-nature: *Tathāgata* (Buddha) is permanent with no change at all.'[5] This well expresses the fundamental standpoint of Mahayana Buddhism. In the passage two important themes are emphasized: 'All sentient beings have the Buddha-nature', and '*Tathāgata* abides forever without change.' These two themes are inseparable from one another.

Against this traditional reading, Dōgen dares to read the passage as follows: '*Issai wa shujō nari*; *shitsuu wa busshō nari*; *Nyorai wa jōjūnishite mu nari, u nari, henyaku nari*': 'All are sentient beings, all beings are (all being is)[6] the Buddha-nature; *Tathāgata* is permanent, non-being, being, and change.'[7] Since gramatically speaking, this way of reading is unnatural and might even be termed wrong, why does Dōgen read it in this manner? It is because this is the only way for Dōgen to express clearly what he believes to be the fundamental standpoint of Mahayana Buddhism. It is more important for him to rightly and correctly convey the Buddhist truth than to be grammatically correct. The crucial point in Dōgen's reading concerns the last four chinese characters of the first part of this passage, – 悉有仏性 – traditionally read [All sentient beings] '*without exception have* the Buddha-nature', which he changes to read '*All beings are* the Buddha-nature.' This change of reading is possible because the Chinese character 有 means both 'to be' and 'to have'. Why did Dōgen believe that this unusual way of reading more appropriately expresses the Buddhist truth? To answer this question I must explain the traditional interpretation of the sentence.

First, the term *shujō*, *sattva* in Sanskrit, means all the living, i.e., living beings which are in samsara, the round of birth-and-death. Buddhist texts show that the term *shujō* is interpreted in one of two ways: in its narrow sense it refers to 'human beings,' and in its broad sense, 'living beings'. Accordingly, *Issai no shujō wa kotogotoku busshō o yūsu* means that not only human beings but also all other living beings have the Buddha-nature. Buddha-nature (*busshō* in Japanese, *buddhatā* in Sanskrit) generally refers to Buddhahood or the nature that enables one to become buddha, that is, to attain enlightenment. The second part of the passage, *Nyorai wa jōjūnishite henyaku arukoto nashi*, '*Tathāgata* is permanent, with no change at all' expresses the unchangeable permanency of a Buddha, a realizer of the truth.

Here one can see that in Buddhism, human beings and other living beings are similar in that they have the Buddha-nature and the capacity for attaining enlightenment. In this understanding, however, Buddhism must imply a basic dimension common to human beings and other living beings. This common dimension may be said to be *shōmetsusei, utpādanirodha*, the generation-extinction nature. Man's 'birth-and-death' (*shōji*) is a human form of 'generation-and-extinction' which is common to all living beings. Although the problem of birth-and-death is regarded in Buddhism as the most fundamental problem for human existence, Buddhism does not only approach this as the problem of 'birth-death' in the 'human' dimension, but rather as the problem of 'generation–extinction' in the wider dimension of 'living beings'.

Unless we are liberated from the very nature of generation–extinction common to all living beings, we human beings cannot be genuinely liberated from the human problem of birth-death. This is the reason why, in Buddhism, it is emphasized that man is in samsara, the endless round of transmigration from one form of life to another, and why people can be said to attain nirvana only by freeing themselves from this endless round, samsara.

According to traditional Buddhist doctrine it is said that *shujō* transmigrate through six realms of existence: *naraka-gati* (the realm of hell), *preta-gati* (the realm of hungry ghosts), *tiryagyoni-gati* (the realm of animals), *asura-gati* (the realm of fighting spirits), *manusya-gati* (the realm of human existence), and *deva-gati* (the realm of heavenly existence). This concept of transmigration was derived from pre-Buddhistic Brahmanism, and was a reflection of the world-view at that time. We need not take the number *six* for the realms of existence seriously. What is essential in this connection is that these six kinds of living beings, human existence included, are all interpreted as transmigrating in *one and the same dimension*, the dimension of generation-and-extinction. Here one can see the dehomocentrism in the Buddhist understanding of the basic human problem and the salvation from that problem. An old Japanese poem says:

> Listening to the voice of a singing mountain bird,
> I wonder if it is my [dead] father
> or my [dead] mother.

The poet expresses his feeling of solidarity with all living beings as they endlessly transmigrate from one form of life to another. A bird thereby may have been one's father or mother, brother or sister in a previous life. This feeling of solidarity is inseparably connected with the realization of the generation-extinction common to all living beings.

In the West and in the East as well, however, the Buddhist idea of transmigration is not always understood as occuring in one and the same dimension as discussed above, but rather is often misunderstood as a transmigration simply from man to animal and from animal to other forms of life in such a way that one views the whole process of transmigration with oneself as the centre – without an awareness of its dehomocentric character. But an understanding of transmigration which does not fully realize its dehomocentric character is inadequate, because in that understanding there is no common basis between human and non-human forms of life, a basis without which transmigration is impossible. Dehomocentricism in this connection means to transcend the dimension of human birth-and-death, thereby arriving at the deeper and broader dimension of the generation-and-extinction of living beings. Transmigration as samsara is emphasized in Buddhism simply because the human birth-death problem is believed to be fully solved only in the dehomocentric or transhomocentric dimension, i.e., the dimension of generation-extinction common to all living beings. Nirvana as the emancipation from samsara is understood to be attainable only on this wider basis.

Accordingly, regarding the dehomocentric character of the Buddhist idea of transmigration, the following two points must be observed. First, the Buddhist idea of transmigration has nothing to do with animism, a theory according to which an *anima* exists apart from human bodies and things, and animates them, (although the poem cited above might be understood to suggest an animistic idea). The Buddhist idea of transmigration is not based on a belief in the independent existence of *spirit*, or *soul*, nor on the idea of the *stream of life*, but on the realization of *generation-and-extinction at each and every moment*. In reality *endless* transmigration is inseparably connected with the realization of *momentary* generation-and-extinction. Here one can see the endlessness of transmigration as regards temporality.

Secondly, the so-called six realms of transmigratory existence are not to be interpreted as meaning that the six different worlds stand somewhat side by side. Rather, for human beings this world is understood to be the human world in which animals and the like are living. For animals, however, this world is the animal world in which humans are living as well. In this sense it is not that there are six worlds existing somewhere concurrently, but that the boundless horizon of generation-extinction opens up, in which six kinds of transmigration are taking place. This shows the boundlessness of transmigration in its spatiality.

Thus, transmigration in terms of dehomocentricism is endless and boundless in time and space. This endless and boundless dimension is nothing but the dimension of generation-extinction in which, as indicated by the phrase *shujō*, humans and other living beings are not discriminated from each other. This means that Buddhism does not give a special or superior position to humans over and against other living things with regard to the nature and salvation of humans.

In this respect Buddhism is quite different from Christianity. As the Genesis story shows, Christianity assigns to humans the task of ruling over all other creatures and ascribes to humans alone the *imago dei* through which they, unlike other creatures, can directly respond to the word of God. Human death is understood as the 'wages of sin', the result of one's own free acts, i.e., rebellion against the word of God. Here, one can see homocentrism among creatures in Christianity. Accordingly, in Christianity there is a clear distinction between humans and other creatures regarding their nature and salvation, with the former having priority over the latter. This homocentric nature is essentially related with Christian personalism in which God is believed to disclose himself as personality and in which a dialogical I-Thou relation between man and God is essential.

Then, does not Buddhism establish any distinction between humans and other creatures? Is it that, in Buddhism, humans have no special significance among creatures? The very realization of dehomocentrism is possible only to human existence, which has self-consciousness. In other words, though it is only by transcending the human limitation that one comes to realize human birth–death as an essential part of a wider problem, i.e., the generation–extinction problem common to all living beings, this self-transcendence is impossible apart from 'self-consciousness' on the part of human beings. Animals, *asura*, and so on, like human beings, are all undergoing transmigration, equally confined by the nature of generation–extinction. Unlike human existence, however, other living beings cannot know transmigration as transmigration. Since only a human, who has self-consciousness, can realize the nature of generation–extinction as such, for a human this becomes a 'problem' to be solved rather than a 'fact'.[8] When a 'fact' becomes a 'problem' the possibility of solving the problem is also present, i.e., the possibility to be liberated from transmigration. Because of this peculiarity of humans, Buddhism emphasizes the need for us to practise Buddhist discipline and attain enlightenment while each of us, though transmigrating endlessly through other forms of life, exists *as a human*. 'The rare state of a human' is, in Buddhism, highly regarded; one should be grateful one is born a human, for it is more difficult to be born a human than for a blind turtle to enter a hole in a log floating in an ocean. Unlike other creatures, a human is a 'thinking animal',[9] endowed with the capability of awakening to the Dharma. Here one can see the Buddhist notion of man's special position among all living beings. In this sense, Buddhism may be said to be not only dehomocentric, but homocentric as well.

Furthermore, the realization of transmigration is a personal realization for one's self (ego), not for human existence in general. Apart from one's self-realization there can be no 'problem' of birth-and-death, generation-and-extinction. Likewise, only through one's self-realization can one attain nirvana by solving the problem of generation-extinction, i.e., the problem of samsara.

Buddhism is, it must be noted, primarily concerned with the liberation of human existence. In this respect it does not differ from Christianity. Yet, what Buddhism believes to be the fundamental problem for human existence, i.e., the problem of man's birth-and-death, can be solved not through a personalistic relationship with the word of God, but, as described above, only when the very nature of generation-extinction common to all living beings is done away with. What has been said up to now about the human dimension and the living dimension and their differences may be described as below in Figure 2.1.

It should be clear then that while both Christianity and Buddhism are concerned primarily with the salvation of human existence, their *ground* for salvation differ:[10] in Christianity it is personalistic, whereas in Buddhism it is cosmological. In the former, the personal relationship between a human and God is axial, with the universe as its circumference; in the latter, personal suffering and salvation reside in the impersonal, boundless, cosmological dimension which embraces even a divine–human relationship.

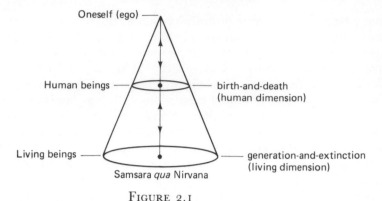

FIGURE 2.1

The Buddhist position indicates that if one attains enlightenment by freeing oneself from generation–extinction, all living beings simultaneously and in like manner are enlightened by being liberated from generation–extinction. This is simply because generation-extinction itself, common both to humans and other creatures, is thereby overcome, and the true Reality is now disclosed universally. According to a Buddhist tradition, upon his enlightenment Śākyamuni exclaimed: 'Wonderful, wonderful! How can it be that all sentient beings are endowed with the intrinsic wisdom of the *Tathāgata?*'[11] Even though one believes one has attained enlightenment, if, from that point of view, other creatures are not enlightened as well, one's enlightenment is not genuine. At the instant one realizes the Buddha-nature, the possibility of which is possessed by every person, all living beings attain their Buddha-nature. This is the meaning of the above quoted phrase from the Nirvana Sutra, 'All sentient beings have the Buddha-nature.'

III

What is Dōgen's position in relation to this traditional understanding?' Why does he reject it and why does he read the phrase from the Nirvana Sutra in his peculiar way? In contrast to the ordinary reading of the passage, 'All *living* or *sentient* beings without exception *have* the Buddha-nature', Dōgen reads it, on the basis of the peculiar twist he gives to the four Chinese characters 悉有仏性 as follows: 'All are sentient beings; all *beings are* the Buddha-nature.' According to the traditional reading, it is understood that all living beings have the Buddha-nature within themselves as the potentiality of becoming a buddha. Naturally this reading implies that, although all living beings are at this moment immersed in illusion, they can all be enlightened sometime in the future because of their potential Buddhahood. The Buddha-nature is then understood as an object which already, as a potentiality, is posessed and which is aimed at in order that it be realized by the subject (living beings). In this understanding, dichotomies of subject and object, potentiality and actuality, within and without, present and future and so on are implied. This results in a serious misunderstanding of the basic standpoint of Buddhism. The traditional understanding of the Buddha-nature not only does not represent the right Dharma of Buddhism which Dōgen mastered and confirmed in himself, but is in fact a violation of it. Thus he rejected the ordinary way of reading the passage with all the above implications, and gave a new reading, even though it meant violating grammatical rules, in order to clarify the right Buddha Dharma. As a result he renders the passage: *shitsuu wa busshō nari*, meaning 'All beings *are* the Buddha-nature.'

This involves a complete, radical reversal of the relation of Buddha-nature to living beings (see Figure 2.2.).

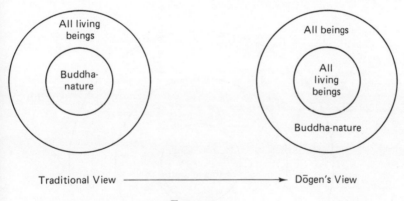

Traditional View ⟶ Dōgen's View

FIGURE 2.2

For, in this understanding of Dōgen, the Buddha-nature is not a potentiality, like a seed, which exists within all living beings. Instead, all living beings, or more exactly, all beings, living and nonliving, *are* originally Buddha-nature. It is not a potentiality to be actualized sometime in the future, but the original, fundamental nature of all beings. In order to elucidate these two different understandings of the Buddha-nature and to clarify Dōgen's unique position, the following four points must be carefully observed: first, the dehomocentric nature of Buddhism; second, the nonsubstantial character of the Buddha-nature; third, the non-duality of 'all beings' and the 'Buddha-nature'; fourth, the dynamic idea of 'impermanence–Buddha-nature.'

1   *The dehomocentric nature of Buddhism*

As stated earlier, in Buddhism the problem of birth-and-death, the fundamental problem of human existence, is not only treated as a birth–death (*shōji*) problem merely within the 'human' dimension, but as a generation-extinction (*shōmetsu*) problem within the total 'living' dimension. It is in this dehomocentric, living dimension that the Buddhist idea of transmigration (samsara) and emancipation from it (nirvana) are understood. By emphasizing 'All beings are the Buddha-nature', Dōgen carries the dehomocentrism of Buddhism to its extreme by going beyond even the 'living' dimension. 'All beings' needless to say, includes living as well as non-living beings.

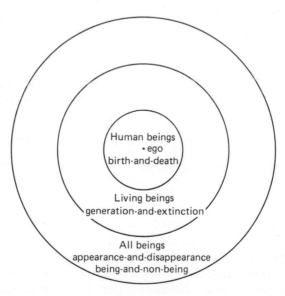

Human beings
• ego
birth-and-death

Living beings
generation-and-extinction

All beings
appearance-and-disappearance
being-and-non-being

FIGURE 2.3

For Dōgen, the dimension of all beings is no longer that of generation–extinction, but that of appearance–disappearance (*kimetsu*) or being–non-being (*umu*). The term 'generation–extinction' is here used to indicate biological producing and dying out, whereas the term 'appearance–disappearance' signifies coming to be and ceasing to be and refers to both living and non-living beings. Thus it is used synonymously with 'being–non-being' (see Figure 2.3). The 'living' dimension, though transhomocentric, has a life-centered nature that excludes non-living beings. The 'being' dimension, however, embraces everything in the universe, by transcending even the wider-than-human 'life-centred' horizon. Accordingly the 'being' dimension is truly boundless, free from any sort of centrism, and deepest precisely in its dehomocentric nature. If we add the 'being' dimension to Figure 2.1, we come to have Figure 2.4 which in turn is a three-dimensional representation of Figure 2.3.

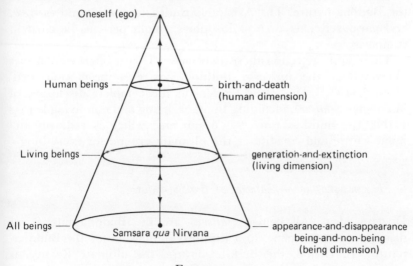

FIGURE 2.4

When Dōgen emphasizes 'all beings' in connection with the Buddha-nature, he definitely implies that a human being can be properly and completely emancipated from samsara, i.e., the recurring cycle of birth-and-death, not in the 'living' dimension, but in the 'being' dimension. In other words, it is not by overcoming generation–extinction common to all living beings, but only by doing away with appearance–disappearance, or being–non-being common to all beings, that the human birth–death problem can be completely solved. Dōgen finds the *basis* for human liberation in a thoroughly cosmological dimension. Here Dōgen reveals a most radical Buddhist dehomocentrism.

Accordingly, one may readily understand why Dōgen refuses the ideas of permanent ego or *ātman*, and of organicism. In the 'Buddha-nature' fascicle of *Shōbōgenzō* Dōgen severely attacks the Senika heresy,[12] as not representing the genuine Buddhist standpoint. That heresy emphasizes the immutability of *ātman* or selfhood and the perishability of the body, a view whose Western equivalent may be the Platonic immortality of the soul or the Cartesian thinking ego. In the same fascicle he also refutes as false the view of those who think 'the Buddha-nature is like the seeds of grasses and trees. When it is well wetted and nourished by the Dharma rain, it may bud and shoot out branches, leaves, and fruit themselves swelled with seeds.'[13] This is a teleological or organicistic view of the Buddha-nature. The Aristotelian idea of *dynamis* and *energeia*, and various Renaissance philosophies, might perhaps be cited in comparison.

Thoroughly rejecting these two views, Dōgen often emphasizes 'Throughout the universe nothing has ever been concealed' (*henkaifusōzō*).[14] This clearly refers to the complete disclosure of 'all beings' (*shitsuu*), including humans, living and non-living beings within the limitless universe, a universe which is radically dehomocentric and constitutes the ultimate ground for everything.

2   *The non-substantial character of Buddha-nature.*

Dōgen's idea, 'All beings (*shitsuu*) are the Buddha-nature', as discussed above, opens up a limitless dimension for the Buddha-nature. In Dōgen, the Buddha-nature, the ultimate Reality, is realized precisely in this infinite and ontological dimension in which all beings can exist respectively as they are. This idea of the Buddha-nature may suggest Spinoza's idea of God as Substance which is also called 'nature' and which is absolutely infinite, with finite beings as His 'modes'. However, despite apparent similarities between them, Dōgen's idea of the Buddha-nature is radically different from Spinoza's idea of God precisely because Dōgen's Buddha-nature is not a substance.

In the 'Buddha-nature' fascicle Dōgen says, 'What is the essence of the World Honored One's (Śākyamuni) words "Everything is a living being: all beings are the Buddha-nature"? They are a verbal preaching of "What is it that thus comes?"'[15] The question 'What is it that thus comes?' is found in the conversation that took place at the first meeting between the sixth Patriarch Hui-nêng (Ja: Enō, 638–713) and Nan-yüeh Huai-jang (Ja: Nangaku Ejō, 677–744), as recorded in the *Ching-tê ch'uan-têng lu*, vol. 5.

The Patriarch asked: "Whence do you come?"
"I come from Tung-shan."
"What is it that thus comes?"
Nan-yüeh did not know what to answer. For eight long years he pondered the question, then one day it dawned upon him, and he exclaimed.
"Even to say it is something does not hit the mark."

The question, '*What* is it that *thus* (*immo ni*) comes?' (*kore shimobutsu immorai*)[16] that Huai-jang took eight years to solve refers to the Buddhist Truth, and in Dōgen's present case, to the essential point of the words, 'All beings are the Buddha-nature.' Even the first question '*Whence* do you come?' is not an ordinary question. Zen often indicates the ultimate Reality by interrogatives as well as by negatives such as 'nothingness' and 'emptiness'. An interrogative 'what' or 'whence' is that which cannot be grasped by the hand, that which cannot be defined by the intellect; it is that which can never be objectified, that which one can never obtain, no matter what one does. Indeed, 'what' or 'whence' is unknowable, unnamable, unobjectifiable, unobtainable, and therefore limitless and infinite. Since the Buddha-nature is limitless and boundless, without name, form or colour, it can be well, indeed best, expressed by such an interrogative. This is the reason Dōgen finds the essence of his idea 'All beings are the Buddha-nature' precisely in the question '*What* is it that thus comes?'
This does not, however, mean that for Dōgen Buddha-nature is *something* unnamable, and unobtainable, *something* limitless and boundless. If the Buddha-nature were *something* unnamable it would not be truly unnamable because it is something *named* 'unnamable'. If the Buddha-nature were *something* limitless it would not be really limitless because it is *limited* by or distinguished from something limited. Therefore, for Dōgen the Buddha-nature is not *something*

unnamable, but *the unnamable*. Yet, at the same time *the unnamable is the Buddha-nature*. The Buddha-nature is not *something* limitless, but *the limitless*, yet at the same time *the limitless is the Buddha-nature*.[17] This simply means that for him the Buddha-nature is *not 'something'* *at all*, even in a negative sense such as something unnamable, something limitless, and so forth. In other words it is *not substantial* at all. Accordingly, an interrogative such as 'what' or 'whence' does not *represent* the Buddha-nature. If it did, then the Buddha-nature would have to be *something* existing *behind* this 'what', and being *represented* by 'what'. Since the Buddha-nature is not substance, 'what' is immediately the Buddha-nature and the Buddha-nature is immediately 'what'.

This being so, the question 'What is it that thus comes?' is totally a question, and the word 'what' is also thoroughly an interrogative. Yet, at the same time 'what' is not a sheer interrogative, but is the Buddha-nature. Again 'What-is-it-that-thus-comes' is not a mere question, but is a realization of the Buddha-nature.

Spinoza's idea of God as Substance is of course not something. Since in Spinoza God is the Substance of so-called substances, He is really infinite and the one necessary being. However Spinoza's idea of God as Substance – though it might be called 'what' from the side of relative substances and finite beings – cannot *in itself* be properly called 'what' because 'Substance' is, according to Spinoza's definition, that which is in itself and is *conceived* through itself; it can be *conceived* independently of the conception of anything else.[18] In other words, for Spinoza God may be said to be 'what' when it is viewed from the outside, from the side of relative substances and finite beings, but it is not that 'what' is God. This is precisely because in Spinoza God is Substance which is conceived through itself.

The difference between Dōgen's idea of the Buddha-nature and Spinoza's idea of God as Substance may be clearer if we take into account their relations to things in the universe. In Spinoza the One God has, in so far as we know, two 'attributes', thought (*cogitatio*) and extension (*extensio*); particular and finite things are called the 'modes' of God, which depend upon, and are conditioned by, the divine and infinite being. This clearly shows the monistic character of Spinoza's idea of God from which everything else is derived and by which everything else is conceived. Yet, the very ideas of 'attribute' and 'mode' involve a duality between God and the World, in Spinoza's terminology, between *natura naturans* (the active nature) and *natura naturata* (the passive nature), a duality in which the former has priority. In sharp contrast to this, Dōgen's Buddha-nature is not *natura naturans* which is distinguished from *natura naturata*, i.e., the created world. Accordingly, particular things in the universe are not 'modes' of Buddha-nature. Nor is there any exact equivalent to Spinoza's idea of 'attribute' in Dōgen's idea of Buddha-nature because the idea of 'attribute' is meaningless in a non-substantial Buddha-nature.

Then, what significance do particular things and particular qualities have for the Buddha-nature? Since the Buddha-nature is non-substantial, no particular thing or particular quality in the universe corresponds to, or is represented by, Buddha-nature. In terms of mode and attribute, for Dōgen each particular thing is a mode of 'what'; each particular quality is an attribute of 'what'. A pine tree, for instance, is not a mode of God as Substance, but a mode of 'what', namely a mode without modifier. Therefore, a pine tree is really a pine tree in itself, no more or less. This refers to the pine tree's *'thus* comes' in the above 'What-is-it-that-thus-comes'. Again, thought is not an attribute of God as Substance, but an attribute of 'what', an attribute not attributed to anything. Accordingly, thought is just thought in itself, no more no less. This again refers to the thought's *'thus* comes'.

When the sixth Partiarch asked Huai-jang *'What* is it that *thus* comes?' the question directly pointed to Huai-jang himself as an independent and individualized personality that will not allow surrogation. Huai-jang is not a creature determined by God as Substance. He may be said to be something coming from 'what', something determined without determinator. Determination without determinator is self-determination, freedom, and selfhood, which are but different terms for the Buddha-nature. If Huai-jang had realized himself as that which *'thus* comes' from 'what', he would have realized his Buddha-nature. It took Huai-jang eight years to solve this question and say, 'Even to say it is *something* does not hit the mark!'

Huai-jang in himself is 'What-is-it-that-thus-comes.' However this is not the case only for him. You and I as well are precisely 'What-is-it-that-thus-comes.' Trees and grasses, heaven and earth, are equally 'What-is-it-that-thus-comes.' *Cogitatio* and *extensio*, mind and body, are respectively 'What-is-it-that-thus-comes.' Everything without exception in the universe is 'What-is-it-that-thus-comes.' This is precisely the meaning of Dōgen's 'All beings *are* the Buddha-nature.' It is for this reason that Dōgen recognized in the sixth Patriarch's question 'What is it that thus comes?' the essence of his idea, 'All beings are the Buddha-nature.'

Like Dōgen's idea of the Buddha-nature, Spinoza's idea of God is eternally infinite, absolutely self-sufficient, self-determining, and self-dependent. However, for Spinoza, the monist par excellence, the relationship between the One Substance and the multiplicity of finite beings is understood *deductively*. In marked contrast to this, in Dōgen the relationship between Buddha-nature and all finite beings is not deductive, but *non-dualistic*, precisely because the Buddha-nature is *not* One Substance. All beings without exception are *equally* and *respectively* 'What-is-it-that-thus-comes.' Even God as the One Substance in Spinoza's sense cannot be an exception to this. In other words, from Dōgen's point of view, God as the One Substance is, prior to being designated as such, 'What-is-it-that-*thus*-comes.' Thus there can be no difference, no deductive relation, between God and finite beings in the universe. This all-embracing, even-God-or-Substance-embracing, 'What-is-it-that-thus-comes' in itself is the Buddha-nature in the sense of Dōgen's words, 'All beings are the Buddha-nature.'

Accordingly, in Dōgen the Buddha-nature is neither transcendent nor immanent. One of the characteristics of Spinoza's philosophy lies in the immanent character of his idea of God – *Deus sive natura* (God or nature). Spinoza rejected the orthodox theological doctrine of a transcendent personal God who creates and rules the world with will and purpose. He emphasized God as the infinite cause of the necessary origination of all entities. In this sense, Spinoza's position is much closer to Buddhism in general, and to Dōgen in particular, than is that of orthodox Christianity. However, as Richard Kroner points out in speaking of Spinoza, 'All individuality is finally swallowed up by the universality of the One God who alone truly Is.'[19] This may be the reason Spinoza's system is called pantheism. In Dōgen, however, the statement 'All beings are the Buddha-nature' does not indicate that all beings are *swallowed up* by the Buddha-nature. Instead, as he stresses 'Throughout the universe nothing has ever been concealed', every particular thing in the universe manifests itself in its individuality simply because the Buddha-nature is not a substance, but a 'what'. For Dōgen, all beings are 'swallowed up' *bottomlessly* by the Buddha-nature; yet at the same time the Buddha-nature is also 'swallowed up' *bottomlessly* by all beings. This is because all beings (*shitsuu*) and the Buddha-nature are non-dualistic and therefore the Buddha-nature is neither immanent nor transcendent (or both immanent and transcendent). Thus, despite frequent misunderstanding to the contrary, one may readily notice that Dōgen is not a pantheist, however pantheistic his words may appear at first glance. Indeed, he is as unpantheistic as he is non-theistic.

IV

3 *Non-duality of 'all beings'* (shitsuu) *and the 'Buddha-nature'*

With the idea 'All beings are the Buddha-nature', Dōgen carries the dehomocentric nature of Buddhism to its ultimate end by transcending the dimension of generation–extinction (traditionally considered the realm of human transmigration and the basis for liberation from it) to the dimension of appearance–disappearance, or the dimension of being–non-being that is common to all beings, living or nonliving. Again, for Dōgen, only on this infinite, ontological basis common to all beings can the human problem of birth-and-death be resolved.

In other words, for Dōgen, the human problem of birth-and-death can be properly and completely resolved and the Buddha-nature fully realized only by moving to and then breaking through this infinite dimension of being–non-being. But 'breaking through' does not imply a mere transcendence or 'going beyond' the dimension of 'all beings' (being–non-being). Even this transcendence must be negated. Thus the 'going beyond' the dimension of 'all beings' is simultaneously a 'return to' that very dimension, so that all beings (*shitsuu*) are truly realized as all beings (*shitsuu*).

However, Dōgen's is not different from the traditional interpretation in the respect that only through human self-consciousness is one's radical transcendence to the dimension of being–non-being possible. For the human problem of birth-and-death is essentially a Subjective problem with which each person must individually and consciously cope. Buddhist dehomocentrism, in Dōgen's case as well, is connected inseparably with its emphasis on one's self (ego) as the subject of self-consciousness. Dōgen insists that, to attain the Buddha-nature, one must transcend one's ego-centrism, homocentrism, and living being-centrism, and thereby ground one's existence in the most fundamental plane, that is, in the 'being' dimension, which is the dimension of Dōgen's *shitsuu*, i.e., 'all beings'. The realization of impermanence of *shitsuu* is absolutely necessary for the attainment of the Buddha-nature.

Accordingly, if one attains the Buddha-nature in oneself by basing one's existence in the all-embracing 'being' dimension, and by then freeing oneself from the being–non-being nature (impermanence) common to all beings, then everything in the universe attains the Buddha-nature as well. For at the very moment of one's enlightenment the being–non-being nature itself is overcome. It is for this reason Buddhist sutras often say, 'Grasses, trees, and lands, all attain Buddhahood', 'Mountains, rivers, and the earth totally manifest the *Dharma-kāya* (Dharma body).' These passages taken objectively without one's own existential awakening seem absurd, at best pantheistic. Dōgen emphasizes *dōjijōdō*,[20] 'simultaneous attainment of the Way', which refers to the fact that everything in the universe attains enlightenment simultaneously at the moment of one's own enlightenment – an enlightenment that opens up the universal horizon of the Buddha-nature. If one cannot rightfully speak of the attainment of Buddha-nature by mountains, rivers, lands and the like, one cannot be said to have realized the Buddha-nature.

This is a crucial point for a thorough realization of the Buddha-nature through emancipation from samsara. Although always latent in Mahayana tradition, this point was clearly realized and explicitly expressed in Dōgen's 'All beings *are* the Buddha-nature.' More important in this connection, however, is that, unlike the dimensions of human beings and living beings, the dimension of *all beings* (*shitsuu*), which Dōgen takes as the basis for the Buddha-nature, is *limitless*. There is no 'centrism' of any sort at all in this dimension. Further, the Buddha-nature which is realized by freeing oneself from the being–non-being nature common to all beings is *non-substantial*. Therefore, even if Dōgen emphasizes 'All beings are the Buddha-nature', he does not mean by this an 'immediate' identity between all beings and the Buddha-nature; rather the identity is established only through the realization of *limitlessness* of the 'being' dimension and the *non-substantiality* of the Buddha-nature – in short, only through the realization of 'What'. This means a complete turnover of the immanent view of the Buddha-nature, which Dōgen doubly denies; first, by transcending the 'living' dimension to the 'being' dimension he denies the immanence of the Buddha-nature within living beings; secondly, by emphasizing the nonsubstantiality of the Buddha-nature he denies its immanence as the one cause of the world, i.e., like Spinoza's idea of God. This double negation of the immanent view of the Buddha-nature brings about a radical reversal in the traditional interpretation of the Buddha-nature. It is the inevitable conclusion to the idea of the Buddha-nature latent in Mahayana tradition, not just a mere explication of its implicit elements. This results in the non-duality of all beings and the Buddha-nature, a Buddha-nature that is neither immanent nor transcendent. '*The Buddha-nature is assuredly all beings*, because all beings are the Buddha-nature',[21] says Dōgen.

To avoid the natural human tendency to objectify and to substantialize everything, and to make clear the nonduality of 'all beings' and the 'Buddha-nature', Dōgen emphasizes two things: (1) the idea of *mubusshō*[22] 'no-Buddha-nature' to indicate the nonsubstantiality of the Buddha-nature, and (2) the bottomlessness of 'all beings' to deny their being objectified.

(1) In the 'Buddha-nature' fascicle, Dōgen often emphasizes the idea of *mubusshō*, no-Buddha-nature, by quoting and reinterpreting various words and conversations of old Zen masters. In one such case he quotes the remark of Kuci-shan Ling-yu (Ja: Isan Reiyū, 771–853), 'All living beings have no-Buddha-nature' and says:

> Śākyamuni preached "All living beings without exception have the Buddha-nature." Kuei-shan preached, "All living beings have no-Buddha-nature." "Having," "not having" are completely different in verbal meaning. People must have doubts as to which grasps the essence. In spite of this, only "All living beings have no-Buddha-nature" excels in the Buddha Way.[23]

In Dōgen the idea of 'no-Buddha-nature' is not understood as peculiar to Kuei-shan alone. 'The Way of no-Buddha-nature' Dōgen says, 'has been taught since long before, from the inner sanctuary of the fourth Patriarch. It was seen and heard by the fifth Patriarch Hung-jên, transmitted in Chao-chou and advocated by Kuei-shan. The way of no-Buddha-nature must be practised. Do not hesitate.'[24] Those who remember Dōgen's emphasis that 'All beings are the Buddha-nature' may be surprised by these words. Dōgen's comment on Kuei-shan's words is also striking.

> The reason in Kuei-shan's words is the reason of "All beings have no-Buddha-nature." He does not speak of vastness beyond rules and regulations. The sutras within one's own house are thus

preserved. One should grope further as to why all living beings are the Buddha-nature, why they have the Buddha-nature. If they have the Buddha-nature they must be confederates of the devil. They bring a devil to add to all living beings.[25]

This is a complete negation of the traditional doctrine which maintains that the Buddha-nature is possessed by living beings. If we penetrate Dōgen's standpoint, however, these words are not merely surprising, but have deep meaning. Dōgen's idea of 'no-Buddha-nature' does not indicate the absence of 'Buddha-nature', but 'no-Buddha-nature' in its *absolute* sense which is free from both 'Buddha-nature' and 'no-Buddha-nature'. Here we find another example of Dōgen's peculiar way of reading traditional texts. In the same fascicle he quotes the following conversation between the fifth Patriarch Hung-jên and Hui-nêng, later the sixth Patriarch, at their first meeting:

"Where are you from?"
"I am from Reinan [in the southern part of China, then considered uncivilized]."
"What did you come for?"
"To become a buddha."
"嶺南人無仏性, *Reinanjin mubusshō* (people from Reinan have no Buddha-nature). How could you become a buddha?"
"Although there is for people north and south, there is no north and south for the Buddha-nature."[26]

Commenting on this conversation, Dōgen dares to say:

This "*Reinanjin mubusshō*" does not mean "people from Reinan have no Buddha-nature," or "people from Reinan have a Buddha-nature," but "people from Reinan, no-Buddha-nature." "How could you become a buddha?" indicates "What buddha is it you expect to become?"[27]

Traditionally, the term *mubusshō* meant living beings have no Buddha-nature within themselves. However, Dōgen is not concerned with *having or not having* the Buddha-nature but with the *Buddha-nature in itself* which is non-substantial. When we concern ourselves with having or not-having the Buddha-nature we thereby objectify it in a positive or a negative way. Since the Buddha-nature is an unobjectifiable and unobtainable 'What', it is entirely wrong to talk objectively about whether or not one *has* the Buddha-nature. With Hung-jên, Dōgen emphasizes: 'Since the Buddha-nature is empty it is called *mu* (no-thing)'.[28]

He also stresses 'The principle of the Buddha-nature is that it is not endowed prior to enlightenment; it is endowed after enlightenment; the Buddha-nature is unquestionably realized simultaneously with enlightenment. This principle should be penetrated in most assiduous, concentrated effort, even for twenty or thirty years.'[29]

If one realizes that living beings are fundamentally the Buddha-nature, there is no need to emphasize 'having the Buddha-nature'. It suffices simply to say that living beings are living beings. To say living beings have the Buddha-nature is like adding legs to a snake, which is the reason Dōgen says 'Why are all living beings the Buddha-nature? Why do they have the Buddha-nature? If they have the Buddha-nature they must be confederates of the devil. They bring a devil to add to all living beings.' Continuing, Dōgen says, 'While the Buddha-nature is the Buddha-nature, living beings are living beings'[30] – a definite statement referring to his idea of 'no-Buddha-nature'. The Buddha-nature is absolutely the Buddha-nature and living beings are absolutely living beings. Yet, in this realization, the Buddha-nature and living beings are not two different things, but simply two aspects of one and the same living reality. Practically speaking, the Buddha-nature is realized as such simultaneously with enlightenment. It is a dellusion to think that the Buddha-nature is or is not endowed in living beings apart from enlightenment. This is why, against the ordinary reading, Dōgen reads *Reinanjin mubusshō* as 'people from Reinan, no-Buddha-nature', meaning that those people in themselves are freed from dichotomous thoughts as to whether or not they have the Buddha-nature. This freedom, no-Buddha-nature itself, is the genuine realization of Buddha-nature.[31] Hence Dōgen emphasizes that both a preaching of having the Buddha-nature and a preaching of having no Buddha-nature involve defamation of Buddhism. Dōgen's idea of 'no-Buddha-nature' clearly indicates the non-substantiality of the Buddha-nature by rejecting both the 'eternalist' view which substantializes and is attached to the idea of the Buddha-nature, and the 'nihilistic' view which also substantializes and is attached to the idea of no Buddha-nature.

(2) For Dōgen, just as the Buddha-nature is non-substantial, 'all beings' (*shitsuu*) are unobjectifiable, limitless and groundless.

As stated earlier, Dōgen emphasizes 'All beings (*shitsuu*) are the

Buddha-nature' by changing the ordinary reading of the passage in the Nirvana Sutra which had been traditionally read as 'All living beings (*shujō*) without exception have the Buddha-nature.' In this case Dōgen broadens not only the meaning of the term 'Buddha-nature', but also that of the term 'living beings' (*shujō*). In the 'Buddha-nature' fascicle, immediately after saying, 'All beings are the Buddha-nature', he continues, 'All beings in their entirety are called *shujō*. Just at the right moment, living beings (*shujō*) both inside and outside are all beings (*shitsuu*) of the Buddha-nature.'[32] This means that Dōgen broadens the meaning of *shujō*, which traditionally referred to living or sentient beings, to include non-living beings or non-sentient beings. In other words, he ascribed life to non-living beings, sentiments to non-sentient beings, and ultimately mind and the Buddha-nature to all of them. Thus he states:

> In what is called in the Buddha Way all living beings (*shujō*), all beings that have mind are *shujō*, because mind is *shujō*; all beings that have no mind must equally be *shujō* because *shujō* is mind. Therefore, all mind is *shujō*; all *shujō* is 'having the Buddha-nature.' Grasses, trees, and lands are mind; being mind, they are *shujō*; being *shujō*, they have the Buddha-nature. Sun, moon, and stars are mind; being mind, they are *shujō*; being *shujō*, they have the Buddha-nature.[33]

Thus we see that for Dōgen, living beings (*shujō*), all beings (*shitsuu*), mind, and the Buddha-nature are ultimately identical.

However strongly Dōgen emphasizes the idea 'All beings are the Buddha-nature' the concept of 'all beings' (*shitsuu*) is not a counter-concept to nonbeing. It is 'all beings' in its absolute sense which is beyond and freed from the opposition between being and nonbeing. This is clearly shown in the following:

> Beings one and all now brought into existence by the Buddha-nature are not 'being' of being-non-being.... The term "all beings" (*shitsuu*) is furthermore not a being that has a beginning (*shiu*), or original Being (*honnu*), or mysterious being (*myōu*), or the like; and it is of course not conditioned being (*en-u*) or illusory being (*mōu*). It has nothing to do with mind-and-object, substance-and-form, etc.[34]

It is noteworthy to point out that in this passage Dōgen insists that 'all beings' (*shitsuu*) does not mean 'original Being', such as might be interpreted as an equivalent to the Heideggerian 'Sein'. Such a comparison between 'original Being' and Heidegger's notion of 'Sein' is instructive because the original Being is that which discloses itself as the place in which beings exist. Heidegger establishes *ontologische Differenz* (ontological difference) which essentially differs from *ontische Differenz* (ontic difference: that which merely distinguishes one being from another). By establishing ontological difference Heidegger thematically questions the meaning of *Sein* (Being), the idea of which is latent in the everyday experience of various beings (*Seiendes*). He thereby constructs *Fundamental-Ontologie* in order to elucidate the significance of *Sein des Seienden* (Being of beings) that is concealed in everyday understanding. In contrast to this, Dōgen does not make an ontological difference, not because he is unaware of the essential difference between Being and beings, but simply because he deliberately denies the idea of *Sein*, which is apt to be considered as something substantial, as ontologically distinguished from *Seiendes*. Hence his emphasis on the idea of 'no-Buddha-nature'.

A question however must remain here. Why, in Dōgen, is *shitsuu* or 'all beings' referred to in the plural form while *shitsuu* is said to be identical with the Buddha-nature? If 'all beings' is not *Sein* in the Heideggerian sense, is not then 'all beings' the ground of *Weltanschuung* in which everything including God, nature, humans, life, and so on, is systematically grasped? Definitely not, as Dōgen's previously quoted words on 'all beings' clearly show. Then what are 'all beings' (*shitsuu*)? Beings (*Seiendes*) are, needless to say, not Being (*Sein*), and vice versa. All beings are, however, just all beings, no more, no less; *nothing* is outside of them. For all beings, there is no possibility even for ontological difference. All beings are really and absolutely all beings – through the mediation of *nothing*. This is precisely the meaning of 'All beings are the Buddha-nature.'

In Heidegger as well nothingness is essential in his quest for Being. *Sein selbst* (Being itself) or *Sein als solches* (Being as such), we are told, must be held down into nothingness; it must appear as nothing, in order to be.[35] In Dōgen, however, it is the *Seiendes als solches* (beings as such) which must appear as nothing in order to be. This is because the dimension of 'all beings' (*shitsuu*) is limitless and bottomless without a further embracing, deeper dimension, without the ultimate ground, even in the Heideggerian sense of *Sein als solches*, or in the traditional Buddhist sense of the Buddha-nature, from which all beings come to be present (*anwesen*).

This may be clearer when we take into account Dōgen's remarks on the term 'thus' (*immo*) which appears in the words 'What-is-it-that-*thus*-comes', words which Dōgen takes as an adequate expression of the Buddha-nature. In the *Immo* book of *Shōbōgenzō*, based on Huai-jang's words, Dōgen emphasizes that *immo* is unobtainable, not-*immo* is unobtainable, both *immo* and not-*immo* are unobtainable. This clearly shows that in the words 'What-is-it-that-thus-comes' 'thus' (*immo*) is not simply affirmative. Rather it is neither affirmative nor negative. The genuine 'thus' is the kind of 'thus' freed from both affirmation and negation. Accordingly, when Dōgen says the essence of 'All beings are the Buddha-nature' is well expressed in the words 'What-is-it-that-thus-comes', all beings appear in this sense of 'thus'. And the very fact that all beings 'thus' appear from 'What' indicates 'All beings are the Buddha-nature'. Zen's household expressions: 'Willows are green; flowers are red,' 'Mountains are really mountains; waters are really waters', simply indicate this. We may fully concur: 'I am really I: you are really you'. Yet, at this very moment – all beings are the Buddha-nature. *Seiendes als solches* 'thus' come to be present (*anwesen*) from 'What'. Only when the Heideggerian idea of ontological difference is overcome can Dōgen's idea of '*All beings* are the Buddha-nature' be truly understood.

V

4   *The dynamic idea of 'impermanence–Buddha-nature'*

I have stated that Dōgen on the one hand insists 'All beings are the Buddha-nature', and on the other emphasizes 'no-Buddha-nature'. This he did to reject the common view that objectifies and substantializes 'all beings' and the 'Buddha-nature', and to clarify their nondualistic and dynamic oneness. Dōgen's characteristic idea of 'no-Buddha-nature' (*mubusshō*) already serves this purpose as it denies both the eternalist view and the nihilistic view of the Buddha-nature. To make, however, definitely clear the nondualistic and dynamic oneness of 'all beings' and the 'Buddha-nature', Dōgen goes further by saying '*mujō* (impermanence) is the Buddha-nature'.

In Hegel the contradistinction of Being and Nothing sets the dialectic in motion, and the unity of Being and Nothing is Becoming (*Werden*). In Dōgen *mujō-busshō* (impermanence–Buddha-nature) is the unity of Buddha-nature and no-Buddha-nature. *Mujō* (*anitya* in

Sanskrit: impermanence, mutability, transiency) has been one of the key concepts of Buddhism from its very beginning, one of the three basic Buddhist principles or Dharma seals[36] – 'Whatever is phenomenal is impermanent.' In Buddhism the impermanence or mutability of phenomena had been emphasized in contrast with permanence or immutability of the Buddha-nature or the Tathāgata (Buddha). Dōgen however insists that impermanence is the Buddha-nature. He makes the following remark concerning Hui-nêng:

> The sixth Patriarch taught his disciple Hsing-ch'ang (Ja: Gyōshō) that impermanence in itself is the Buddha-nature, that permanence is good and evil, each and every phenomenal thing, and discriminating mind.[37]

This again may sound surprising to the ear of one who holds to a stereotyped understanding of Buddhism, according to which the task of Buddhism is to emancipate oneself from impermanence or samsara and to enter nirvana by realizing the Buddha-nature. However, if nirvana is sought for simply *beyond* impermanence it is not true nirvana because it stands against impermanence and thereby is still related to and limited by impermanence. The true nirvana is attained only by emancipating oneself even from nirvana as transcendence of impermanence. In other words, it is realized by a complete return from nirvana to the world of impermanence through liberating oneself from both impermanence and permanence, from both samsara so-called and nirvana so-called. Therefore genuine nirvana is nothing but realization of impermanence as impermanence. If one remains in 'nirvana' by transcending samsara one must be said to be still selfish because that person loftily abides in his or her own 'enlightenment' apart from the sufferings of other samsara-bound sentient beings. True compassion can be realized only by transcending 'nirvana' to return to and work in the midst of the sufferings of the ever-changing world. This is the characteristic realization of Mahayana Buddhism, which emphasizes 'Do not abide in samsara or nirvana.' This complete no-abiding is the true nirvana in the Mahayanist sense. Hui-nêng's words quoted above are one Zen expression of this idea.

When Dōgen quotes Hui-nêng to the effect that '*mujō* (impermanence) in itself is the Buddha-nature' he carries the Mahayanist standpoint to its ultimate end. As stated before, by stressing 'All beings are the Buddha-nature' Dōgen goes beyond the dimension of living beings to that of beings, and makes explicit the implication of Mahayana Buddhism that even non-living, non-sentient beings can attain Buddhahood. As discussed earlier, the dimension of beings is that of appearance–disappearance or being–non-being. This dimension, embracing all beings, sentient and nonsentient, may be said to be the most thoroughgoing dimension of *mujō* (impermanence). In other words, it is only in Dōgen's emphasized dimension of 'all beings' that the time-honoured Buddhist idea of *mujō* is fully and completely realized because not only living beings but also all beings, living and non-living, are without exception impermanent. It is precisely through the realization of impermanence in this sense that one can properly state of one's own enlightenment that grasses, trees, and lands disclose the Buddha-nature.

Not only that, by emphasizing 'All beings are the Buddha-nature', Dōgen radically turned over the traditional view of the Buddha-nature. The dimension of 'all beings' is limitless and bottomless to such an extent that it cannot properly be called a measurable dimension. For Dōgen, who grounded his own existence in this dimensionless–dimension of all beings, there is a mutual interpenetration between the 'Buddha-nature' and 'all beings': the Buddha-nature is neither immanent nor transcendent in relation to all beings (see Figure 2.5).

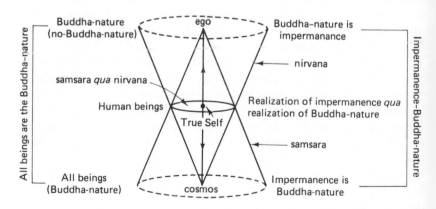

FIGURE 2.5 The dynamic and non-dualistic structure of 'All beings are the Buddha-nature' or 'impermanence–Buddha-nature'.

Figure 2.5 is a further and final development of Figures 2.1 and 2.4. Figures 2.1 and 2.4 were each cones. Figure 2.5 shows the crossing or intersection of two opposing cones. The cone which stands upright with 'all beings' or 'cosmos' as its bottom and with 'ego' as its top indicates the realm of samsara. On the other hand, the inverted cone with 'Buddha-nature' as its base signifies the realm of nirvana.

The intersection of these two opposing cones, i.e., the realms of samsara and nirvana, indicates the complete mutual interpenetration between the 'Buddha-nature' and 'all beings', and the dynamic oneness of the 'Buddha-nature' and 'impermanence'. This mutual interpenetration and dynamic oneness are possible because the Buddha-nature is non-substantial (and thus no-Buddha-nature) and because all beings are limitless and boundless. The non-substantial character of the Buddha-nature and limitlessness of all beings (which is described above as the 'dimensionless-dimension of all beings') are here in Figure 2.5 indicated by the circles in dotted lines as the bases of the two cones. Since the bases of the two cones are non-substantial and limitless – or, as it were, bottomless, these two opposing cones can be freely overturned so that neither cone is fixed to either the upright or the inverted position. This 'turning over' from samsara to nirvana, from nirvana to samsara, as well as the realization of the dynamic oneness of the Buddha-nature and all beings, or the Buddha-nature and impermanence, are possible only through human beings, specifically through a person who attains his or her true Self by awakening to the realization of impermanence *qua* the realization of Buddha-nature. In Figure 2.5 this crucial fact is represented by the middle circle at the intersection of the two cones. The figure especially attempts to show the true Self as the pivotal point of the dynamism of samsara and nirvana, the realization of impermanence qua the realization of Buddha-nature.

Restated in connection with the idea of impermanence, when Dōgen reaches the dimension of 'all beings', impermanence common to all beings is thoroughly realized *as impermanence*, no more, no less. Apart from this thorough realization of impermanence there is no realization of Buddha-nature. However, in this very realization that underlies Mahayana Buddhism, Dōgen achieves a complete and radical reversal, a reversal from the realization of 'impermanence itself is the Buddha-nature' to the realization of 'the Buddha-nature in itself is impermanence'. His idea of *mujō-busshō*, i.e., 'impermanence–Buddha-nature', is the outcome of this reversal. It can also be seen in the following passage in which he develops the words of the sixth Patriarch:

The very impermanence of grasses, trees, bushes, and forests is the Buddha-nature; the very impermanence of people, things, body, mind is the Buddha-nature; states, lands, mountains, rivers are impermanent, because they are the Buddha-nature. The supreme and complete enlightenment is impermanent because it is the Buddha-nature. Great nirvana is the Buddha-nature because it is impermanent. Those holding various narrow views of the two vehicles [the hearer and the self-enlightened], Buddhist scholars of the scriptures and commentaries and the like may be suspicious of, surprised and frightened by these words of the sixth Patriarch. If they are they are a confederation of devil-heretics.[38]

For Dōgen, impermanence itself is preaching impermanence, practising impermanence, and realizing impermanence, and this, as it is, is preaching, practising, and realizing the Buddha-nature.

Spinoza looked at everything under the aspect of eternity (*sub specie aeternitātis*). In marked contrast, Dōgen looked at everything under the aspect of impermanence. In Spinoza, time seems to be effaced or conquered by the one Substance. Transiency is surpassed by the perfect stability of truth in its ultimate sense. But for Dōgen transiency is indispensable; apart from it there is no such thing as eternal substance. Time is realized as 'being' which is beyond both continuity and discontinuity. As discussed below, for Dōgen time as being is neither continuity nor discontinuity. Rejecting the eternalist view Dōgen states:

To learn, in speaking of essential nature, there is no flowing for water and no growth and perishing for trees, is to learn heresy. Śākyamuni Buddha said "Such is form; such is essential nature." Accordingly, flowers opening, leaves falling in themselves are suchness of their essential nature. Nevertheless fools think there can be no flower opening, no leaf falling, in the realm of true Reality.[39]

In emphasizing change and motion Dōgen is more akin to Hegel than Spinoza. As 'Becoming' in Hegel is the unity of Being and Nothing, '*mujō-busshō*' (impermanence–Buddha-nature) in Dōgen is the unity of the Buddha-nature and no-Buddha-nature.

One cannot doubt that negation and contradiction are the vital notions in Hegel's account of the dialectic. For Hegel neither pure Being nor pure Nothing is true, and only Becoming as their unity (*Einheit*) or unseparateness (*Ungetrenntheit*) is their truth. In his *Science of Logic*, referring to Being and Nothing he says:

> The truth is not their lack of distinction, but that they are not the same, that they are absolutely distinct, and yet unseparated and inseparable, each disappearing immediately in its opposite. Their truth is therefore this movement, this immediate disappearance of the one into the other, in a word, Becoming: a movement wherein both are distinct, but in virtue of a distinction which has equally immediately dissolved itself.[40]

This is strikingly similar to Dōgen's idea of *mujō-busshō*. However, despite Hegel's emphasis on the unseparateness and the mutual passing over (*Übergehen*) of Being and Nothing, it cannot be overlooked that in his system Being is prior to Nothing. In Hegel the Beginning (*Anfang*) of everything is Being as such, and his dialectical movement develops itself in terms of Being (thesis), Nothing (antithesis), and Becoming (synthesis). In this way Being as such is the supreme principle of Hegel's metaphysical logic. In so far as Being is thus given priority over Nothing, however dialectical 'Becoming' as the unity may be, it is not a genuine Becoming but a quasi-Becoming which is after all reducible to Being because in Hegel Becoming is a synthesis of Being and Nothing in which 'Being' is always the thesis. In addition, by asserting that there is a final synthesis, his system cut off all further development: it swallowed up the future and time itself. For all its dynamically fluid, dialectical character, his system is consistently formulated in an irreversible, one-directional line with Being as the Beginning.

On the other hand, Dōgen's idea of 'no-Buddha-nature' is already freed from the contradiction between Buddha-nature and no Buddha-nature. Herein 'Buddha-nature's possible priority over 'no Buddha-nature' is overcome. When he goes further and comes to the point of 'impermanence–Buddha-nature', Dōgen consciously denies any possible trace of final duality, i.e., the possible priority of 'no Buddha-nature' over 'Buddha-nature' that could be implied in the very idea of 'no-Buddha-nature'. Hence in the idea of *mujōbusshō*, i.e., 'impermanence–Buddha-nature' every kind of duality and every sort of priority of one against the other is completely overcome. There is no irreversible relation. Everything is dynamically interrelated yet distinct. Thus Dōgen's idea of 'impermanence-Buddha-nature' is not a Becoming that can be reduced either to Being (Buddha-nature) or to Nothing (impermanence). Rather it is a genuine 'Becoming' of which we can, after Hegel, legitimately say:

> They [the impermanence of all beings and the Buddha-nature] are not the same. They are absolutely distinct, and yet unseparated and inseparable, each disappearing immediately in its opposite. Their truth is therefore this movement – in a word, Becoming.

Becoming in this sense is seen in the following words of Dōgen:

> To think the Buddha-nature exists only during one's life and ceases to exist at death is the utmost in ignorance and superficiality. During life there is the 'Buddha-nature' and 'no Buddha-nature'. In death as well there is the 'Buddha-nature' and 'no Buddha-nature'.... Nonetheless the attachment to false views that the Buddha-nature exists or not according to whether there is motion or not, that it functions or not in proportion to consciousness or no-consciousness, or that it ceases as the Buddha-nature or does not cease according to whether it is perceived or not, is heretical.[41]

Therefore, 'Becoming' in Dōgen's sense is not a *synthesis* which *presupposes* any duality as its basis such as Being and Nothing, Buddha-nature and impermanence, and so forth. Rather, this 'Becoming' itself takes place in the boundless, dimensionless–dimension of 'all beings' which is truly cosmological. This leads us to sum up the essential differences between Hegel and Dōgen as follows:

1. Taking the 'absolute Spirit' as its philosophical foundation, the *basis* of Hegel's system is still personalistic, not completely dehomocentric or cosmological while the *basis* of Dōgen's system is completely dehomocentric and cosmological.[42]

2. Accordingly, in Hegel the development of concept (*Begriff*), though dialectic, is *ultimately* a one-dimensional and closed system; in Dōgen everything is reversible and mutually inter-

penetrating, thereby forming an open system. The more cosmological the basis, the more personalistic the mind, and vice versa. In other words, if the basis on which one attains the Buddha-nature is limited to the living-dimension, or more narrowly to the human dimension, that is to say, is limited to a narrow cosmological framework, then the Buddha-nature which is attained on that basis will also be limited in its personalistic depth. Conversely, a realization reached in a broader cosmological framework will be one of greater personalistic depth. This may be termed 'cosmo-personalistic'.

3. In Hegel, because emphasis on the final synthesis is stronger than contradictory opposition, an individual finally loses his individuality. This is seen in his term *List der Vernunft* (trick of reason) which manipulates individual figures through passion in history.[43] Since for Dōgen the Buddha-nature is thoroughly nonsubstantial, all beings are all beings, inseparable from each other yet without losing individuality.

4. Despite his emphasis on 'The truth is the Whole' and 'The ultimate truth is Subject' there is working in Hegel's system a hidden objectification which *speculates* the whole. In marked contrast to this, Dōgen insists that through Zen *practice*, which for him is seated meditation, every objectification is overcome and dynamic nonduality between 'subject' and 'object', self and the universe, is fully realized.

5. Again, despite his emphasis on time and history, Hegel's speculative dialectic, which is often called panlogicism, ultimately turns them into motionless eternity. In Dōgen, however, time is being and being is time. Becoming as 'impermanence–Buddha-nature' involves the paradoxical unity of time and eternity at each and every moment.

All of these differences stem from a completely radical turning over of the priority of Being over Nothing, a turning over which is lacking in Hegel. In Dōgen's case, there is a turning over of the priority of the Buddha-nature over impermanence – a reversal from 'impermanence is the Buddha-nature' to 'the Buddha-nature is impermanence'. For Dōgen, all beings, impermanence, and the Buddha-nature are identical, with the realization of impermanence as the dynamic axis.

VI

The four preceding sections, set forth Dōgen's idea of the Buddha-nature in its ontological structure. His position, however, is not exhausted by an ontology of the Buddha-nature nor by a philosophy of 'all beings'. Not solely a thinker, Dōgen was essentially an ardent religious practitioner who emphasized *shikantaza*, just sitting, and devoted himself fully to the Buddha Way. The *mujō* (impermanence) of all things was not, in Dōgen, the nature of the world viewed with a philosophical eye but the pain and suffering of all sentient beings in the universe felt by a religious mind. In fact, it was this impermanence that drove him as a youth to renounce the world and seek the truth. *Mujō-busshō*, i.e., 'impermanence–Buddha-nature', was the consummation of his final realization 'All beings are the Buddha-nature.'

Dōgen's idea of 'All beings are the Buddha-nature' cannot be fully understood apart from his idea of 'oneness of practice and enlightenment' (*shushōitto*).[44] These two ideas constitute the solution, realized in his own enlightenment, to the question that he encountered as a young monk: 'Both exoteric and esoteric Buddhism teach the primal Buddha-nature and original enlightenment of all sentient beings. If this is the case, why then do all buddhas and bodhisattvas arouse the longing for enlightenment and engage in ascetic practice?'[45] This concerns the ideas of 'original awakening' (*hongaku*) and 'acquired awakening' (*shikaku*) which stand in contrast in T'ien-t'ai Buddhism. 'Original awakening' is an awakening with which one is originally endowed, an awakening innate in everyone, whereas 'acquired awakening' is an awakening attained or acquired only through religious practice. Why should people engage in religious practice to overcome delusion if they are already endowed with the Buddha-nature and are originally enlightened?

An emphasis on an 'original awakening' that is *a priori*, fundamental to all living beings, and eternal is apt to become pantheistic or mystical, neglecting ethical and religious practice. On the other hand, an emphasis on an 'acquired awakening' which an unenlightened one can attain *a posteriori* only through various stages of practice is inclined to become idealistic or teleological, setting enlightenment far afield as an end. The relationship between original and acquired awakening is a dilemma in Mahayana Buddhism, particularly in the T'ien-t'ai school in which Dōgen started his Buddhist studies. It is, however, not theoretical problem. It is *the* practical problem par excellence.

After struggling seriously with this problem, Dōgen, on the basis of his Zen practice and his own enlightenment, rejected sheer original awakening as a naturalistic heresy[46] that regards the human mind itself as buddha by identifying the given human self-consciousness with true awakening. Accordingly, he emphasizes the importance and necessity of practice: 'Although this Dharma [the Buddhist truth] is amply present in every person, unless one practices, it is not manifested; unless there is realization, it is not attained.'[47] At the same time Dōgen also rejects the idea of a mere acquired awakening as an unauthentic Buddhist teaching which distinguishes practice and enlightenment, taking the former as a means to the latter as an end. Dōgen instead emphasizes oneness of practice and enlightment saying, 'To think practice and realization are not one is a heretical view. In the Buddha Dharma, practice and realization are identical. Because one's present practice is practice in realization, one's initial negotiating of the Way in itself is the whole of original realization. Thus, even while directed to practice, one is told not to anticipate a realization apart from practice, because practice points directly to original realization.'[48] Thus by rejecting both the naturalistic-pantheistic and the idealistic-teleological views of the Buddha-nature, Dōgen breaks through the relativity of 'original' and 'acquired' awakening and opens up a deeper ground that is neither *a priori* nor *a posteriori*. This very ground is the original awakening in its absolute sense because it is prior to and liberated from any dualistic thought, any discriminatory view. For Dōgen it is the 'immaculate' Buddha-nature that is realized in *zazen*, seated meditation, which he calls 'body-and-mind-casting-off' (*shinjindatsuraku*). The original awakening as understood by Dōgen is not an original awakening which is looked at and aimed at from the point of view of acquired awakening. Rather Dōgen's 'original awakening' is deeper than both original and acquired awakening in their relative sense, and takes them as aspects of itself. This is the reason Dōgen emphasizes that 'one must practice in attaining the Way',[49] and that 'as enlightenment is already in practice, enlightenment is endless: as practice is enlightenment, practice is beginningless'.[50] For Dōgen the Buddha-nature manifests itself regardless of human delusions and enlightenment. Both practice and enlightenment are beginningless and endless. There is nothing standing against the Buddha-nature in its immediacy. Throughout the universe nothing has ever been concealed; all beings ceaselessly manifest the Buddha-nature while they are ever-changing.

Accordingly, Dōgen's position of 'oneness of practice and enlightenment', combined with 'All beings are the Buddha-nature', completely overcomes the following three dualities:

1. The duality of subject and object. When Dōgen emphasizes 'All
    beings *are* the Buddha-nature' instead of 'All living beings *have*
    the Buddha-nature', the subject-object structure is already
    overcome. The Buddha-nature is no longer an object with
    which one is endowed and which is to be realized by a subject
    (living beings); rather subject (all beings) and object (Buddha-
    nature) are identical – the verb *are* indicating their non-dual
    relationship. Yet their identity is dynamic rather than static
    because all beings are limitless and the Buddha-nature is
    non-substantial. Through the realization of impermanence they
    are dynamically nondualistic. Here the realizer and the realized
    are one and the same. Even a distinction between creator and
    creature does not exist, for the realization of 'All beings are the
    Buddha-nature' is based on the dehomocentric, cosmological
    dimension. The oneness of practice and enlightenment, an
    exceedingly human and personal problem, is realized not on a
    personalistic basis but on the limitless cosmological basis.
    Hence there is the simultaneous attainment of the *zazen* practi-
    tioner and everything in the universe. This is also the reason
    Dōgen emphasizes self-enlightenment *qua* enlightening others.[51]

2. The duality of potentiality and actuality. The Buddha-nature is
    not a potentiality to be actualized sometime in the future but
    originally and always the basic nature of all beings. At each and
    every moment in the ever-changing movement of all beings, the
    Buddha-nature manifests itself as 'suchness' or 'thus-comes'.
    Since 'suchness' or 'thus-comes' is the Buddha-nature, Dōgen
    says, as stated before, that 'The principle of the Buddha-nature
    is that it is not endowed prior to enlightenment.... The
    Buddha-nature is unquestionably realized simultaneously with
    enlightenment.' Therefore, for Dōgen, the distinction of Bud-
    dha-nature (potentiality) and Buddha (actuality) is also over-
    come. The simultaneity of the Buddha-nature and enlighten-
    ment (Buddha) is realized only *here and now* at each and every
    moment. From this point of view the theological ideas of
    'participation' and 'anticipation' are not acceptable because,
    though dialectical, they imply an ultimate Reality beyond 'here
    and now'. They seem to be well aware of human finitude, but
    are lacking a keen realization of the impermanence common to

all beings, which is fully realized only 'here and now' at each
and every moment in the ever-changing world.

3. The duality of means and end. Practice in itself, as a means
approaching enlightenment as an end, is an illusion. With such
a practice one may infinitely approach and approximate but
never reach the 'end', thereby falling into a false endlessness
(*schlechte Unendlichkeit*). In the very realization of the illusory
character of such a practice one may find oneself at the real
starting point for life because in this realization one realizes that
the Buddha-nature is not the end but the *basis* of practice. Even
in an initial resolution to attain enlightenment Buddha-nature
fully manifests itself. Dōgen says, 'Both the moment of initial
resolution and the moment of attaining highest enlightenment
are the Buddha Way.'[52] For Dōgen religious conduct, i.e.,
initial resolution, practice, enlightenment, and nirvana, consists of an infinite circle where every point is its starting point
as well as its end.

Accordingly, Dōgen's rejection of a mere 'acquired awakening'
and of a practice–enlightenment duality does not involve a negation of ethical and religious practice. Rather it implies a strong
emphasis on the importance of pure practice, because for him
realization is fully functioning at every step of practice in so far as it
is undefiled.[53] Practice as such is a manifestation of realization.
Dōgen's apparently contradictory emphasis on 'Do not intend to
become a buddha'[54] refers to a realm free of human agency in which
practice (*zazen*) is pure practice. This pure practice, undefiled *zazen*,
in itself is realization – simply because it is the practice (*zazen*) of
body-and-mind-cast-off. On the other hand, Dōgen's rejection of a
sheer 'original awakening' and emphasis on practice does not deny
authentic original awakening as the fundamental basis for practice.
It simply denies the notion of given enlightenment or innate
Buddha-nature. It involves a recognition that people are immersed
in the midst of delusion and suffering in this floating world and that
there is no self-existing Reality apart from this fact. Here we should
notice Dōgen's words, 'Buddhism has never spoken of nirvana
apart from birth-and-death.'[55] Delusions and sufferings originate
from a lack of right and full realization of the impermanence of man
and the world, and from a false idea of Reality apart from this impermanence. A rejection of the defiled idea of 'original awakening'
conceived as something beyond impermanent phenomena and a
direct realization of impermanence as impermanence immediately

enable one to awaken to Reality here and now, liberated from
delusions and sufferings. This awakening is *originally* functioning
precisely in the impermanence of the world. It is through undefiled
practice that this original awakening in its authentic sense is
awakened to. The oneness of practice and enlightenment is realized
only in the realm of undefiled practice and awakening – practice
undefiled by an intention to become a buddha, and awakening
undefiled by illusory projective thinking which posits enlightenment
as a goal beyond the realm of impermanence. In other words, only
by being freed from aim-oriented human action, both in practice
and in enlightenment, is Dōgen's idea of oneness of practice and
enlightenment realized. However, this undefiled standpoint is not
static but highly dynamic, because through *zazen* it opens up
authentic original awakening directly at the feet of one's existence,
here and now at each and every moment.

Practically speaking, in Dōgen this freedom from aim-oriented
human action indicates faith in the Buddha Way, religious spirit,
and compassion. This is expressed clearly in the following passages
taken from his writings:

> One who practices the Buddha Way above all should have
> faith in the Buddha Way.[56]

> To begin with, the practice of the Buddha Dharma is not done
> for one's own sake. And of course not for the sake of fame and
> wealth. One should simply practice the Buddha Dharma for its
> own sake.[57]

> The resolve to attain supreme enlightenment is the issuance
> and act of a vow to save all sentient beings prior to one's own
> salvation.[58]

> The *zazen* of buddhas and patriarchs is a prayer to gather and
> appropriate the entire Buddha Dharma from the time of initial
> resolution. Accordingly, their *zazen* does not forget or reject living
> beings; their compassionate thought always extends even to
> insects, and their earnest desire is to save them and transfer all
> merits to all things.[59]

However, the realm of undefilement with its accompanying faith
and compassion is not merely the goal but the starting point of
Buddhist life, because without the realization of faith and compassion one cannot have a real point of departure for this life. And only

in the undefiled realm in which oneness of practice and enlightenment is realized is the idea 'All beings are the Buddha-nature' as
well rightly realized.

VII

Dōgen's idea of 'oneness of practice and enlightenment' necessarily
leads us to an examination of his view of *time*, because that idea
overcomes another important duality – time and eternity. His view
of time in connection with the Buddha-nature is clearly seen in still
another example of his peculiar way of reading traditional texts.
In the 'Buddha-nature' fascicle Dōgen quotes the following
passage from the Nirvana Sutra:

欲知仏性義當觀時節因縁　時節若至仏性現前

(*Busshō no gi o shiran to omowaba masani jisetsu no innen o kanzubeshi:
Jisetsu moshi itareba busshō genzen su.*)
(To wish to know the meaning of the Buddha-nature one should
contemplate the causal relation of time and occasion. If the time
come the Buddha-nature will manifest itself.)[60]

This traditional reading implies waiting for the time of the Buddha-
nature's manifestation sometime in the future through present
practice: unless the time comes the Buddha-nature is not manifested, however one may engage in practice. This reading presupposes the Buddha-nature as a potentiality like a seed contained
within living beings, a view Dōgen adamantly rejects. Accordingly
he changes the reading: 當觀時節因縁 *tōkan jisetsu innen*, '*Just see* the
causal relation of time and occasion',[61] instead of 'one *should
contemplate* the causal relation of time and occasion', and 時節若至
jisetsu nyakushi, 'the time and occasion *thus* come',[62] instead of '*if* the
time and occasion come'. Dōgen's aim is clear. He rejects such an
attitude as anticipation of Buddha-nature's future manifestation
and clarifies the presence of the Buddha-nature. There is no time
that is not the right time.
Dogen's emphasis on the idea of 'All beings are the Buddha-
nature' may be regarded as referring to spatiality. This idea
developed into 'no-Buddha-nature' and then into 'impermanence
–Buddha-nature' which implies temporality. As indicated earlier,
the dimension of all beings is that of appearance–disappearance or

mutability. However, this does not mean that first there is time and then within this time, for example, spring comes. Nor is it that there is a time named spring and then, in it, flowers bloom. Rather the flower blooming in itself is the coming of spring, i.e. time called 'spring'. Apart from the facts of flowers blooming, birds singing, grass growing and breezes blowing there is not 'spring'. Apart from mutable phenomena of the world there is no 'time'. Dōgen says, 'Times have colour such as blue, yellow, red, and white.'[63] He also says, 'Mountains are time, oceans are time. If they were not, there would be no mountain, no ocean. One should not think there is no time in the absolute present of mountains and oceans. If time decays, mountains and oceans will also decay. If time does not decay mountains and oceans will not decay either.'[64] There is no time apart from mutability or appearance–disappearance of things in the universe. Nor is there anything apart from time. Thus emphasizing *uji* (being-time) Dōgen says, 'Time in itself is being; all beings are time.'[65]

Dōgen does not, however, simply identify being and time. Their common denominator is mutability or impermanence. For Dōgen, all beings without exception are impermanent; just for this reason all beings are the Buddha-nature, for he rejects an immutable Buddha-nature beyond impermanence. Here we have seen a radical turnover of the traditional understanding of the Buddha-nature. Similarly, Dōgen makes a radical change in the common understanding of time. For him, time does not simply flow.

> Time should not be understood simply to fly away. Flying away should not be learned as the only function of time. If time is subject to flying there may be an interval [between coming and going]. It is because time is understood as merely passing that the truth of *uji* is not truly grasped. In short, all beings of the universe are joined together, and each is time. Precisely because it is *uji* it is one's own time. *Uji* has the characterastic of *kyōryaku*[66], i.e., seriatim passage.[67]

Against the ordinary understanding, for Dōgen, time is flying, yet not flying; flying-*qua*-not flying is time's passage. Seriatim passage as flying-*qua*-not flying is always the *present* in which the Buddha-nature manifests itself. In other words, the Buddha-nature always manifests itself as time, specifically as present time.

Accordingly, with the realization of mutability or impermanence as the dynamic axis, being and time are identical. The realization of universal impermanence involves the unity of spatiality and temporality. And just as all beings are the Buddha-nature all times are the Buddha-nature. This the Zen maxim 'Every day is a good day' expresses well. Dōgen himself expressed the same realization in the following poem written shortly after his return from Sung China:

Morning after morning the sun rises from the east,
Every night the moon sinks in the west;
Clouds disappearing, mountain ridges show themselves,
Rain ceases, surrounding mountains are low.

When Dōgen emphasizes a new reading '*Just seeing* the causal relation of time and occasion' instead of the traditional reading 'One *should contemplate* the causal relation of time and occasion' he strongly rejects such ideas as anticipation, hope, and expectation that look for eternity beyond the present moment. Even an idea of anticipation or hope that involves a dialectic of 'already' and 'not yet' is not an exception, because the very dialectic is based on the future-oriented idea of divine will or a Supreme Being. Dōgen denies continuity of time and emphasizes the independence of each point of time as seen in his following words:

Once firewood turns to ash, the ash cannot turn back to being firewood. Still, one should not take the view that it is ashes *afterward* and firewood *before*. He should realize that although firewood is at the dharma-stage of firewood, and that this is possessed of before and after, the firewood is beyond before and after. Ashes are in the stage of ashes, and possess before and after. Just as firewood does not revert to firewood once it has turned to ashes, man does not return to life after his death. In light of this, it being an established teaching in Buddhism not to speak of life becoming death, Buddhism speaks of the unborn. It being a confirmed Buddhist teaching that death does not become life, it speaks of non-extinction. Life is a stage of time and death is a stage of time, like, for example, winter and spring. We do not suppose that winter becomes spring, or say that spring becomes summer.[68]

This indicates complete discontinuity of time which is realized through negating a transition from one state to another, immortality of the soul, and eternal life after death. Life is absolutely life, death is absolutely death; spring is absolutely spring, summer is absolutely summer; each in itself is no more and no less – without the slightest possibility of becoming. This refers precisely to Dōgen's idea of 'just seeing' (*tōkan*) the causal relation of time and occasion. When we 'just see' time and occasion at each and every moment there is nothing beyond it, nothing apart from it. Thus Dōgen says, 'The causal relation of time and occasion should be seen by the causal relation of time and occasion.'[69] There is no room for God as the ruler of time and history, the one Substance, or even the Buddha-nature. To realize time as time is to attain the Buddha-nature. For Dōgen time is the Buddha-nature and the Buddha-nature is time.

This is the reason he changes the reading of the phrase *jisetsu nyakushi* from '*if* the time and occasion come' to 'the time and occasion *thus* come'. In Dōgen's realization it is not that the fullness of time occurs at a particular time in history but that any moment of history is the fullness of time because for him at every moment time fully manifests itself. This is inseparably connected with his idea of the complete discontinuity of time and the independence of each moment. The criticism may be voiced that time and history are spatialized by such ideas and thereby lose their meaning. But, conversely, the idea of anticipation or waiting for the fullness of time in the future, however dialectic it may be, is not entirely freed from a naturalistic view of time. This is because the idea of anticipation is still lacking the thorough realization of discontinuity of time and is, in the final analysis, based on the nature of time (continuity) as conceived by man. Time and space are, however, completely contradictory. Space is fully realized as space only through the negation of time which is in turn realized as the negation of space. Likewise, time is fully realized as time only through the negation of space which is in turn realized as the negation of time. Accordingly, the negation of space as well as the negation of time are necessary for the full realization of space; and the negation of time as well as the negation of space are necessary for the full realization of time. For Dōgen the complete discontinuity of time, that is, the negation of temporality, is not a mere spatialization of time, but rather an essential element for the full realization of time itself. Only by the realization of the complete discontinuity of time and of the independent moment, i.e., only by negation of temporality, does time become real time. For Dōgen there is no time that is not the fullness of time. '*Jisetsu nyakushi* indicates the time and occasion have already come. There is nothing to doubt.... You should know *jisetsu nyakushi* never involves passing time in vain.... Since the time and occasion have arrived, this is the manifestation of the Buddha-nature.... There has been no time and occasion that does not 'thus come'. There is no Buddha-nature that does not manifest itself.'[70]

However, in spite of the complete discontinuity of time and independent moment, time flows. This is *kyōryaku*, i.e., seriatim passage as flying-*qua*-not flying and not flying-*qua*-flying simultaneously. Therefore time's passage is not one-directional but completely reversible.

Uji (being-time) has the virtue of seriatim passage; it passes from today to tomorrow, from today to yesterday, from yesterday to today, from today to today, and from tomorrow to tomorrow. Since seriatim passage is the virtue of time, time past and time present are neither piled up nor congregated linearly. Therefore Ch'ing-yüan (Seigen) is time; Huang-po (Ōbaku) is time; Ma-tsu (Baso) is time; Shih-t'ou (Sekitō)[71] is time. Because self and others are already time, practice and enlightenment are time.[72]

There are great similarities between Dōgen's view of time and Heidegger's. Both of them emphasize the identity of being and time. In Heidegger, through the analysis of *Dasein* (man) in terms of *Sorge* (care), *Angst* (dread), and being-toward-death, temporality is regarded as the essential nature of human existence. In Dōgen it is through human self-consciousness that the problem of life-and-death, of generation-and-extinction, and of being-and-nonbeing, in short, the problem of impermanence, is realized as the problem to be solved. However, at least the following three differences must be noticed:

1. In Heidegger, temporality is grasped particularly through the analysis of human existence, while in Dōgen impermanence is realized emphatically as the universal nature of all beings in the universe. This is because Dōgen grounds his existence on the radically dehomocentric, cosmological dimension whereas Heidegger is not altogether freed from homocentrism, though he emphasizes transcending towards the world.

2. In Dōgen, through the realization of impermanence of all beings, the dimension of which is limitless and bottomless, not only is it clearly realized that being is time but also that time is

being. On the other hand, in Heidegger it is clear that being is time but not clear that time is being even in the thought of his later period.[73]

3. Dōgen's idea of 'impermanence-Buddha-nature' results in the realization of simultaneous enlightenment for humans and nature. His idea of reversible seriatim passage involves the realization of the contemporaneity of an infinite past and infinite future in terms of the Buddha-nature; progression is regression and regression is progression – in the awakening to 'what'.

We cannot, however, find the equivalent of these ideas in Heidegger.

In Dōgen the impermanence of the universe and the passage of time are inseparable. The mediating point of these is sustained practice and realization. His ideas of the oneness of being and time and the fullness of time at each and every moment are based on severe religious practice, especially *zazen*. At the culminating point of religious practice 'All times are the Buddha-nature' is fully realized. Through *zazen* all beings in the universe are enlightened and all times in history manifest eternity. Yet this takes place here and now in the absolute present. Apart from the here and now, apart from the realization, right now, of 'body-and-mind-casting-off', this can not take place. Time elapses from present to present. Things in the universe are mutually interpenetrating, with self and others being undifferentiated yet distinct. This is Dōgen's world of manifestation of the Buddha-nature. It must, however, be repeatedly emphasized this is not merely the goal but the starting point of Buddhist life.

In the 'Sansuikyō' fascicle Dōgen quotes Fu-jung Tao-k'ai's (Fuyō Dōkai n.d.) words, 'A stone-woman bears a child at night'[74] to indicate that Beginning (*Anfang*) springs from the Absolute and free Subjectivity. A 'stone-woman' refers to the undifferentiated 'what' as the Buddha-nature. 'Bear a child' may be taken as differentiated multitude coming out of the undifferentiated 'what'. It happens 'at night' because it is beyond analytic reasoning. These words excellently symbolize the Beginning of all things and freedom in Zen.

Freedom in Zen, particularly in Dōgen, is different from that in Spinozism. In Spinoza God as the one Substance is free because he is *causa sui* (self-cause) and self-determined, while humans can be free by seeing themselves as part of God's self-determined being. On the other hand, as has been repeatedly stated, since Dōgen's idea of the Buddha-nature is non-substantial, empty, and no-Buddha-nature, humans themselves are *causa sui* and completely free in the sense of 'What-is-it-that-thus-comes.' 'A stone-woman bears a child at night' is simply another expression of this. However, the 'night' is not the same as 'the night in which . . . all cows are black', so stated by Hegel as criticism of Schelling's idea of the undifferentiated identity. Hegel attacked Schelling in that manner because for the latter the law of identity A = A is supreme, whereas the distinction between subject and object is formal and relative. In Dōgen, on the contrary, the distinction between subject and object, self and others, becomes clear through the realization of all beings' limitlessness and the Buddha-nature's nonsubstantiality. One statement, 'All beings are the Buddha-nature', may be rendered into two inseparable statements, 'All beings are absolutely all beings' and 'the Buddha-nature is absolutely the Buddha-nature'.

In this sense the 'night' in which 'A stone-woman bears a child' is much closer to 'a bright night of nothingness of dread'[75] in Heidegger's philosophy. By referring to 'onto-theo-logy', Heidegger rejects the whole Western metaphysical tradition and emphasizes nothingness instead of substance. Beings in totality are opened up through the 'night of nothingness of dread'. However, Heidegger's emphasis on the nothingness of dread does not necessarily lead him to the completely dehomocentric, cosmological dimension alone in which the impermanence of all beings in the universe is fully realized. Only in this dimensionless-dimension is a complete radical reversal from 'impermanence is the Buddha-nature' to 'the Buddha-nature is impermanence', from 'being is time' to 'time is being', possible. 'A stone-woman bears a child at night' indicates the cosmo-personalistic freedom based on the realization of this reversal. It is self-determination without determinator that takes place at each and every moment of the absolute present with the boundless cosmological dimension as its basis. This freedom is realized in the infinite circle of the religious way of life in which practice and enlightenment are not two but one.

Let me conclude this lengthy discussion on Dōgen's idea of the Buddha-nature by quoting the following conversation between Zen master Ch'ang-sha Ch'ing-ts'ên (Ja: Chōsha Keishin n.d.) and Minister Chu (Ja: Jiku Shōsho n.d.) which Dōgen discusses at the end of the 'Buddha nature' fascicle.

'An earthworm being cut, becomes two. Both of them move.
I wonder which part contains the Buddha-nature?'
The master replied,
'No illusions!'[76]

3 True Person and Compassion – D. T. Suzuki's Appreciation of Lin-chi and Chao-chou

I

In memory of Daisetz Teitarō Suzuki (1870–1966), I would like here to consider his appreciation and interpretation of the *Lin-chi Lu*[1] and the *Chao-chou Lu*[2] on the basis of what Suzuki regarded as the idea of 'man' or 'person' (*nin* in Japanese, *jên* in Chinese), an idea he found common to both works. The *Lin-chi Lu* and *Chao-chou Lu* are two Zen classics recording respectively the sayings of Lin-chi I-hsüan (Ja: Rinzai Gigen, d. 866) and Chao-chou Ts'ung-shen (Ja: Jōshū Jūshin, 778–897). Traditionally called 'King of Zen Records',[3] Suzuki once remarked that the *Lin-chi Lu* is 'regarded by many as the strongest Zen treatise we have.'[4] Yet, the collection of Zen sayings and anecdotes he prized most was the *Chao-chou Lu*, which, in Suzuki's evaluation not only possesses the same vital Zen realization as does the *Lin-chi Lu*, but also expresses vividly the compassionate aspect of Zen.

In 1949, Suzuki published in Japanese *Rinzai no Kihon Shisō: Rinzai-roku ni okeru 'nin' shisō no kenkyū* (*The Fundamental Thought of Lin-chi: a Study of 'Person' in the 'Lin-chi Lu'*).[5] This represents one of Suzuki's most important writings in either Japanese or English. In this book he presents an original and penetrating approach to the *Lin-chi Lu* in which the idea of 'Person' is elucidated as the key to the entire work and as the nucleus of genuine Zen spirit. An English translation of the *Lin-chi Lu* was a long cherished project of Suzuki.

It is unfortunate that he passed away before his wish could be realized.[6]

Suzuki did not publish a separate volume of interpretation on the *Chao-chou Lu*, although he quoted it as often as the *Lin-chi Lu* in his writings. In 1962, however, Suzuki published a critically edited text of the *Chao-chou Lu* with Japanese translation,[7] his last work of this type.

Before going on, it would be well to note that Suzuki was more concerned with Lin-chi and Chao-chou as Zen personalities than he was with the *Lin-chi Lu* and the *Chao-chou Lu* as collections of Zen sayings and anecdotes. And yet, even more than the Zen personality of these two figures, what concerned him was the genuine and vivid 'Zen' which manifests itself in Zen texts or in and through Zen masters, and which can and should manifest itself in every one of us. So, what moved Suzuki above all was that in these two works can be found that living 'Zen' which is the true way of human existence.

Throughout his extensive writings Suzuki used Zen texts only to show what genuine and vital Zen is. It was simply because he believed genuine Zen was well expressed in these two texts that he appreciated the *Lin-chi Lu* and especially the *Chao-chou Lu*.

II

One day Rinzai (Lin-chi) gave his sermon: "There is the true man of no rank in the mass of naked flesh, who goes in and out from your facial gates (i.e., sense organs). Those who have not yet testified (to the fact), look, look!"

A monk came forward and asked, "Who is this true man of no rank?"

Rinzai came down from his chair and, taking hold of the monk by his throat, said, "Speak, speak!"

The monk hesitated.

Rinzai let go his hold and said, "What a worthless dirt-stick this (true man of no rank) is!"[8]

This is one of the famous events from the *Lin-chi Lu*, one to which Suzuki attached great importance. The subject matter of this sermon is 'the true man of no rank'. It is here that Suzuki found the pivotal point of the *Lin-chi Lu* and the culmination of Zen thought. He says, 'The true man of no rank is Rinzai's term for the Self. His teaching is almost exclusively around this Man, or Person, who is sometimes called the 'Way-man' (*dōnin, tao-jên*). He can be said to be the first Zen master in the history of Zen thought in China who emphatically asserts the presence of this Man in every phase of our human life-activity. He is never tired of having his followers come to the realization of the Man or the real Self'.[9]

Suzuki's idea, that Lin-chi's 'Man' or 'Person' is the culmination of Zen thought in China, may be clarified by summarizing his discussions in the *Rinzai no Kihon Shisō* as follows:

While the 'Mind' (*shin, hsin*) was transmitted as being the core of Zen by Bodhidharma, 'Seeing into one's Self-nature' (*kenshō, chien-hsing*) was emphasized by the Sixth Patriarch, Hui-nêng. This is probably because 'Mind' was and is apt to be understood as static when grasped only in terms of *Dhyāna* (meditation). It may not be wrong to say that Hui-nêng emphasized the oneness of *Dhyāna* and *Prajña* (wisdom) in 'Seeing into one's Self-nature' as the nucleus of Zen in order to avoid the static implication of the term 'Mind'.[10] Hui-nêng's 'Seeing', because of its emphasis on *Prajña*, was replaced with 'knowing' (*chi, chih*) by Shên-hui (Ja: Kataku Jinne, 688–760). 'Knowing', however, has a tendency to become conceptual and abstract, and this is incompatible with the nature of Zen.[11] To guard against this, Hui-nêng's 'Seeing' was developed on the other hand by Ma-tsu (Ja: Baso Dōitsu, 707–86), into 'Activity' (*yū, yung*). While the school of Shên-hui which emphasized 'Knowing' declined, that of Ma-tsu prospered with great vigour. This is because 'Activity' is nothing other than Zen itself.[12]

To emphasize 'Activity' alone, however, is not entirely satisfactory. There must be something living behind 'Activity'. At the root-source of 'Activity' there must be the 'Person'. In Ma-tsu's Zen, 'Person' although working behind 'Activity', was not clearly realized as 'Person'. It is Lin-chi who vividly grasped and pointed to 'Person' as 'Person'. This is clearly seen in Lin-chi's grabbing the monk and demanding that he 'Speak, Speak!' in response to the question 'Who is the true man of no rank?' Thus Suzuki says, 'In this "Man", "Seeing", "Knowing", and "Activity" are integrated in a concrete way. In this respect Lin-chi may be said to be a great thinker.'[13]

According to Suzuki, the *Lin-chi Lu* is a record of the sermons and activities of this 'Person': it is exclusively upon this 'Person' that Lin-chi established his religion. The historical success of the Lin-chi school may be said to have essentially derived from its realization of

'Person' and its future destiny as well will depend on its *living* grasp of this realization.[14] Now, what really is 'Person'?

III

Let us return to Lin-chi's sermon as quoted above.

There is the true man of no rank in the mass of naked flesh, who goes in and out from your facial gates (i.e., sense organs). Those who have not yet testified (to the fact), look, look!

This is Lin-chi's declaration of 'Person' as the most concrete and living Self. He also calls him 'the One who is, at this moment, right in front of us, solitarily, illuminating, in full awareness, listening to this talk on the Dharma'.[15] If one, however, takes the concreteness of this 'Person' for the concreteness of sensory experience unmediated by intellect, he is entirely off the mark. It is likewise erroneous to understand 'the true man of no rank who goes in and out from your facial gates' as a psychological self.[16] Interpreting Lin-chi's 'Person' as the real Self, Suzuki says, 'The real Self is a kind of metaphysical self in opposition to the psychological or ethical self which belong in a finite world of relativity. Lin-chi's "Man" is defined as "of no rank" or "independent of" (*mu ye, wu i*), or "with no clothes on', all of which makes us think of the "metaphysical" Self.'[17]

If one, however, in considering the term 'metaphysical Self', assumes 'Person' to be consciousness in general or an abstract humanity, one's view is 'dead wrong'.[18] Neither consciousness in general nor an abstract humanity are a living 'Person', a concrete existence. Being intellectualizations, they are abstractions, devoid of vital activity. On the contrary, Lin-chi's 'Person' is 'The One who is, at this moment, right in front of us, listening to this talk on the Dharma.' He is neither a philosophical assumption nor a logical postulate, but one who is working, fully alive, here (right in front of us) and now (at this moment). This is why Lin-chi says, 'Look, look!' and 'Speak, speak!'

In order to realize Lin-chi's 'Person' therefore, one must transcend the discriminative consciousness. Human consciousness is always imprisoned in objectivity and relativity. Zen urges us to 'advance further from the top of a hundred foot pole';[19] it urges human consciousness or human intellect to move to the far edge of its own field, and then to leap, effecting a 'turning-over', called *parāvrtti*[20] in Buddhist terminology.

This turning-over as a leap from the very field of consciousness is the realization of absolute Subjectivity which itself cannot be objectified – it being the root-source of one's objectification in terms of the consciousness or intellect. In other words, the realization of absolute Subjectivity takes place at the moment one realizes that the intellect's endless advancing is nothing but its complete turning back. Lin-chi's 'true man of no rank' is this absolute Subjectivity. Since 'Person' in Lin-chi's sense is the very root and source of one's objectification, he himself has no further root and yet is most active and creative as the source of one's objectification.

Thus Lin-chi says of 'Person', 'He is the most dynamic one except that he has no roots, no stems whatever. You may try to catch him, but he refuses to be gathered up; you may try to brush him away, but he will not be dispersed. The harder you strive after him the further he is away from you. When you no more strive after him, lo, he is right in front of you. His supersensuous voice fills your ear.'[21] Suzuki characterizes this 'Person' as absolute Subjectivity, *'reiseiteki-jikaku'*,[22] 'the Cosmic Unconsciousness'[23] or *'prajñā*-intuition'.[24]

Lin-chi's 'Person' is not a person who stands over and against nature, God, or another person, but is rather one's absolute Subjectivity, as *prajñā*-intuition, which goes beyond the dualism of all forms of subject and object, self and world, being and non-being. 'If the Greeks', says Suzuki, 'taught us how to reason and Christianity what to believe, it is Zen that teaches us to go beyond logic and not to tarry even when we come up against "the things which are not seen". For the Zen point of view is to find an absolute point where no dualism in whatever form resides. Logic starts from the division of subject and object, and belief distinguishes between what is seen and what is not seen. The Western mode of thinking can never do away with this eternal dilemma, this or that, reason or faith, man and God, etc. With Zen all these are swept aside as something veiling our insight into the nature of life and reality. Zen leads us into a realm of Emptiness or Void where no conceptualism prevails'.[25] In so saying, Suzuki does not mean that Christianity, for instance, is dualistic in the ordinary sense. He says this only by way of comparison with Zen's 'Emptiness' or 'Void', the realization of which is called *Satori*, 'Seeing into one's self-nature' (Hui-nêng) or testifying 'Person' (Lin-chi).

This can be seen when one takes seriously the following question raised by Suzuki: 'Who was it that heard God speak and then wrote down, "God said, 'Let there be light' and there was light"?'[26] There must be a witness of God's creation who is hidden in the Biblical account. The Christian idea of God is certainly beyond the duality of subject and object, transcendence and immanence, being and non-being. He created the universe out of nothing – by His word. There is, however, a hidden duality between God, who is creating the universe, and a veiled seer of His creation. Even when 'God before creation' is talked about, who is it who talks about 'God before creation'? This hidden and final dualism is a great and serious problem which Zen believes must be thoroughly overcome for us to attain a complete liberation. Zen is properly concerned with the very origin before duality takes place. Since the hidden duality is the final one, one which is concerned with God Himself, the veiled 'seer' of God's creation can be neither God nor a human as a creation. This seer is, in Lin-chi's terms, 'the true man of no rank'. Such terms as 'Emptiness', 'Void', 'Mind', 'Seeing', 'Activity', and 'Knowing', have also been traditionally used in Zen to indicate that seer.

The veiled seer is called 'Emptiness' or 'Void' because, as the ultimate seer, it cannot be objectified and cannot be anything whatsoever. It is called 'Mind', 'Seeing', 'Knowing', 'Activity' and so on because, although it cannot be objectified, it is not sheer emptiness but rather the absolute Subjectivity at the root-source of human objectification. Lin-chi calls the ultimate seer 'Person' or 'the true man of no rank' to express its living concreteness.

In his Song of Enlightenment, Yung-chia Ta-shin (Ja: Yoka Daishi, 665–713) describes the spiritual awakening as follows: 'You cannot take hold of it, nor can you get rid of it; while you can do neither, it goes on its own way.'[27]

This 'it' is precisely the ultimate seer, or 'Person' in Lin-chi's sense. The ultimate seer or 'Person' can neither be taken hold of nor forsaken. Yet, right in the midst of these impossibilities 'it' or 'Person' already *is*. So Lin-chi's 'true man of no rank' as the ultimate seer 'stands' neither before God's creation nor after God's creation. He is standing and working right here and now 'prior to' *any* form of duality such as before and after, time and eternity, God and humanity, seer and the seen. The ultimate seer is nothing but 'Seeing' itself. 'Seeing' is the absolute Activity prior to both personification and deification. 'Seeing' in this sense, however, is nothing other than 'Emptiness' or 'Void'. For this very reason 'Seeing' is really the absolute Activity which can never be objectified. As absolute Activity, 'Seeing' does not see itself just as an eye does not see itself. 'Seeing' is *non-seeing* in regard to itself. It is because seeing is *non-seeing* in regard to itself that 'Seeing' is 'Seeing which is absolutely active' – pure 'Seeing' without a seer.

From this 'Seeing' as the absolute Activity spring God's words 'Let there be light' – that is, God Himself and His creation. In the 'Seeing', God sees the light and the light sees God; God sees God and the light sees the light. Since 'Seeing' is *always* working regardless of *before* and *after*, and thereby is working right *here* and *now*, Lin-chi, taking it in the most existential way, calls it 'Person'. Hence he addresses 'The One who is, at this moment, right in front of us, listening to this talk on the Dharma' and shouts 'Look, look!' and 'Speak, speak!' seizing the monk by the throat.

Accordingly, Suzuki emphasizes that Lin-chi's 'Person' is supra-individual[28] as well as individual.[29] 'Person' is supra-individual because Lin-chi's 'Person' is identical with 'Emptiness', 'Seeing', or to use Suzuki's terminology, 'Cosmic Unconsciousness'. At the same time, 'Person' is an individual, a concrete living existence such as Lin-chi, Tê-shan, you or I.

'Person' has two aspects – one exists as a finite individual, and at the same time, one is a 'bottomless abyss'. It is not possible to take hold of 'Person' on the plane of the individual alone. For, the finite individual inevitably goes hand in hand with the 'bottomless abyss', and we must break through this 'abyss' (aspect of 'Person') if we are to be individuals in the true sense.[30] The bottomless abyss is, needless to say, 'Emptiness', 'Void' or 'Cosmic Unconsciousness' which is supra-individual. One often mistakes Emptiness, Void or Cosmic Unconsciousness as something separated from an individual existence. Lin-chi, however, says that it 'goes in and out from your facial gates. Those who have not yet testified to the fact, look, look!' The supra-individual Emptiness or Cosmic Unconsciousness cannot manifest itself directly unless it materializes in an individual existence. On the other hand, an individual existence is really individual only insofar as the supra-individual Emptiness or Cosmic Unconsciousness manifests itself in and through it. Lin-chi's 'Person' is nothing but a living individual who *is* always (therefore, right here and right now) *Emptiness, Cosmic Unconsciousness* or *Seeing*. In other words, the living non-duality of the individual and the supra-individual is 'Person'.

Hence Lin-chi's saying. 'O Followers of the Way, the One who, at this moment, right in front of us, brightly, in solitude, and in full awareness is listening [to this talk on the Dharma] – this Man (*jên*) tarries nowhere wherever he may be, he passes through the ten quarters, he is master of himself in the triple world. Entering into all situations, discriminating everything, he is not to be turned away [from what he is].'[31]

This is the liberated and creative activity of 'Person'. Acting through the five senses, 'Person' goes beyond them without being trapped by them. Acting in accord with consciousness, 'Person' transcends consciousness without being confined by it. 'When conditions arise let them be illuminated. You just believe in the One who is acting at this very moment. He is not employing himself in any particularly specified fashion. As soon as one thought is born in your mind, the triple world rises with all its conditions which are classifiable under the six sensefields. As you go on acting as you do in response to the conditions, what is wanting in you?'[32] Thus Lin-chi says, 'He is master of himself wherever he goes. As he stands all is right with him.'[33]

The above gives a brief insight into Lin-chi's 'Person' which Suzuki elucidates as the core of the *Lin-chi Lu* and as the most concrete basis of Zen. Here we can see what Suzuki thinks to be the true way of human existence.

IV

As I said earlier in this essay, Suzuki believes that Chao-chou places as much emphasis on the necessity of awakening to 'Person' as does Lin-chi, although the former does not use the term 'Person' so explicitly as does the latter. Suzuki illustrates this by the following *mondo* (question and answer) from the *Chao-chou Lu*:

> Chao-chou was once asked by a monk, "What is my self?"
> Chao-chou said, "Have you finished the morning gruel?"
> "Yes, I have finished", answered the monk.
> Chao-chou then told him, "If so, wash your bowl."[34]

Chao-chou's instruction here is not simply to wash a bowl after a meal, but to awaken to the 'Self' in eating and washing. Commenting on the *mondo* Suzuki says, 'The eating is an act, the washing is an act, but what is wanted in Zen is the actor himself: the eater and the washer that does the acts of eating and washing; and unless this person is existentially or experientially taken hold of, one cannot speak of the acting. Who is the one who is conscious of acting and who is the one who communicates this fact of consciousness to you and who are you who tells all this not only to yourself but to all others? "I", "you", "she", or "it" – all this is a pronoun standing for a somewhat behind it. Who is this somewhat [behind it]?'[35]

We may also see from the following *mondo* that Chao-chou clearly grasped the same core of Zen as Lin-chi.

Chao-chou once asked a new monk: "Have you ever been here before?"

The monk answered, "Yes, sir, I have."

Thereupon the master said, "Have a cup of tea."

Later on another monk came and he asked him the same question, "Have you ever been here?"

This time the answer was quite opposite. "I have never been here, sir."

The old master, however, answered just as before, "Have a cup of tea."

Afterwards the Inju (the managing monk of the monastery) asked the master, "How is it that you make the same offering of a cup of tea no matter what a monk's reply is?"

The old master called out, "O Inju!" who at once replied, "Yes, master." Whereupon Chao-chou said, "Have a cup of tea."[36]

I think I am right in saying that Chao-chou's 'Have a cup of tea' is the same as Lin-chi's 'Look, look!' or 'Speak, speak!' in that both are trying to help another to awaken to his true 'Self' – that is, to 'Person'.

Of Chao-chou it was said, 'His Zen shines upon his lips', because the utterances he made were like jewels that sparkled brightly. This characteristic of Chao-chou is often contrasted with the somewhat militant attitude of Lin-chi and Tê-shan as seen in their use of the shout (*katsu!*) and stick (*bō*) respectively. Suzuki's appreciation of Chao-chou's Zen may be said to depend partly on his personal affinity for Chao-chou's verbal skill. But the more important and more essential reason for his appreciation of Chao-chou's Zen is of course beyond any such personal predilection on the part of Suzuki.

That reason can be found in the following words from his writings: 'It ought to be said that the most distinguishing characteristics of Chao-chou's Zen lies in his teaching of "suffering by taking upon oneself myriad evil passions for the sake of all living beings". Other Zen men, of course, say the same thing, because those who do not declare this cannot be Zen men. In Chao-chou's Zen, however, the emphasis is striking.'[37]

In this connection Suzuki quotes the following *mondo* involving Chao-chou:

Jōshū (Chao-chou) was approached by an old lady who said, "Women are considered to be heavily laden with the five obstructions. How can I be freed from them?"

The master said, "Let all the other people be born in Heaven, but may I this old woman be forever drowned in the ocean of suffering."[38]

A literal translation of the last words of Chao-chou in this *mondo* is, 'May *the* old woman be forever drowned in the ocean of suffering', referring to the other party of the *mondo*. In so saying Chao-chou, though apparently pitiless, is trying to save the old woman by cutting off her attachment to her own liberation from the 'five obstructions'. Chao-chou's seemingly harsh reply springs from great compassion in which no distinction between Chao-chou and the old woman exists and in which Chao-chou himself is willing to suffer much more than or in place of anyone else. I understand it was to emphasize this point that, identifying Jōshū with the old woman, Suzuki translated this portion as 'May *I this* old woman be forever drowned in the ocean of suffering.'

Another *mondo* concerning Chao-chou goes like this:

Someone asked, "You are such a saintly personality. Where would you find yourself after your death?"

Jōshū the Zen master replied, "I go to hell ahead of you all!"

The questioner was thunderstruck and said, "How could that be?"

The master did not hesitate: "Without my first going to hell, who would be waiting there to save people like you?"[39]

Referring to the first *mondo*, Suzuki says, 'This expresses the *praṇidhāna* (original Vow) or vicarious suffering.'[40] As for the second *mondo*, he makes the comment, 'This is, indeed, a strong statement, but from Jōshū's Zen point of view he was fully justified. He has no selfish motive here. His whole existence is devoted to doing good for others. If not for this, he could not make such a straightforward statement with no equivocation whatever. Christ declares, "I am the Way." He calls others to be saved through him. Jōshū's spirit is also Christ's. There is no arrogant self-centred spirit in either of them. They simply, innocently, wholeheartedly express the same spirit of love.'[41]

In the view of Suzuki, a Zen person is apt to seem to make too much of *prajñā*, the great wisdom, rather neglecting *karunā*, the great compassion. However, Suzuki emphasizes that 'What makes Zen as such is that various *upāya* (good devices for salvation) naturally come out of the great compassion with the quickness of the echo following a sound.'[42] In Zen, properly speaking, *prajñā* and *karunā* are not two but one. Says Suzuki, 'Vimalakīrti's words, "I am sick because my fellow beings are sick", expresses the essence of religious experience. Without this there is no religion, no Buddhism, and accordingly, no Zen. It must be said that Jōshū's Zen well expresses this insight in a most thoroughgoing fashion.'[43]

One can be rightly called 'The true man of no rank' when in the person the great wisdom is rooted in the great compassion and the great compassion is rooted in the great wisdom. As proof of the clear realization of this idea in Chao-chou, Suzuki quotes another *mondo*.

> Somebody asked Jōshū, "Buddha is the enlightened one and teacher of us all. He is naturally free of all the passions (*kleśa*), is he not?"
> Jōshū said, "No, he is the one who cherishes the greatest of all the passions."
> "How is that possible?"
> "His greatest passion is to save all beings!" Jōshū answered.[44]

From this point of view Suzuki stressed, especially in his later years, affinity between Shin Buddhism (Pure Land True Buddhism) and Zen Buddhism. Indeed, he emphasized the basic oneness of the very root of Amida's *pranidhāna* (original Vow) and Zen's Realization of the true 'Person'.

With heartfelt sympathy, Suzuki often quoted in his writings and lectures Chao-chou's story of the stone bridge.

One day a monk visited Jōshū and said: "O Master, your stone bridge is noted all over the empire, but as I see it, it is nothing but a rickety log bridge."

Jōshū retorted, "You see your rickety one and fail to see the real stone bridge."

The monk asked, "What is the stone bridge?"

Jōshū: "Horses pass over it; donkeys pass over it."[45]

The following comment by Suzuki on this story well expresses his view of Zen and of the true human way of life.

Jōshū's bridge resembles the sands of the Ganges, which are trampled upon by all kinds of animals and incredibly soiled by them, and yet the sands make no complaint whatever. All the footprints left by creatures of every description are effaced in no time, and as to their filths, they are all effectively absorbed, leaving the sands as clean as ever. So with Jōshū's stone bridge: not only horses and donkeys but nowadays all kinds of conveyances, including heavy trucks and trains pass over it and it is ever willing to accomodate them. Even when they abuse it its complacency is not at all disturbed. The Zen man of the "fourth step"[46] is like the bridge. He may not turn the right cheek to be struck when the left one is already hurt, but he works silently for the welfare of his fellow beings.[47]

Suzuki, in my view, not only appreciated Chao-chou's story of the stone bridge; he himself was a stone bridge over which men and women, scholars and laymen, artists and psychoanalysts, Easterners and Westerners, all passed for the extraordinary length of his life of ninety-five years. He, or 'The true man of no rank' realized in him, will serve timelessly as a stone bridge, spanning East and West, for all his fellow beings.

Part II
Zen, Buddhism, and
Western Thought

4 Zen and Western Thought

'Zen and Western Thought' is one of the intellectual areas which must by all means be studied and elucidated in today's world. And yet it is an extremely difficult subject. To deal, in all its ramifications, with this theme which is so vast and difficult to grasp in its core, is quite beyond the powers of the present writer. I shall attempt here only a preliminary sketch with the hope that I can revise it in the future after I have obtained the criticisms of my learned readers.

I

In both the present and the past, in both the West and in the East, man has not been satisfied with living only in immediate actuality, only in the phenomena of sensation, only in the present world. He feels eternal beauty even in the falling petals of a flower. Looking up to the starry heavens above, he senses a universal law. Perceiving his own evil and that of others, he seeks ideal forms of man. In the face of life which ends in death, he longs for the existence of an imperishable world. These are all sentiments rooted in man's nature. The human heart does not rest from its quest for an invisible world behind the visible world, for law at the basis of phenomena, for meaning behind events, and for ideals on the other side of actualities. This incessant quest originates in an essential demand of man which compels him to search for something which transcends the present world precisely because he lives within the present world, for something universal precisely becaue he is concerned with individual phenomena, for something unchanging and eternal since he experiences the ceaseless changes of birth and death. The philosophers have said that man is a metaphysical animal, and it can be said that this definition is fundamental and common to East and West, past and present. But precisely because man is a metaphysical animal, he comes also to reveal a perspective which

83

denies the existence of ideals which transcend the reality of the present, and of the eternal behind things, and to manifest a standpoint which insists that this present world of individual events is the one and only existing world.

Consequently, this opposition and tension between actualities and ideas, immanence and transcendence, individual and universal, temporal and eternal, runs incessantly through human existence, ever making human life itself *problematic*. I shall here call this the opposition and tension between *ji* and *ri*.[1] Human existence is penetrated through and through by the opposition and tension of *ji* and *ri*, and precisely thereby, humanity cannot help but be aware of itself as a *problem* – this is the fate and essence of man.

This usage of *ji* and *ri* is of Buddhist origin, in which *ji* means the actual, phenomenal, particular, temporal, and differentiated; *ri* connotes the ideal, noumenal, universal, eternal, and undifferentiated. In this essay these two Japanese words are used as the key terms to discuss both Buddhist and Western thought. As discussed below, Buddhist and Western thought differ greatly in their *concrete understanding* of what the ideal and universal are. Similarly, as even within the context of Western thought, there are a multiplicity of philosophical viewpoints, the following study will explore *differences of nuance* in terms connoting the notions of *ji* and *ri* as they occur in such philosophies as those of Plato, Aristotle, Kant or as found in Christianity.

There are standpoints which attempt to grasp and comprehend the totality of the opposition and tension between *ji* and *ri* by taking the former (*ji*) as foundational. These are the various empiricist positions common to both East and West. In contrast to them, other standpoints endeavor to grasp and comprehend the same totality of the opposition and tension between *ji* and *ri* by taking the latter (*ri*) as foundational. These are the various idealist positions which are also common to East and West (see Figure 4.1).

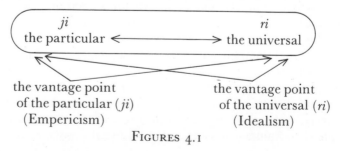

FIGURES 4.1

But neither empiricism nor idealism can be said to provide a fundamental solution to the problem of man as long as either attempts, in a one-sided way, to grasp and comprehend the opposition between *ji* and *ri* by taking one pole of that opposition as its basic principle, thus remaining within the opposition and tension rather than transcending it. For the standpoint which will give a true solution to such an opposition and tension must be one which breaks through that opposition and tension. It must be a *metaphysical* standpoint in the best sense of the word.

Accordingly, I will try, on the basis of such a metaphysical standpoint, to bring under one purview the philosophical thought of the West and East, representing the latter by Buddhist thought in particular.

In the philosophy of Aristotle, which can be called the highest peak attained by Greek thought, and especially in his *Metaphysica*, 'Being' as such, i.e., absolute *Sein*, which is the ground of the existence of beings, is established as the fundamental principle. The history of Western metaphysics after Aristotle has been erected on the extension of this concept of 'Being'. It was Kant who, attacking all these metaphysical positions as dogmatic, raised the question, 'How is metaphysics as a science (*Wissenschaft*) possible?', and who made use of his own critical method to indicate the possibility of metaphysics on an entirely new foundation. This new foundation was the transcendental law of pure practical reason, i.e., the absolute 'Ought' (*Sollen*). In Kant, the philosophical thought of the West reached a definite turning point. The metaphysics of substantive 'Being' became that of the subjective 'Ought'.

It can also be said that the process of Western philosophical thought since Kant has taken a wandering and groping course in the attempt to circumvent the tension or polarity between Aristotelian 'Being' and the Kantian 'Ought', either drawing to one side or the other of that polarity, or contriving to harmonize the two, or attempting to transcend them in some form or other. Among these philosophical endeavours, those of Nietzsche and Heidegger especially have seriously dealt with the question of 'Non-being' or 'Nothingness' (*Nichts*) which cannot be categorized as either 'Being' (*Sein*) or 'Ought' (*Sollen*).

However, the apprehension of 'Nothingness' (*Nichts*) as a primary metaphysical principle commensurate with 'Being' in Aristotle and 'Ought' in Kant (each of which had an absolute character, transcending relativity and forming the fundamental principle of the possibility of metaphysics) did not make a dominating appearance in the history of Western philosophy for over two thousand years. In the East, on the other hand, Nāgārjuna[2] of India already in the second century A.D. clearly realized the concept of 'Nothingness' in this sense and established it as a basic philosophic principle. Constituting the highest point of Indian Mahayana Buddhism, Nāgārjuna's view of 'Emptiness' (*śūnyatā*) was not merely philosophical but rather was the outgrowth of profound religious experience. Rooted in the tradition of religious self-realization going back to the time of the Buddha, Nāgārjuna philosophically established the standpoint of absolute 'Nothingness' which transcends both being and non-being. Nāgārjuna's thought became the basic point of departure of Mahayana Buddhist thought thereafter.

'Being' (*Sein*), the 'Ought' (*Sollen*), and 'Nothingness' (*Nichts*), or, in Japanese, *U*, *Ri*, and *Mu*,[3] as introduced by Aristotle, Kant, and Nāgārjuna, all have an *absolute or non-relative character* and have all, respectively, *in principle*, transcended the above discussed opposition between *ji* and *ri*. The opposition between *ji* and *ri* can be surmounted only when *u*, *ri*, or *mu* is absolutized. *Ri*, or the 'universal' in its relative sense as a pole of the opposition discussed above, when absolutized, naturally becomes *Ri* or the 'Universal' (in Kant, 'Ought') in its absolute sense. On the other hand, *ji* or the 'particular', as the other pole of the opposition, is itself a synthesis or mixture of relative being and relative non-being. Therefore, if the absolute be derived from *ji*, then *ji* will be reduced to *U* (Being) or *Mu* (Nothingness) in their absolute sense (see Figure 4.2).

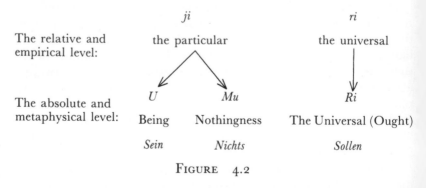

FIGURE 4.2

It can also be said that Aristotle, Kant, and Nāgārjuna, while differing in time and place, have each in their own way arrived at some kind of absolute realization. I think we should call 'Being' (*Sein*), the 'Ought' (*Sollen*), and 'Nothingness' (*Nichts*), each taken in the absolute sense, the three *fundamental categories* for human thought, and accordingly, for human existence itself. For they can be understood as the three possible categories which in principle have transcended the opposition between *ji* and *ri* which runs through human existence and forever makes human life problematic. They can be understood as the three possible *answers* to the essential problematic of human existence. Since these three categories each have a transcendental and absolute character, irreducible either to one another or to anything else, these three categories alone can be considered to be truly *fundamental* (see Figure 4.3).

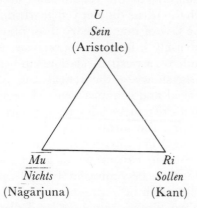

FIGURE 4.3 Three fundamental categories for human thought and existence realized either in Western thought or Buddhism

In the intellectual history of mankind, these three fundamental categories have been enunciated philosophically by Aristotle, Kant, and Nāgārjuna respectively. However, in order to clarify their fundamental character, further inquiry is necessary.

II

As is well known, Plato, who preceded Aristotle, posited Ideas (ἰδέα) behind the objects of sensation and things which come into being, pass away, and change, as that which transcends sensation and does not come into being, pass away or change. In Japanese terms, behind phenomena as *ji*, Plato posited Ideas as *ri*. Moreover, Plato conceived phenomena (*ji*) to be copies of the Ideas (*ri*) which are the original prototypes in which they participate. For Plato, the Ideas (*ri*) had more than a merely theoretical and ontological character as principles of natural existence. The Ideas also possessed an extremely ethical and practical character and were the *eros* ever driving man toward the supreme Idea which was the Good. In Plato, the Ideas as *ri* were the true realities which formed the phenomena – as *ji* – into phenomena. In these Ideas, the laws of nature and of man, theory and practice, reason and will, were grasped as not yet differentiated, i.e., without a clear realization of their distinction or duality.

Plato's understanding of the relationship between phenomena and Ideas in which the Ideas did not yet clearly differentiate the law of nature from the law of man, theory from practice, reason from will, yet were intensely ethical and practical in coloration, was replaced in Aristotle by a posited relationship between matter and form which clearly shows a theoretical and ontological nature rather than an ethical and practical one. Moreover, unlike Plato's Ideas which as self-existent entities transcended phenomena and were their prototypes, the forms of Aristotle were not separated from individual things. They existed inherently in individual things themselves as the basic causes by means of which matter (as *dynamis*) is formed, thus becoming individual things (as *energeia*). While Plato's Ideas essentially pre-existed in relation to the phenomena, Aristotelian form – which is itself distinguishable from the matter of individual things – was always co-existent with the individual thing and could be discovered only in the individual thing. Resting on but surmounting the Platonic world of Ideas (those universal principles which transcend the world of phenomena, yet make it possible), Aristotle saw the forms as inseparable from individual phenomena or individual things. It was by truly surmounting this kind of Platonic theory of Ideas that Aristotle attained to the concept of 'Being', i.e., *ousia*, which makes beings the beings they are. (This should not be taken to mean that Aristotle attributes the origin of being to the prime mover in the Christian sense of *creatio ex nihilo*.) In his achievement, we can see a radical overcoming of the opposition between *ji* and *ri*. 'Being', and especially the supreme Being as God realized by Aristotle, was 'Being' of an essential and absolute character which in this sense had risen above relativity. Accordingly, it may be considered *one of*

the fundamental categories of human thought, as I have said above.
When we look back upon Greek thought from the perspective of
the opposition and tension between *ji* and *ri*, we see that Plato's
thought considered that behind phenomena as *ji* there were Ideas as
the *ri* which made it possible for phenomena to be phenomena. The
Ideas constituted the world of true existence; phenomena constituted the world of temporal existence. In other terms, the very *ri*
which made *ji* to be such was taken to be the truly existent entity. In
surmounting this Platonic position, Aristotle in a certain sense
reversed the relationship between *ji* and *ri*. To Aristotle, individual
things were substances. Individual facts were themselves true
'Being'. This, however, should not be said in the sense of simple
immediacy. Instead, by denying the Ideas as universal *ri* which
transcended individual *ji*, and especially by denying their transcendent and separate character, Aristotle returned again to the *ji*
(phenomena) themselves – under the name of *eidos* rather than
Ideas – and therein realized the concept of 'Being'.

According to Aristotle, form should be called 'being' or *u* rather
than the 'universal' or *ri*. Only by thus denying universal *ri* that
transcended individual *ji* was Being (*ousia*), which Aristotle took as
the basis of metaphysics, realized as 'Being' that makes *ji* (particulars) to be *ji*. However, this 'Being' as form was in motion and never
at rest. God, as the supreme Being, was also the prime mover, the
pure first form (*proton eidos*) which had no trace at all of the shadow
of matter. Ultimate Being was pure activity itself.

The colourful history of Western metaphysics since Aristotle has
been the history of the different variations played on the theme of
Aristotle's notion of 'Being'. But Kant's critical philosophy put a
full stop to this history of variations on the theme of 'Being', and
was intended to be the prelude to a new metaphysics which would
strike an entirely different keynote. This new keynote was not *Sein*
but *Sollen*, i.e., the transcendental *Ri* or the 'Universal Principle' of
the law of pure practical reason.

Although Kant repudiated all ancient metaphysics since Aristotle
as dogmatic, he hardly denied man's irrepressible metaphysical
interest, i.e., his metaphysical concern itself which attempts to cognize transcendent, metaphysical objects beyond sensations. Moreover, he considered that that concern, as a disposition inherent
in man, must be fulfilled. From this standpoint, Kant raised the
critical question, 'How is metaphysical knowledge possible?' and
took as his own theme the critque of the very faculty of reason. As is

well known, what his critical philosophy made clear was that cognition of metaphysical objects was impossible through theoretical reason. It was only possible through pure practical reason and faith based on it. Here an essential distinction was made between theoretical reason (the theoretical use of reason) and practical reason (the practical use of reason), which had not been distinguished with adequate clarity since the days of Plato. Yet reason thus used in these two ways was not taken simply as reason innately given to man, but as a *transcendental pure reason* which made this natural reason possible in principle and yet established it in actuality.

In this Kantian position there emerged an entirely new tension between *ji* (particular, phenomenal) and *ri* (universal, noumenal) not seen since the days of ancient Greece. It was an extreme tension between *ji* as one pole and a new form of pure reason, *ri* – which makes *ri* as universal reason possible – as another pole. Since the Kantian transcendental pure reason makes universal reason possible, it may be called the *ri* of *ri* or the 'principle of principles'. *Ji* is legitimately able to be such only on the basis of this kind of *ri* of *ri* (transcendental principle in the Kantian sense). Moreover, what Kant clarified was that despite such a transcendental character of pure reason, as long as it is used *theoretically*, metaphysical ideas may be speculated about but their validity cannot be recognized. Only when pure reason is being used *practically* is it possible to recognize the validity of metaphysical ideas through moral faith. Kant established the possibility of metaphysical knowledge not by employing theoretical reason concerned with objects in external nature, but only by appealing to reason in its practical use. Such practical use turns pure reason deeply within and roots Subjective moral determination in one's own will. This standpoint of the primacy of practical reason constitutes a return to the standpoint of the moral and practical nature of the Platonic theory of Ideas and a displacement of the rationalistic, ontological standpoint of Aristotle. But, needless to say, it was not simply a return to the Platonic *ri* as Idea. Emphatically denying Aristotelian ontology, i.e., the standpoint of 'Being' which had in turn transcended the standpoint of Plato, Kant gave a transcendental foundation to the standpoint of pure reason, the *ri* of *ri* as stated above.

As mentioned above, Kant clearly distinguished the theoretical and practical uses of reason, and considered that metaphysical ideas could be recognized not by the former but only by the latter, i.e., only *practically* through moral faith. Therefore, Kant's fundamental principle of the possibility of metaphysics, even if called the 'principle of principles', was not that of *Müssen* (must) i.e., natural necessity, which in principle establishes the laws of nature in general, but that of *Sollen* (Ought), i.e., moral necessity, which is the foundation of the moral law in general.

Incidentally, the good, and accordingly the ought, was one focus of Aristotle's attention as well. But for Aristotle, that which is good in value ontologically meant the middle, i.e., the 'mean' (*to meson*) of things or of a situation. He grasped both the good, and virtue too, ontologically. In contrast to this position, Kant moved the problem of morality to the field of the human will, and thereby established the 'Ought' as the principle of pure practical reason. For Kant, reason is practical in essence; moreover, precisely thereby it is metaphysical. Thus through investigating the critical theme, 'How does pure reason legislate for the will?' the possibility of the categorical imperative, the standpoint of the autonomy of reason, and the epistemological foundation of such metaphysical ideas as freedom, immortality, and God, were all established on the basis of the moral reason. This position was clearly different both from Platonic *ri* or 'Idea' and from Aristotelian *u* or 'Being' which transcended Platonic *ri*. It was an entirely new standpoint of *ri* – i.e., *Ri* in the absolute sense as the truly Subjective and practical 'Ought' which self-consciously transcends the dimension of substantiality. It is precisely this Subjective *Ri*, as the transcendental moral law established by Kant as the fundamental principle, which can be viewed as the *second* basic category of human thought and existence. It thus stands in contrast to the first basic category as substantive 'Being' that was the foundation of Aristotelian metaphysics.

III

'Being' and 'Ought' were thus established as fundamental principles in an absolute sense by Aristotle and Kant respectively. However, 'Nothingness' or 'Non-being' has not come to be regarded as a basic principle of metaphysics in the West.[4]

In ancient Greece, non-being was regarded as the privation of being, i.e., *me on* or non-existence, just as darkness was considered to be the privation of light, and evil the privation of good. Non-being was not taken as existing itself as such. It was only taken as a problem in a secondary sense as the negation and privation of being. It can be said that the phrase 'nothing comes from nothing' (*ex nihilo nihil fit*) was the thought of ancient Greece, including Aristotle.

Kant, in rejecting metaphysics since Aristotle as dogmatic, also rejected moral philosophy since the time of Greece as an erroneous moral philosophy which had not critically studied the foundation of moral principles themselves. He himself critically established the standpoint of pure practical reason. Before Kant, moral reason and moral sentiment had come to be understood as innate in man. Kant, however, was reluctant to take human nature, including both moral reason and moral sentiment, as a moral principle. He firmly believed that the ethical reason and moral sentiment inherent in man could not become universal moral principles.

But this hardly led him to despair over human nature or to a realization of sin. Nor did it lead him to deny the possibility of morality. Rather, Kant was led to a new understanding of pure practical reason by asking the question: 'Can pure reason determine the will by itself?' His perspective took the morality of man neither as being nor as non-being, but as that which 'ought to be'. As the standpoint of a Subjective practical principle (more accurately, a 'principle of principles', or *ri* of *ri*), it found its basis in a transcendental ethical ought which in every case unconditionally commanded what 'you really ought to do'. Therefore, this 'ought', which Kant took to be the only principle by which metaphysics is possible, denied Aristotelian *U* or 'Being', but did not take *mu* or 'non-being' as the basic principle. Kant instead took the position of the Subjective, practical *ri* of *ri*, which regards precisely the performance of duty for duty's sake as true freedom. In his religious philosophy, Kant regarded radical evil as a profound problem, but there too he hardly abandoned this Subjective standpoint of the *ri* of *ri*. Rather, he thought to surmount even the problem of radical evil in terms of the *ri* of *ri* by deepening the meaning of that concept.

As I have stated above, it was Nāgārjuna who accomplished in an extremely radical form the grounding of 'Non-being' or 'Nothingness' as the fundamental principle of all things. But, of course, even Nāgārjuna's philosophy of 'Non-being' – more accurately, of Emptiness (*śūnyatā*) – did not emerge suddenly.

The theory of dependent origination, *pratītya-samutpāda*, which the Buddha expounded, advocated that anything experienced by us arises through dependence on something else. It involved a denial of the concept of substantiality, i.e., the concept that anything has a true substantial nature through which it can exist independently. The statement that phenomenal beings have no true selfhood (that there is nothing which has a permanent, true nature), a statement which is considered to be one of the basic teachings of Buddhism, well expresses this philosophy. Herein we can see a clear bud of the philosophy of 'Emptiness'. In early Buddhism, however, the theory of dependent origination and the philosophy of emptiness were still naively undifferentiated. It was Abhidharma Buddhism which awakened to a kind of philosophy of emptiness and set it up in the heart of Buddhism. But the method of its process of realization was to get rid of concepts of substantiality by analysing phenomenal things into diverse elements and thus advocating that everything is empty. Accordingly, Abhidharma Buddhism's philosophy of emptiness was based solely on *analytic* observation – hence it was later called the 'analytic view of emptiness'.[5] It did not have a total realization of emptiness of the phenomenal things. Thus the overcoming of the concept of substantial nature or 'being' was still not thoroughly carried through. Abhidharma fails to overcome the substantiality of the analysed elements.

But beginning with the *Prajñāpāramitā-sūtra*, Mahayana Buddhist thinkers transcended Abhidharma Buddhism's analytic view of emptiness, erecting the standpoint which was later called the 'view of substantial emptiness'.[6] This was a position which did not clarify the emptiness of phenomena by analysing them into elements. Rather, it insisted that all phenomena were themselves empty in principle, and insisted on the nature of the emptiness of existence itself. The *Prajñāparamitā-sūtra* emphasizes: 'not being, and not not being'. It clarified not only the negation of being, but also the position of the double negation – the negation of non-being as the denial of being – or the negation of the negation. It thereby disclosed 'Emptiness' as free from both being and non-being. That is, it revealed *prajñā*-wisdom.

But it was Nāgārjuna who gave this standpoint of Emptiness found in the *prajñāpāramitā-sūtra* a thorough philosophical foundation by drawing out the implications of the mystical intuition seen therein and developing them into a complete philosophical realization. Nāgārjuna criticized the proponents of substantial essence of his day who held that things really exist corresponding to concepts. He said that they had lapsed into an illusory view which misconceived the real state of the phenomenal world. He insisted that with the transcendence of the illusory view of concepts, true Reality appears as *animitta* (no-form, or non-determinate entity). But Nāgārjuna rejected as illusory, not only the 'eternalist' view, which took phenomena to be real just as they are, but also the opposite 'nihilistic' view that emptiness and non-being are true reality. He took as the standpoint of Mahayana Emptiness an independent stand liberated from every illusory point of view connected with either affirmation or negation, being or non-being, and called that standpoint the *Middle Way*.

Therefore, for Nāgārjuna, Emptiness was not non-being but 'wondrous Being'. Precisely because it is Emptiness which 'empties' even emptiness, true Emptiness (absolute Nothingness) is absolute Reality which makes all phenomena, all existents, truly *be*. The opposition and tension between *ji* and *ri* which runs through human existence and ever makes human life problematic was for Nāgārjuna to be resolved by 'Nothingness' (*Mu*) which transcends the opposition between being and non-being, that is, by 'Emptiness'. 'Nothingness' thus made absolute by Nāgārjuna as the basic principle which truly discloses reality as such is here affirmed to be the *third* fundamental category, differing from both Aristotelian 'Being' and the Kantian 'Ought'.

It may sound strange to take 'Nothingness' as one of the fundamental categories for human thought and existence in the sense of having an absolute character. For in the West 'nothingness' is always negative and is derived through the negation of 'being' as the positive principle – as expressed in terms like *me on*, *non-being*, *non-être*, *Nichtsein*, etc. However, it is precisely one of the points of this essay to elucidate, through comparison with the Western idea of non-being, the Buddhist ideas of *Mu* and Emptiness (*śūnyatā*).

Now, *mu* is not a negative form of *u* (being) and is not, like *me on* or non-being, one-sidedly derived through a negation of *u*. Being the complete counter-concept to *u*, *mu* is a more powerful form of negation than 'non-being'. In other words, *mu* is on equal footing with and is reciprocal to *u*. Accordingly, it can both be said that *mu* is the negation of *u*, and also that *u* is the negation of *mu*. But if *mu* is absolutized in principle, it can transcend and embrace within itself both *u* and *mu* in their relative senses. The Buddhist idea of Emptiness may be taken as *Mu* in this absolute sense.

In Sanskrit, equivalents to *me on* or non-being are *asat* or *abhāva* which are negative forms of *sat* or *bhāva*. To this extent it does not differ from Greek and other related Western languages. (This is due to the fact that Sanskrit is an Aryan language.) However, unlike

Greek and so forth, as Hajime Nakamura points out, 'The Indians think a negative form is not only negative but also positive and affirmative. So in Indian logic the universal negative judgment (E) is not used, and it is discussed after being changed into the universal positive judgment (A); e.g., "All the speeches are non-eternal" (*anityah śabdah*).'[7] Accordingly in Indian thinking, *sat* and *asat*, *bhāva* and *abhāva*, instead of having a simple before-after relationship, are rather understood to be, not only opposed to one another, but even contradictory to one another.

In Buddhism, which propounded 'dependent origination', *sat* and *asat*, *bhāva* and *abhāva*, are also taken to be mutually dependent with the understanding that *sat* or *bhāva* is non-self-existent reality (*asvabhāva*). Nāgārjuna's idea of 'Emptiness' was firmly established through the idea of 'dependent origination' – as the fundamental and creative principle which transcends both *sat* (or *bhāva*) and *asat* (or *abhāva*).

IV

I have discussed above how 'Being' (*Sein*), 'Ought' (*Sollen*), and 'Nothingness' (*Nichts*), which may be called the three fundamental categories of human thought and existence, were realized by Aristotle, Kant, and Nāgārjuna in absolute senses which respectively transcended relativity, and accordingly, as metaphysical principles, transcended the opposition between *ji* and *ri*. If this viewpoint can be accepted, then let me proceed to the next point: the question of why in Western thought the concept of non-being never reached the stage of realization in the radical sense of Emptiness realized by Nāgārjuna as a principle transcending the opposition between *ji* and *ri*. We must also inquire whether in Eastern thought, and especially in Buddhism, *u* (being) and *ri* (ought) were entertained as problems and investigated as basic principles which transcended the opposition between *ji* and *ri* with the same depth and radicalness which is found in Aristotle and Kant. This inquiry may provide a basic perspective from which to clarify the theme of this essay, 'Zen and Western Thought'. But before going into these questions, we must say a few words, in relation to the perspective noted above, about Hebrew thought, which was another source of Western thought, and especially about Christianity, which has deeply nourished Western philosophy for two thousand years.

Needless to say, Christianity is not a philosophy. Neither is it exhausted by thought. For Christianity is not something attainable by human reason. Rather it is a faith which earnestly follows the Word of the living God as revelation. It is not any conclusion of rational judgement, but is a life of grace, or a life in the Holy Spirit, which meets God beyond the collapse of all thought; a life in which the old man dies and is resurrected by the love of God as the new man.

But even though Christianity is faith in revelation and life in the Holy Spirit, as long as it is related to man, it is profoundly rooted in human existence and consequently it is essentially related to human thought. In this sense, it is not altogether inappropriate to consider Christianity in relation to the afore cited three basic categories of human thought, namely 'Being', 'Ought', and 'Nothingness'. This is especially so because in this essay we are attempting to view Christianity as *Christian thought* which, together with philosophical thought since the Greeks, has constituted 'Western thought.' But at the same time we must never lose sight of the fact that Christianity itself transcends Christian *thought*.

Christian religious thought, along with Greek thought, are said to constitute the two main fountainheads of 'Western thought'. But the two have extremely different natures. Generally speaking, in Greek thought, with the exception of Greek tragedy, we can see a simple and open-minded affirmation of man and the world; but in Christian thought and Hebrew thought which preceeded it, there runs a deep and keen realization of the negative aspects of human life. In that more than anything else there can be seen a despair in regard to man's intellectual and moral nature and with it a realization of being cut off from the transcendent Being. The story of the Garden of Eden indicates that man is prohibited from knowing the truth as God knows it. Indeed, the snake in the garden of paradise, which caused man to desire to know good and evil like God, was perhaps the spirit of intelligence and self-consciousness. But the episode of the expulsion from the garden also indicates that human independence based on self-consciousness is a sin and that obedience to the Word of God is the only path given to man. The God of the Hebrews is a transcendent living God who cannot be enshrined in any temple of speculative systems. Not contemplation, but faith; not metaphysics, but abandonment of intellect in favour of revelation, was required. Moreover, the Greeks had no consciousness of original sin. But the Hebrews stood trembling with fear before the justice of God. They felt compelled to consider themselves as being entirely devoid of justice, and as sinful. In that attitude there was an extremely deep and acute opposition and tension between *ji* and *ri*. Yet it was of an entirely different dimension than the corresponding opposition and tension in Greek thought.

No matter how transcendent and metaphysical in themselves were the Platonic 'Ideas' and Aristotelian 'Being', they were still immanent in comparison with the justice of the God of Christianity. They were still merely *ji* (particular events) immanent in man in comparison with the sacred 'Truth' or *Ri* of God's justice. For both Platonic Ideas and Aristotelian metaphysics were ultimately only 'the wisdom of the world' (I Cor., 1:20), which is considered to be foolishness by God. The 'wisdom of God' (ibid., 2:7) which is an inscrutable mystery, and the 'justice of God' (Psalms, 98–9) which governs the universe, entirely transcend worldly wisdom, including metaphysical concepts and human justice. In Christianity, the justice of God is *ri* in a new sense, as the *logos* of God which judges as foolishness and sin the Greek solution itself to the opposition between *ji* and *ri*, formulated in such terms as the Idea of the Good, the virtue of human justice, or the metaphysics of 'Being'.

This *Ri* as the divine *logos* is hardly a theoretical and ontological characteristic. It is an extremely practical, volitional, individual personality who appears as judging, or angry, or redeeming. And the *Ri* as the justice of God and the divine *logos* is not simply transcendent. It itself, having *become flesh*, is immanent in history in order to save mankind which had turned its back on the justice of God. The justice of God is now conferred as grace on repentant sinners. This *logos* made flesh is Jesus Christ. Those who believe in the new revelation of the Justice of God through the crucifixion of Christ are justified by means of that faith. The *logos* becoming flesh is the *Ri* becoming *ji* (the particular). The *Ri* as the *logos* of God which transcended even the cosmos had thus become *ji* in the cross of Christ. Moreover, it was an historical event which occurred only once. The Christian faith stood on the *Ri* which was revealed when this single historical 'event' took place. Consequently, the *ji* – the 'event' of the crucifixion of Christ – was a fact established in the abnegation of transcendent, eternal, divine *Ri*. It was *ji* which was inseparable from history and time.

V

Therefore, the standpoint of Christianity must be said to be an entirely independent one, which differs from both *ri* as Platonic Ideas and *U* (Being) as Aristotelian *ousia*. But in Western intellectual history, Christian theology from its comparatively early stages found a certain affinity with the Platonic position of the clearly transcendent *ri*. Augustine erected a great theology which manifested Christian faith under the decisive influence of the Platonic *ri*. This was simply because Christianity, while grounded in a dimension differing from that of Platonic philosophy and based on the historical *ji* of the incarnate Son, Christ, took as its basic principle the transcendent *Ri* of the justice of God, the Father.

Again, Thomas Aquinas went beyond Augustine by synthesizing Aristotelian philosophy with Christianity. He thereby erected a new theology which was rationalistic and ontological. Aristotelian philosophy, which at first glance seems to be extremely foreign to the Christian faith, was employed instead of Platonic thought to illuminate that faith. One main reason for this can be said to have been that knowledge of the connection of the divine with the phenomenal world, which was not altogether clear in Plato, had been clearly theoreticized in the rationalistic metaphysics of Aristotle. Again, Aristotelian philosophy, which attached importance to actual facts, had an attraction for Christianity which is not a mere idealism. For Aristotle, God was not an Idea on the infinitely unattainable other shore. As pure form, the divine itself both transcends motion and is the 'unmoving first mover' which moves the entire universe and toward which the universe ever moves. Here there emerged a metaphysical principle which dynamically linked transcendence and immanence. Thomistic theology, which thus employed Aristotelian concepts, was accordingly not a theology of Platonic 'Idea' but of Aristotelian 'Being'.[8] Moreover, it was not a theology of static 'Being' (*ens*), but of dynamic 'Being' (*esse*).[9] Here Christian thought attained one of its loftiest heights.

However, there was the danger that Christian theology thus linked to Greek philosophy – whether in Augustine or in Thomas – glossed over *ji* or the 'event' of the cross that is essential to Christianity and concealed the sacred *Ri* as the justice of God which functions at its foundation. With the Reformation, Luther overturned the Thomistic theology of 'Being', and even surmounted the Augustinian theology of the *ri*. Luther reestablished the sacred *Ri* as the *justice of God* which was inherent in the Christian teaching. Hence it was a movement to restore the *ji* (the event) of the Cross, which had been glossed over by Greek thought, back into the hands of faith. In Luther's theology, the *Ri* as the justice (*Gerechtigkeit*) of God was realized in a purity and strictness never seen before.

The history of Christianity just discussed gives evidence that Christian thought, while centring around *ji* (the event) of the Cross, has had an intense pendulum movement from *ri* to *u* and back again (see Figure 4.4).

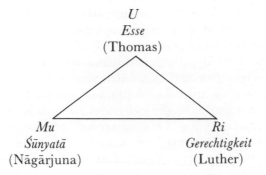

U
Esse
(Thomas)

Mu   *Ri*
Śūnyatā   *Gerechtigkeit*
(Nāgārjuna)   (Luther)

FIGURE 4.4   Three fundamental categories for human thought and existence realized either in Christianity or Buddhism

In the history of modern Protestantism, this pendulum movement can again be seen in the movement from Hegelian philosophy, which constructed a new synthesis of Greek thought and Christianity, to that of Kierkegaard, who, as he criticized Hegel, endeavoured to clarify the transcendent nature of God through a dialectic of paradox imbued with a sense of guilt and anxiety.

If this extremely rough sketch is acceptable, then we can conclude that in both the development of Christian thought and in the history of Western philosophical thought, there has always been opposition and tension in the pendulum movement between *ri* (the ideal) and *u* (being) as metaphysical principles. The concept of 'nothingness' (*mu*) articulated above was not, in the last analysis, taken as a basic metaphysical principle in Western philosophical thought. It was always understood as a secondary, negative principle. The same was true in Christian thought.[10]

Now we can draw the following conclusion from the above consideration. The opposition and tension between *ji* (the particu-

lar) and *ri* (the universal), which runs through human existence and
ever makes human life problematic, was resolved in the West in the
concepts of *u* or *ri* – *u* in the sense of Being or *esse*, or *ri* in the sense
of Idea, Ought, or divine justice – insofar as thought, and accordingly the metaphysical dimension, was concerned. It was not
ultimately resolved in the concept of 'non-being' or 'nothingness'
(*mu*) in a sense commensurate with *u* or *ri*. Therefore, in this
metaphysical dimension itself, *u* and *ri* each insisted, as positive
principles, on its own absolute nature over against the other, while
'non-being' continued to be understood as a merely negative
principle. The whole of Western intellectual history achieved its
dramatic development centering around the opposition and tension
between these two basic positive principles.

In the West, the two standpoints which since ancient times have
been called Platonism and Aristotelianism – represented in the
middle ages by Augustine and Aquinas respectively – and again,
from the modern world on, the two standpoints of Kantianism and
Hegelianism, have often been regarded as contrasting ones.
Although differing in nuance, they may be understood in the sense
of opposition between the contrasting standpoints grounded in the
above discussed *ri* and *u* as their metaphysical basis. And considering their history as a whole, it has been my interpretation that
'Being' (*U*) in Aristotle's metaphysics which transcended Plato, and
the 'Ought' (*Ri*) in Kant's critical philosophy which in turn overturned the metaphysical tradition of Aristotelian 'Being', were
each taken to be basic principles in the purest and most fundamental sense.

However, as a religion, Christianity was not exhausted by
Christian thought. By taking either *u* or *ri* as the basis of its religious
thought, the *ji* (event) of the Cross was covered over. It became too
speculative in the first instance (*u*), and too legalistic in the second
instance. Therefore, in order to recover the *ji* (event) of the Cross,
Christianity has come to develop a pendulum movement between
these two basic principles.

VI

Nāgārjuna's view of Emptiness was also not exhausted by philosophical thought. As I have said above, Nāgārjuna refuted both the
substantialists of his time and the analytic and 'nihilistic' view of

emptiness taught by Abhidharma Buddhism. He thereby demonstrated the standpoint of true Mahayana Emptiness articulated in
the *Prajñāpāramitā-sūtra* which extinguishes the opposition between
being and non-being. This emphasis took its departure from the
religious and practical intention of the salvation of all sentient
beings by criticizing the Abhidharma Buddhists for taking the
negative state of *keshin metchi* ('turning the body to ashes and
annihilating consciousness') as the ideal state of deliverance, i.e., of
nirvana, and he showed the path of true deliverance. For Nāgārjuna, the path of true deliverance involved neither attachment to
fleeting phenomena as true being, nor falling into the 'nihilistic'
view which regards everything as illusory. Rather, it was precisely
the Middle Path which transcends these two extremes. If I may say
so, by making the mystical intuition of the *Prajñāpāramitā-sūtra*
logically self-conscious, Nāgārjuna renewed, within his own historical context, the Buddha's emphasis on saving all sentient beings.
At the same time, it cannot be denied that Nāgārjuna formulated a
thoroughly philosophical and profoundly metaphysical position.

Not only in Nāgārjuna, but in the history of Mahayana Buddhism in general, there has been a struggle against both those
standpoints which take all phenomena (*ji*), including man and
human consciousness, to be true being, and those standpoints
which in contrast take phenomena as non-being. In other words,
there has been a struggle against both substantialists and nihilists.
The Buddha himself had developed the doctrine of Buddhistic non-
ego (nothing has an inherent self) and of dependent origination
(all things arise by dependence on something else), by transcending
both the philosophy of the *Upanishads* of the orthodox Brahmans,
who considered Brahman to be the only reality, and the standpoint
of the free thinkers of that time, among whom were pluralists,
skeptics, and nihilists. The Buddha's doctrine of non-ego and
dependent origination from the beginning stood in practice on the
foundation of free absolute Nothingness (emancipation), which is
free from the very opposition between being and non-being.

That Nāgārjuna's view of Emptiness keenly realized this doctrine
of non-ego and dependent origination of the Buddha, and retermed
it the Middle Way, has already been stated. We may say that such
post-Nāgārjuna concepts as the 'absolute middle' of the San-lun
School, the 'perfect true nature' of the Vijñaptimātra School, the
'perfect harmony among the three truths of the empty, the pro-
visionally-real, and the mean' of the T'ien-t'ai Sect, and 'the realm

of unhindered mutual interpenetration of phenomena and phenomena' of the Hua-yen Sect, while differing in their respective
positions, each endeavoured to fathom the standpoint of Emptiness
and non-ego essential to Buddhism. Each completely eliminated
both the 'eternalist' view which is attached to being and the
'nihilistic' view which is attached to non-being.

Attachment to something means *substantializing* that thing. Accordingly, Buddhism's search for the standpoint of Emptiness and
non-ego liberated from both being and non-being swept away both
the substantialization of being and non-being. In so doing, it meant
the denial of substantive thinking itself. When he formulated the
standpoint of true Emptiness, Nāgārjuna realized that unless he
abandoned and transcended substantive thinking itself, he could
not truly attain Subjective freedom. Because substantive thinking is
deeply rooted in the very nature of human thought, delusions and
attachments arise from it which are difficult for man to overcome.
By thoroughly negating substantive thinking, Nāgārjuna clearly
discerned, in both logical and practical terms, the Way of Buddha
who had taught deliverance from illusion and attachment when he
explained that everything arises through dependent origination.

To overcome substantive thinking completely, it was necessary to
achieve the victory over both being and non-being. For this purpose
it was essential to realize an absolute negation which 'negates even
the negation (non-being)'. But since substantive thinking is essentially rooted in man's daily egocentric way of doing things, this
realization of absolute negation, if expressed in practical terms,
means a fundamental negation of man's egocentricity, i.e., the
realization of non-ego. But the 'non-ego' here mentioned is something more than a mere subjective non-ego of each individual. Being
attained through the denial of subjective thinking itself, the 'non-
ego' is nothing less than the realization of the non-substantiality of
all things, including one's own self. The expressions 'phenomenal
things have no ego' or 'all is empty' make this same point.
Consequently, the standpoint of non-ego in Mahayana Buddhism
represented by Nāgārjuna was not simply a subjective one. It was at
the same time cosmological. Indeed, it was the position of
Mahayana Buddhism that it can only truly be Subjective by being
cosmological, and vice versa.[11]

When one develops substantive thinking beyond its habitual use
in daily human life into a logic, one thereby creates a logic of
self-identity, which tries to eliminate contradictions. Aristotle's

logic brought about a thorough refinement of substantive thinking. As we have seen, his metaphysics is grounded in 'Being' as ultimate substance, *ousia*. In ancient India, logical thinking based on substantive thinking also emerged, but it is doubtful whether 'Being' as such was realized in the same radical sense as in Aristotle. In any case, Nāgārjuna rigorously attacked the substantive thought that was influential within and outside of Buddhism at that time. Nāgārjuna thus established a standpoint of true Emptiness unique in the history of human thought. In that sense, Nāgārjuna's concept of 'Emptiness' or 'Nothingness' can be said to stand in absolute opposition to the 'Being' of Aristotle.

Even though Nāgārjuna's doctrine of 'Emptiness' has a common element with Kant's Subjective standpoint of the 'Ought' in that they both absolutely opposed Aristotle's metaphysics of substance, the position of Kant and that of Nāgārjuna are far from identical. Indeed, the doctrine of 'Emptiness' in another sense is in absolute opposition even against the *Ri* as the Kantian 'Ought'.

The notion of *ri* is often found in Buddhism too. It usually means the universal and eternal, which is not subject to birth, death, or change, in contrast to *ji*, which denotes individual phenomena that are subject to birth, death, and change. In that restricted sense, the relation between *ri* and *ji* is not unlike terms employed in Western thought to indicate the universal and the particular. However, even if the term *ri* denotes that which is universal and eternal, etc., its *content* conspicuously differs from the 'universal' in Western thought. For the universal in Western thought is something noumenal and rational such as Plato's *Idea* and Kant's pure reason, whereas *ri* in Buddhism, while expressing the unchanging nature of things, actually means *tathatā* or *thusness*, i.e., everything is truly *as it is*. This thusness or as-it-is-ness is nothing but another term for *Dharmatā*, that is, the universal nature of the dharmas (particular things). Further, in Buddhism, *tathatā* and *Dharmatā* as the universal is realized as nonsubstantial and non-rational 'Emptiness'. As *ri* or the universal in the Buddhist sense is thus nonsubstantial Emptiness, it is entirely nondual with *ji* as the particular. In this sense *ri* as the Buddhist universal is radically different from the universal in Western thought which is not nondual with the particular because of its transcendent and noumenal character.

The Japanese term *risei*, while its non-Buddhist meaning is 'reason', is also read *rishō* with the same characters in Buddhism and means 'dharma nature' or 'true thusness', as just stated. It does not mean *nous, ratio, Vernunft,* or human 'reason'. The concepts which most nearly correspond to *ratio, Vernunft,* or human reason in the history of Western thought were grasped in Buddhism as *vijñāna* ('consciousness'), *mananā* ('thinking'), and *vikalpa* or *parikalpa* ('discrimination'). They were always understood pejoratively as delusions which cannot absolutely realize the truth, and as something to be either overturned or abandoned in order to reach true wisdom. Even *nous* and *intellectus,* which were regarded in the West as faculties which truly intuit the supra-sensible divine truth, still had a kind of objectivity (or again, they still were intellectual). Under that limitation, they can be understood as negated by Nāgārjuna's theory of true Emptiness which severely repudiates all substantive and objective thinking, whether it refers to being or non-being, and which is thus based on the Subjective *nirvikalpa-jñāna* ('non-discriminating Wisdom').

To take the standpoint of Subjective 'Emptiness' which rejects all substantive thinking means to deny both the faculty of human reason represented by *nous* and *ratio* and also the ideal reality attained by *nous* and *ratio.* It means definitely not to regard them as positive principles. Again, Mahayana Buddhism, represented by Nāgārjuna's theory of true Emptiness in which all artificiality is done away with and in which 'each thing as it is in its suchness' is realized, can be understood to stand at the opposite pole from Kant's position of the pure ethical Ought – i.e., absolute *Sollen* as the foundation of the moral law in general – which unconditionally commands that 'you ought to do such and such'. Needless to say, Nāgārjuna's concept of 'Emptiness' and the Mahayana doctrine of 'naturalness' are extremely foreign to the sacred *Ri* as the justice of the God of Christianity.

In summary, the standpoint of 'Emptiness' in Mahayana Buddhism represented by Nāgārjuna took its central theme to be the realization of a free, Subjective standpoint which was liberated from the opposition and tension between being and non-being, by transcending them at their source. In Buddhism as a whole, the solution to the above discussed opposition and tension between *ji* and *ri* was sought by taking 'being' as the ultimate as in the case of *Sarvāstivāda,* or by taking 'nothingness' or 'emptiness' as the ultimate as in *Prajñāpāramitā-sūtra,* the *Mādhyamika* (the Middle Way School), etc. But, while 'being' or 'nothingness' were thus taken as ultimate principles, *ri* was not so strongly emphasized. In fact, *ri* as an universal principle in the Western sense – i.e., human reason, intellectual reality, the laws of the universe, and particularly moral principles in terms of Ought – was never taken as an ultimate principle. It was always apprehended as something secondary.

VII

We have at last reached the point of taking up the question of Zen in relation to Western thought. Zen, of course, is also not exhaustible by philosophical thought. Even if we call it religion, it is not religion in the same sense as the Mādhyamika of Nāgārjuna, or the T'ien-t'ai, or Hua-yen Schools, etc. Calling these forms of Buddhism 'doctrinal', Zen grounds itself on the principle of 'an independent transmission apart from doctrine or scripture'. When this is emphasized, it means that Zen differs from all Buddhism which stands within the doctrinal teaching. Zen is neither dependent on any sūtras (scriptures) nor shackled by any creed or tenet. It 'directly points to man's Mind.'[12] Zen holds that 'man's Mind' is itself the basic source from which all the sutras derive and is the foundation of truth which makes every teaching to be such.[13]

That 'man's Mind' – the 'Mind' initially awakened in the Buddha himself as his own inner confirmation of himself as the authentic truth – is the source of the sutras and the foundation of the teaching may be a point which not only Zen, but even the various forms of Buddhism which stand within the teaching, may equally recognize insofar as they are Buddhist. But Buddhism within the teaching attempts to reach the Mind realized by the Buddha through reliance on the sutras, that is, through teachings (believed to have been) expounded by the Buddha. Moreover, in that way does it attempt to attain the Mind initially realized by the Buddha. In contrast to this, Zen endeavours to reach the same Mind realized by the Buddha without utilizing scriptures and the teaching, and insists that in that way only is it possible to realize Mind in the true sense. (The question of whether the teachings and sutras which Buddhist schools within the teaching rely on were directly expounded by the Buddha, is not the essential issue here. The essential point, whatever the origins of the sutras may have been, is whether or not such schools utilize the teaching in general as the authoritative truth.)

Utilizing the 'teaching' means utilizing 'words' in which 'Mind' is expressed. Such a practice presupposes the premise that to reach the 'Mind' or in order for 'Mind' to be transmitted, 'Mind' must be transformed into 'words'. Even if 'Mind' is here realized to be essentially incapable of transmission outside of a transmission from mind to mind, it is still not necessarily in principle a *direct* transmission from mind to mind, but one mediated by words, i.e., through the teaching. After the Buddha attained enlightenment, he expounded various teachings, but as his reputed utterance 'For forty-nine years I have not preached a single word' suggests, preaching in Buddhism is always a non-preaching. In Buddhism, the 'word' – in no matter how fundamental a sense – essentially contains a self-negation. Buddhism standing within the teaching was not, of course, unmindful of this. Rather it depended on preaching, and accordingly on teaching, while standing on the realization that preaching was always non-preaching. Unlike other forms of Buddhism, however, it may be said that Zen, while grounded on the realization that preaching is always non-preaching, takes its stand on non-preaching itself, and accordingly, stands 'outside of scripture'.

But the Zen position goes further. Even if Buddhism within the teaching was based on preaching, and accordingly on teaching, while realizing that preaching was always non-preaching, when it regarded itself as striving to reach 'Mind' by depending on and utilizing the teaching, that Mind meant Mind of *Gautama the Buddha*, i.e., Mind realized in *Gautama the Buddha*.[14] Of course, so far as it is the *Mind* of the Buddha, for the one who has attained it, the Mind of the Buddha was immediately his own, i.e., Self-Mind. But therein the fundamental premise that the realization of Self-Mind was accomplished through the mediation of the Mind of *Gautama the Buddha* was adopted. That the Mind of Gautama the Buddha is necessary as mediator demonstrates the essential meaning of the notion of 'utilizing the scriptures.'

In contrast to this, that Zen stands on the basis of 'non-preaching' and accordingly 'apart from the scripture' while realizing that preaching is always non-preaching, does not mean the realization of Self-Mind through the mediation of the Mind of Gautama the Buddha. The Zen position rather signifies becoming free even of the Buddha himself. Therefore Zen stands outside of his teaching and his 'word'. The Zen position is that the 'Self-Mind' of the individual must *immediately* attain to *self-realization of 'Self-Mind' itself*. When the individual's own Self-Mind immediately awakens to its Self-Mind as such, the individual becomes aware that his Self-Mind is entirely one and the same with the Mind of Gautama the Buddha. Herein lies the reason that 'an independent transmission apart from the scriptures' means 'directly pointing to man's Mind' and 'awakening to his (original) Nature, thereby actualizing his Buddhahood'. This is also the reason that in Zen, 'Mind' is preferably called 'man's Mind' rather than 'Buddha Mind'.

This immediate self-realization of Self-Mind by Self-Mind itself is nothing other than the realization of 'Emptiness'. When Self-Mind immediately awakens to Self-Mind itself, the world is simultaneously awakened to as the world itself, and therefore everything in the world is revealed and realized as itself in its true (or formless) form, not as something objectified. This is the reason that true 'Emptiness' is regarded as 'wondrous Being' and as 'true thusness', and again as 'unhindered mutual interpenetration of phenomena and phenomena'. It is thus evident that Zen stands in the tradition of the *Prajñāpāramitā-sūtra* and of Nāgārjuna's view of true Emptiness, and of the Hua-yen teaching concerning 'the realm of unhindered mutual interpenetration of phenomena and phenomena'. However, Zen is not concerned with the *concepts* of 'wondrous Being of true Emptiness' and of 'unhindered mutual interpenetration of phenomena and phenomena'. Rather it straightforwardly causes their realization by destroying even these concepts. Indeed, Zen often expresses itself simply by 'raising one's eyebrows and winking one's eyes', by 'carrying brushwood and water', by 'sitting on the top of the solitary peak', and by 'working to save others at the crossroads'.

Therefore, Zen must be said to transcend any one of the three fundamental categories of 'Being', (*Sein*), 'Ought' (*Sollen*), and 'Nothingness' (*Nichts*). It is for this reason that Zen insists that 'by abandoning the four terms and wiping out the hundred negations, say what the Buddha-dharma is!'[15] And this is why in response to the question 'What is the Buddha?' it answers that it is 'a shit-wiping stick.'[16] Or, conversely, seizing the questioner himself, it answers: 'You are Etchō.'[17] But if one is to give philosophical expression to the realization of the ground of this kind of Zen activity, it must be said to be based on the 'Nothingness' of the three fundamental metaphysical categories enunciated above.

VIII

The standpoint of 'Nothingness' or 'Emptiness', which was firmly established by Nāgārjuna and constitutes the philosophical background of Zen, transcends both the theory of substantial being and the theory of nihilism. But in *the historical process* of its victory over the theory of substantial being, it can hardly be said to have confronted the kind of perspective of 'Being' realized in an absolute sense by Aristotle when he transcended Plato's Ideas. Aristotle's concept of Being, and especially Being as pure activity, uniquely and absolutely grasped in ancient Greece, can be said to have been unknown to Nāgārjuna in his discussion of 'Emptiness'. In this *historical sense*, Aristotelian 'Being' has the significance of rising above Nāgārjuna's view of 'Emptiness.'

At the same time, Mahayana Buddhism's position of 'Emptiness', represented by Nāgārjuna, has the converse significance of having *essentially* transcended Aristotelian 'Being'. For Aristotle, not the universal Idea but actually existing being, i.e., the individual, was the real substance and was regarded as real. This kind of Aristotelian 'Being' may be thought at first glance to be identical with the 'wondrous Being' of Mahayana Buddhism. But this is not so in actual fact. For Mahayana Buddhism's standpoint of 'the wondrous Being of true Emptiness' is established by radically overthrowing 'Being' in the Aristotelian sense.

Actually existing being is never pure being. Pure being is an abstract concept. For being (*Sein* or *u*) is always related to non-being (*Nichts* or *mu*). Being can be being only in contrast to non-being. Existing being always faces the non-being of extinction. Actually existing being is simultaneously being and non-being. Being and non-being are, therefore, mutually inseparable and relative concepts, and actually existing being is always being in which being and non-being are inseparable. (With *u* and *mu* in the Buddhist sense this is exactly the case.)

Ancient Greece, of course, also understood this fundamental nature of actually existing being. Plato understood this relation of being to non-being as the participation (*methexis*) of the phenomena in the Ideas. Aristotle grasped it as motion (*kinēsis*) in which matter as *dynamis* is linked to form and actualized in *energeia*. In either case, non-being (a Western equivalent to *mu*) was regarded as the privation or non-existence of being, so that a dualistic standpoint which gave priority to being resulted. Of course, in Aristotle, God as the highpoint of this motion was absolute 'Being' which transcends the duality of being and non-being. God was pure form which transcends all matter and was the *entelechy* in which all matter is actualized. But this was the perspective of absolute 'Being' attained by realizing to an ultimate point the dualistic standpoint of the primacy of being over non-being articulated by Plato. Therefore it had the character of both *overcoming* the duality of the primacy of being over non-being, and of being its *fulfilment*. As its overcoming, Aristotelian 'Being' was liberated from the duality of the primacy of being over non-being on the one hand, but as its fulfilment, it was an absolute affirmation of the same primacy of being over non-being on the other. This indicates that Aristotle's concept of absolute 'Being' was attained through the complete elimination of 'non-being' (*mu*) by bringing to a final conclusion the position of regarding *mu* as non-existence.

The problem lies in Plato's philosophy which was Aristotle's point of departure. The relational nature of being to non-being in which *actually existing being* always faces the non-being of extinction was grasped by Plato in terms of a participation in the Ideas in such a manner that being always has primacy over non-being. However, Plato's solution is not acceptable. For the relational nature of being (*u*) and non-being (*mu*) is one of mutual contradiction in which neither being nor non-being has priority.

Some Western thinkers such as Paul Tillich would insist that we cannot speak of the *mutual contradiction* of being and non-being because non-being is, logically and ontologically, dependent on being and not vice versa. Hence the priority of being over non-being.[18] But we *must* talk about the *mutual contradiction* of u and *mu*, because in reality they are interdependent and mutually negating. The mutual contradiction between *u* and *mu* is not only logically but also ontologically true. The priority of (*u*) being over (*mu*) non-being is not *ontologically* justifiable with regard to things in general and humans in particular. This is the position held by Buddhism. Herein, we see the essential difference in understanding the *negativity* of beings, including human existence, between the West and the East, especially as exemplified in Buddhism.[19]

The Buddhist idea of 'Emptiness' presents a solution of the mutual contradiction of u and *mu* inherent in actually existing being.

The position of Mahayana Buddhism expressed by Nāgārjuna took its own point of departure from such a realization of actually existing being. For Nāgārjuna, actuality was not something affirmative from which, taken as the starting point, transcendence and true Reality could be sought. Rather it was something negative which could not be taken as the point of departure in this sense. This is the reason that Nāgārjuna first of all insisted on the doctrine of the 'eightfold negation'.[20] By grasping the relational nature of being and non-being as a mutual contradiction, Nāgārjuna denied actuality itself and the nihilistic view established thereby as well. What was realized in this two-fold negation was precisely the standpoint of true 'Emptiness' (*Śūnyatā*). It was therefore the standpoint of *absolute actuality* in which actually existing being is itself realized as truly such through double negation. Hence transcendence is not something beyond, but exists immediately *here* and *now*. That 'Emptiness' was expressed as the 'Middle', as 'wondrous Being', and as 'the unhindered mutual interpenetration of phenomena and phenomena' was precisely due to this position of absolute actuality which has gone through this two-fold negation.

Speaking from the standpoint of this 'Emptiness', it must be said that in ancient Greece the absolutely contradictory nature of the opposition between being and non-being within actually existing being was not realized. Accordingly it must also be said that in Aristotle's case, even though individual entities were real substances, they were not absolute reality realized through the two-fold negation. Aristotelian 'Being' would seem to have been a fabrication projected by a human mind unable to endure actuality, in which being and non-being are mutually negating. In other words, as long as the absolute contradiction of being and non-being was not realized, actuality was grasped with the dualistic standpoint of the primacy of being as its point of departure. Consequently Aristotle's view would also seem to have been an illusory one which, in order to attain true Reality, i.e., 'wondrous Being', had to be overturned from that starting point itself.

This point will be clearer when we further consider that Aristotelian 'Being' was essentially linked to a teleological theory. In Aristotle, the universe is the process of movement in which matter as *dynamis* is actualized as *energeia* by the energy of the form as *telos* (end). It is considered in a teleological system in which God as pure form is the highest end. But does not this point tell the same story, that his real substance – the standpoint of 'Being' – is still not thoroughly carried through to a standpoint of absolute actuality such as expressed in the phrase 'the unhindered mutual interpenetration of phenomena and phenomena'? For the individual, though a real substance containing form within itself, moves from potentiality to actuality while seeking the form of a higher dimension outside itself.

Zen rejects this sort of quest for the foundation of the real in teleological terms. In the *Hsin-hsin-ming* ('On Believing in Mind'), it is written: 'Pursue not conditioned existence, nor dwell in the recognition of emptiness. When all kinds [of discrimination] come to rest, [duality] ceases of its own accord.' And Ta-chu Hui-hai (Ja: Daiju Ekai) taught:

> To seek the great Nirvana is [to make] the very karma of birth-and-death. To have realization and have enlightenment is the very karma of birth-and-death. Not to transcend the remedial means [practices to extinguish the evil passions] is the very karma of birth-and-death (*Ching-tê ch'uan-têng lu*, vol. 6).

Nirvana is usually understood as the goal of the Buddhist life. Even so, if nirvana is sought simply as the end, one must fall into the karma of transmigration of birth-and-death. For in seeking nirvana as the end by overcoming samsara, in aiming to attain enlightenment by extinguishing the evil passions, one is not free from a dualistic separation of samsara and nirvana, passions and enlightenment. Nirvana or enlightenment is, in this approach, objectified and conceptualized – karma is thus created. True nirvana cannot be objectified and should not be sought for teleologically. It is absolute actuality realized here and now which is beyond the duality of means and end, subject and object, being and non-being.

That Zen insists upon a thorough overcoming of duality, including the duality of being and non-being, is witnessed also in the statement:

> Because both being (*u*) and non-being (*mu*) are originally and essentially Nothingness (*Mu*), the various teachings concerning my true Form proclaim that being and non-being are both empty. And why? Because without being there is no non-being: thus, being and non-being are both Nothingness (*Pai lun*, vol. 2).

Therefore, this total Nothingness which transcends being and non-being is not a mere negative vacuity. As the Sixth Patriarch, Hui-nêng (Eno), wrote: 'Not a single thing obtainable, the ten thousand things are established.' The realization of total 'Nothingness' (*Mu*) is truly the Subjective fountainhead of free creative activity.

True 'Emptiness' and the Zen perspective which, realizing the absolute contradiction of being and non-being, stands on an absolute actualism or radical realism which transcends it, is therefore established by radically overturning the position of Aristotelian 'Being' that has a teleological character after taking its point of departure from the dualistic nature of the primacy of being. Zen is the standpoint of complete 'Formlessness' which destroys even the form of pure *eidos*. It thus indicates a thorough repudiation of 'being'. But such a repudiation is in fact a rejection of 'thinking' at the same time. For 'being' is always connected with 'thinking'. And 'thinking' is such insofar as that being continues to exist. In this respect we may recall what we have already related to Nāgārjuna, i.e. that his rejection of both the view of being and the view of non-being signified a rejection of substantive thinking itself which substantializes being and non-being. The perspective of substance or being is essentially linked to substantive thinking which objectifies and substantializes things. In negating the perspective of being, Zen stands on the ground of Non-thinking.

Non-thinking is a position which transcends both relative thinking and relative not-thinking. Indeed, for that very reason, Zen Non-thinking is unshackled ultimate thinking. Therefore, it transcends thinking in the usual sense. This does not mean a simple lack of understanding in respect to thought. It is rather based on a fundamental critique of the nature of thinking asserting that human thinking is essentially a substantive one. However, when Zen thus rejects thinking, does not Zen abandon human thinking without fully realizing its *positive* aspects which in the ancient Greek and the Western world broadly considered have been developed in the fields of knowledge of nature, mathematics, science, law, morality, etc.? In Zen, the positive and creative aspects of human thinking have been neglected and only its dualistic and discriminative aspects have been clearly realized as something to be overcome.

Here we may see the reason why *ri* in the Western sense was always grasped as only a negative principle in Buddhism and in Zen. Essentially, the standpoint of Non-thinking should be able to be said to have the *possibility* of giving life to the positive aspects of human thinking which have been developed in the West. But this possibility has not yet been *actualized*. Precisely the actualization and existentialization of this possibility must be the theme of the future for the standpoint of the true 'Emptiness' of the Eastern tradition.

IX

The elimination of thinking by the Zen position becomes a more serious question when we consider the perspective of ethical 'reason' represented by Kant's law of pure practical reason.

As stated above, Kant rejected as dogmatic the entire tradition of the metaphysics of 'Being' since the time of Aristotle. This implied the denial of the very position which grasps the relational nature of being and non-being in terms of the duality of the primacy of being. He attacked the very point of departure of the Aristotelian metaphysics of 'Being'. This Aristotelian position must be said to be itself based on a hidden assumption, namely a dogmatic assumption which had not been criticized. Kant's critical philosophy acutely realized this dogmatic assumption hidden at the root of the metaphysics of 'Being'. Kant's focus of attack may be said to have been a critique of the ground of that thinking which was connected with being, i.e., substantive thinking itself. Kant grasped the contradictory character of being's relation to non-being and rejected the attempt to conceive this relation in terms of a duality which gave primacy to being. For this reason, Kant established his critique on Subjectivity rather than substance.

At the same time it signified that Kant had moved, not, of course, to the perspective of 'Nothingness', the 'wondrous Being of true Emptiness', by transcending the mutually contradictory character of being and non-being in that double negation realized in the 'eightfold negation' of Nāgārjuna, but to the perspective of 'pure reason'. We have previously called it the standpoint of the *ri* of *ri* or the 'principle of principles', i.e., the transcendental foundation of the *ratio juris* of moral principle. The standpoint of the *Subject*, which was firmly established by Kant through negation of Aristotelian *substance*, was not the Subject of Nothingness (*Mu*) seen in Mahayana Buddhism. It was rather the *Subject* of the *moral principle* (*Ri*) in the sense that pure reason can determine the will by itself. For Kant pioneered the perspective of *pure reason* which entirely transcended the connection with being through his critique of the ground of substantive thinking linked to being. Moreover, by limiting its theoretical, objective function, he took metaphysics to be possible only in its practical, Subjective function. This was Kant's standpoint of the autonomy of reason, of practical freedom which takes the highest good to be the moral postulate.

We have referred above to the point that Zen, in taking the position of Non-thinking by rejecting being and thinking as well, might be abandoning, without realizing it, the positive aspects of human thinking which were developed in the West. Kant's standpoint of *moral and Subjective pure thinking* based on pure reason, which was realized only by overturning the basis of substantive thinking and which allowed for the possibility of metaphysical knowledge only to its practical, Subjective employment, must be said to have been even more unrelated to the Zen perspective of Non-thinking. It must be said that the Kantian position of the 'principle' of moral 'principles' which commands the performance of duty for duty's sake was one entirely unknown to Zen in the sense of being a metaphysical standpoint which opened up a *third* dimension that was neither the substantive 'Being' of Aristotle nor the Subjective 'Nothingness' of Zen.

But this hardly means that Zen was entirely unconcerned with the problem of good and evil. The *gatha* (verse) of the Seven Buddhas' Injunctions: 'Cease to do evil, perform all that is good', has always been honoured by Zen as well. These first two lines can be reduced to the third: 'Cleanse thy heart by thyself.'

In the statement of the text entitled *Tun-wu-yao-men lun* (*On the Essentials of Sudden Awakening*) it is said, 'thinking of good and thinking of evil is called "wrong-mindedness"; thinking not of good and evil is called "rightmindedness".' In Zen, to distinguish good and evil and to think of matters on the basis of their discrimination is itself evil or illusory thinking. Awakening to 'Mind' – which because it is free from and essentially prior to such discrimination, does not contemplate their difference – that is the true foundation. This 'Mind' is also called 'right-mindedness', 'pure Mind', 'straightforward Mind', 'one Mind', 'No-mind'. Therefore the statement 'Cease to do evil, perform all that is good' also taught not to reprove vice and encourage virtue in the moral dimension of the opposition of good and evil, but to act from the 'straightforward Mind' or 'No-mind' which transcends every discrimination, including this kind of distinction between good and evil. The third sentence, 'Cleanse thy heart by thyself', indicates this.

Zen agrees with Kant on the necessity of transcending the dimension of the opposition between good and evil. Kant also hardly focused upon the moral law in the dimension of the relative opposition between good and evil. But Zen and Kant completely part company in *how* they transcend the dimension of the opposition between good and evil. Kant grasped this problem of good and evil as that of the *determination of the will*. Seeking the basic principle which makes the will the good will, he established the law of pure practical reason which transcends all experience. This is what we have called the standpoint of the Subjective 'principle of principles' in Kant. In contrast to this, Zen grasped the problem of good and evil not as a problem of free will, but as that of the *discriminating mind* which distinguishes the two dimensions of good and evil. Zen advocated that we must awaken to No-mind itself which transcends all discrimination. This was the Zen position of Subjective 'Nothingness' (*Mu*) which is not *ri*.

In Zen, therefore, the problem of good and evil is of course a real one, but it is grasped, not as a problem of the moral will and its laws, but as one of the discriminating mind and, in the last analysis, of objective-substantive thinking which establishes the duality. Together with and in the same way as is the problem of life and death, the problem of good and evil is transcended in Non-thinking which is liberation from the discriminating mind itself. This means that the Kantian 'Ought' (*Ri*) goes beyond the Zen standpoint of 'Nothingness' (*Mu*) in the sense of squarely taking up the question of the moral law and of clarifying its transcendental foundation. But at the same time, as the standpoint of Non-thinking, Zen has the significance that it transcends the Kantian 'Ought' as well. But in what sense?

In saying that 'Reason is practical and metaphysical in essence', Kant took his stand, not on a contemplative position which saw the world as a process of motion aiming at pure form, as in Aristotle, but on that of the practical 'Ought' in which the categorical imperative 'You ought to act' ever reverberated at the root of human existence in an interminable struggle between sensuality and reason. Here the objectivity, the non-subjectivity, of Aristotelian 'Being' was transcended. But in Kant even though the transcendental ground of the subject was grasped in a deeply Subjective manner as expressed by pure 'Ought', it cannot be said to have entirely overcome objectivity. For Kant's 'Ought' is still something standing against us and thereby something objective in the sense that the 'Ought' is an unconditional moral imperative imposed upon our being. As pure 'Ought', his position was most Subjective, but at the same time non-Subjective. This may be clearer when we consider that Kant's critical philosophy, while severely rejecting Aristotelian teleology, established its own kind of teleology which was not a cosmological but a moral one.

Zen stands on the basis of 'Non-action' and 'no-business'[21] by transcending every 'ought'. It says: 'He neither seeks the true nor severs himself from the defiled; he clearly perceives that dualities are empty and have no reality' (*Ch'eng-tao ke, Song of Enlightenment*). Again it says: 'The true nature of ignorance is the Buddha-nature; the empty body of illusory transformation is the Dharma-body' (ibid.). It further says: 'Buddha Mind is seen to accord with ordinary mind' (*Pi-yen-chi*. Case 62). Zen destroys the commonly understood view that the Buddha Mind is something which 'ought' to be sought somehow beyond 'this shore.' By transcending the standpoint which *seeks* anything – which seeks anything *externally* – it returns to the absolute actuality which is the 'interior of the interior' of the self. The very point of 'Non-action' which cannot be the 'ought' is nothing but the 'not thinking of good, not thinking of evil', at which time 'the Original Face' becomes manifest.[22] Herein lies the Zen position which takes as its practical ground the 'Non-abiding Origin' which is free from every moral law and moral principle by radically overturning all practical teleologies. It is the unconventional, free and easy, open-minded state of 'the Great Activity which presents itself independent of rules'. It is also the basis of the eternally expressed pledge: 'However innumerable beings are, I vow to save them.[23]

Thus the Zen position of 'Non-action' and 'no-business' transcends the standpoint of the 'Ought'. But it did not necessarily experience a self-conscious confrontation with the moral and ethical 'Ought' so keenly realized in the intellectual tradition of the West. The fact that, as a result, Zen often harboured the danger of losing its own authentic freedom, of falling into a non-critical dilettantism, and of sinking into a mere non-ethic or anti-ethic is one that must not be minimized. If Zen feels a mission as a true 'world religion', then an open-minded confrontation with the standpoint of the 'principle' of moral 'principles' realized by Kant and a confrontation with various problems contained therein – such as free will, the autonomy of reason, realization of transcendental moral laws, radical evil, etc. – must be said to be inescapable.

X

In both the Aristotelian 'Being' and the Kantian 'Ought', which represent Western philosophical thought, objectivity – not in the usual sense of objectivity, but in a profound sense as a kind of non-subjectivity – was discovered. This may be seen in the fact that both these perspectives, while differing in their respective meanings, have a teleological character. That they still have a kind of objectivity, even though not in the usual sense, and are teleological, implies that these perspectives have some sort of *form*, i.e., are *not* completely formless. That they have 'form' means that neither 'Being' or 'Ought' is free from *thinking*. The Aristotelian 'Being' and the Kantian 'Ought' differ in that one is substantive, the other Subjective; but both are essentially linked to 'thinking'. In order to transcend every kind of objectivity and stand on a *truly* Subjective ground, *emancipation must be made from thinking itself*. This implies a radical conversion of the standpoints of 'Being' (*U*) and 'Ought' (*Ri*)

The Zen position, which is grounded on Non-thinking, essentially has such a meaning. Non-thinking, to speak of it in terms of action, means Non-attachment. Therefore, it is the 'Non-abiding Origin' through which all things are established. Because it is a Subjective position which cuts across all thinking and transcends the objectivity connected with *u* and *ri*, it thinks purely and freely, and wills and acts completely unshackled by anything. Thus it is activity which, without being in any sense teleological, functions creatively according to things confronted in the given situation. This is the reason Lin-ch'i (Rinzai) said that 'If you are master of yourself, wherever you go, all is right with you. No matter what the circumstances are they cannot dislodge you', and also:

> When host and guest meet they vie with one another in discussion. At times, in response to something, they may manifest a form; at times they may act with the entire body; or they may, by picking up a device, [make a display] of joy or of anger; or they may reveal the half of the body; or again, they may ride upon a lion or ride a kingly elephant (*Lin-ch'i lu*).

As long as we are attached to the standpoint of thought, no matter how much we have purified and internalized it, we cannot avoid seeing the self from the outside, i.e., cannot avoid some kind of objectivity, or non-subjectivity. No matter how well the eye can see everything else, it cannot see itself; similarly, even if it can think of everything else, thinking cannot think of thinking itself as long as it goes no further than the standpoint of thinking. When it attempts to do so, it inevitably falls into a self-bind. This self-limitation from which thinking cannot extricate itself is, as long as thinking is attached to the standpoint of thinking, not realized by thinking itself. This self-bind is nothing less than the manifestation of a blindspot which thinking has simply because thinking is the activity of thinking.

Aristotle discerned the concept of 'Being' which causes existing things to be such by bringing substantive thinking concerning existing beings to a final conclusion. Here he discovered God as thought thinking itself (*noēsis noēseōs*). But that God was the ultimate foundation of every existing being and yet simultaneously regarded as the supreme end to be attained meant that 'thought thinking itself' *was still thought* in some way, i.e., was regarded as an object of thought, although not in the usual sense.

By the self-critique of reason, Kant clearly recognized this blind-spot which ran through Aristotle's metaphysics of 'Being' and through all metaphysics subsequent to Aristotle. The result was his doctrine in which the thing-in-itself was said to be unattainable by theoretical reason. Kant's so-called antinomies of pure reason exposed the self-bind which substantive thinking unconsciously harboured in the area of metaphysics. Through his critique, Kant thus shifted the ground of the possibility of metaphysics from substantive (theoretical) thinking to Subjective (practical) thinking. As far as metaphysics was concerned, thought linked to 'being' was severed and thought linked to the Subjective 'Ought' (*Sollen*) was taken up. In this way he firmly established a Subjective standpoint liberated from objectivity connected with 'being'. Therefore, Kant keenly realized the self-bind and the blind-spot harboured by *substantive thinking* connected with being on which Western metaphysics since Aristotle had been grounded. But it may be thought that Kant did not necessarily realize the self-bind and the blind-spot which *thinking itself* possesses. At the least, he may have thought that he could avoid the self-bind and blind-spot by thoroughly purifying thinking to the standpoint of pure reason – indeed, of Subjective pure reason.

In Western thought, the first philosopher who clearly realized the cul-de-sac of thinking itself would seem to have been Nietzsche. This was hardly unconnected with the fact that Nietzsche was the first philosopher in Western intellectual history to grasp 'non-being' in a positive sense, i.e., in the form of an active nihilism. It is well known that Nietzsche overturned the traditional Western value system which was rooted in Platonism and Christianity, and announced the arrival of nihilism. In respect to philosophical thought, he regarded the entire 'true world' established by traditional metaphysics to be a fabrication. He destroyed thinking linked not only to being but to ideal (ought) as well, and took 'life' and the 'will to power' as his own position.

Heidegger then in a sense brought Nietzsche's position to its final conclusion. In contrast to Nietzsche who, in overturning the standpoint of thinking itself, focused his attack rather on thinking linked to *ri* or ought – therefore critiques of Platonism and Kant's ethical theory were striking – Heidegger attempted to transcend traditional Western thinking in general by especially attacking thinking linked to *u* or being, thereby undermining the very foundation of Western metaphysics. Heidegger, like Nietzsche – indeed, more radically than Nietzsche – focused upon the problem of 'nothingness' and thereby opened up a standpoint extremely close to Zen. This may be said to have derived from his intention to trace back the hidden root of traditional Western thought represented by Aristotle and Kant, i.e., Western thought itself which, taking on a teleological character, had not avoided some kind of non-subjectivity. Considering the history of Western metaphysics as the history of the forgetfulness of 'Being', Heidegger tried to ask the meaning of 'Being' itself (*Sein selbst*) which is disclosed by passing beyond Aristotelian 'Being' to its root source through the realization of 'nothingness'. At the same time, however, he did not depart from thinking itself, and tried to the last to stay in a kind of thinking – the *Denken des Seins* in a sense intrinsic to Heidegger. To that extent he must be said still to differ from Zen which is grounded on Non-thinking. Indeed, it would seem that Heidegger's intention was rather to open up a new path of thinking following the traditional course of Western metaphysics without departing from the standpoint of thinking and to make the forgotten 'Being' present itself truly as 'Being' as such.

Zen is grounded in Non-thinking which is not shackled by either thinking or not-thinking and yet freely uses both of them. But precisely because of its standpoint of Non-thinking, Zen has in fact not fully realized the positive and creative aspects of thinking and their significance which have been especially developed in the West. Logic and scientific cognition based on substantive objective thinking, and moral principles and ethical realization based on Subjective practical thinking, have been very conspicuous in the West. In contrast to this, some of these things have been vague or lacking in the world of Zen. Because Zen (at least Zen up until today) has thus not fully realized the positive and creative aspects of human thinking, its position of Non-thinking always harbours the danger of degenerating into mere not-thinking. In fact, Zen has frequently degenerated into this position. That Zen today lacks the clue to cope with the problems of modern science, as well as individual, social, and international ethical questions, etc., may be thought partly to be based on this.

If Zen intends to be a formative historical force of the human world as a new 'world religion' in the 'one World' which is coming, Zen must take up as its historical task to place substantive thinking and Subjective thinking, which have been refined and firmly established in the Western world, within the world of its own Non-thinking, and to make them function from 'the Origin of Non-attachment', so as to establish various things in their particularity. However, to carry out this task, just as the Western notions of 'Being' and 'Ought' are being forced into a basic reexamination through present dialogue between Zen and Western thought, Zen too must internally embrace the standpoints of Western 'Being' and 'Ought' which have been foreign to itself. And it must grasp again and renew its own standpoint of 'Nothingness' so as to be able truly to concretize and actualize its Non-thinking in the present moment of historical time.[24]

5 Non-Being and *Mu* – the Metaphysical Nature of Negativity in the East and the West

In Volume I of his *Systematic Theology*, Paul Tillich says, 'Being precedes nonbeing in ontological validity, as the word "nonbeing" itself indicates.'[1] Elsewhere, he says 'Being "embraces" itself and nonbeing',[2] while 'Nonbeing is dependent on the being it negates. "Dependent" points first of all to the ontological priority of being over nonbeing.'[3] Tillich's statements reflect a tendency among some Christian thinkers to take God as Being itself. The same understanding of the relation of being to non-being can be discerned in major strands of Greek philosophy in the ideas of *to on* and *me on*. Although Greek philosophy and the Christian movement have different starting points in time, in geographical locale, and in conceptual orientation, Tillich's statements demonstrate the way in which the two strands have to a significant degree merged, and his comments reflect a basic understanding (if not *the* basic understanding) of being and non-being in the West.

An objection must be made to this understanding of being, however, for in reality there is no ontological ground on which being has priority over non-being. It is assumed that being embraces *both* itself *and* non-being. But the very basis on which *both* being *and* non-being are embraced must not be 'Being' but 'that which is neither being nor non-being'. That being has priority over, is somehow superior to, and more fundamental than, non-being, has been assumed, perhaps uncritically, not only by Tillich in particular but for quite some time by the West in general.

I

In ancient Greece, just as darkness is considered to come to exist where light is lacking, non-being is understood to 'appear' when being is lacking. Non-being is understood as *sterēsis, privatio*, or privation of being, that is as *me on*. Parmenides said, 'What is, is; what is not, is not.' Plato distinguishes 'what is not' into *me on* as the relative negation of being and *ouk on* as the absolute negation of being. He rejects the latter as unthinkable and unknowable whereas he understands the former in correlation with *to on*. For Plato, actual existence is always comprised of both being and non-being as illustrated by the fact that phenomena cannot escape coming into being, changing, and passing away. But pure being is unchangeable and eternal as the *idea* which is the original prototype for which phenomena are copies. Again, for Plato, *eidos* or form, which determines an actual existence, is 'being', whereas *hyle* or matter, which is formed by *eidos*, is 'non-being' because it is undetermined and formless in itself. Further, from the ethical point of view, 'being' is identified with good (*agathon*) while 'non-being' is regarded as the metaphysical source of evil. In short, the ancient Greeks understood non-being merely as the privation of being and hence exhibited an affirmative attitude toward this life.

Christians have always believed in God as the creator who transcends his creation and his creatures. God did not create the universe out of some 'given' matter but created everything, including matter itself. Tillich says, 'The *me-ontic* matter of Platonism represents the dualistic element which underliēs all paganism – Christianity has rejected the concept of *me-ontic* matter on the basis of the doctrine of *creatio ex nihilo*. Matter is not a second principle in addition to God.'[4] Thus, the *nihil* out of which God creates is *ouk on*, the absolute negation of being. According to Tillich, God, who has revealed himself in terms of 'I am that I am' (*'ehyeh 'asher 'ehyeh*: *'hāyāh'* as the root of *'ehyeh'* means happen, become, be), is being itself or the ground of being which has the power of resisting non-being.[5] On the other hand, all creatures, being created out of nothing, are always facing the abyss of nihility. Further, within the Christian tradition, God is not a philosophical principle but the living personal God who is love and justice. So, for that tradition, the issue of being and non-being is not only an ontological issue but also a practical and religious one in which notions like fidelity, sincerity, falsehood, deception, sin, faithfulness and rebellion, justice and injustice are integrally involved. Accordingly *nihility*, being a part of a person as a finite creature, indicates the negative aspect of human being. In the ethical dimension, it functions as the source of *evil* as the privation of good. But in the religious dimension peculiar to Christianity, which is based on personal God, *nihility* is not merely a privation of good, but is rather the source of *sin* as the rebellion against the will of God, the negative principle in human life which constantly tries to undermine God's essential goodness.

In comparison with Platonism, Christianity takes the ideas of being and non-being (both *me on* and *ouk on*) more existentially and more profoundly. Yet, the notion that being in some way has priority over non-being is common to both Platonism and Christianity. However, as stated above, there is in reality no ontological ground on which being has priority over non-being; being need not be assumed to be superior to, or more ultimate than, non-being. The point at issue lies in how the *negative principle* should be understood in relation to the positive principle. The objection mentioned above might become more cogent in the light of the following two observations:

First, being-and-non-being can be taken as an ontological category corresponding to life-and-death, good-and-evil, and other polarities. Therefore, it must be asked: what is the ontological ground for the superiority of life over death? Is the Western presumption that good is superior to evil fully justifiable in the final analysis? It is needless to say that life is more *desirable* than death; good *should be* superior to evil. However, whether *human actuality* can be controlled by the desire for life and a moral imperative is another problem.

Secondly, since being prevails in the balance of being and non-being, to overcome the opposition between being and non-being means to approach Being with a capital 'B' as the end. In the same way, to overcome the opposition between life and death means to attain Eternal Life, and to overcome the opposition between good and evil means to move toward and finally arrive at Supreme Good. But since the idea of the priority of the positive principle over the negative principle must be called into question, the ideas of Being itself, Eternal Life, and Supreme Good must also be subjected to severe scrutiny (see Figures 5.1 and 5.2).

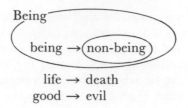

life → death
good → evil

FIGURE 5.1   'Being precedes non-being in ontological validity.'
'Being "embraces" itself and non-being.'

Paul Tillich

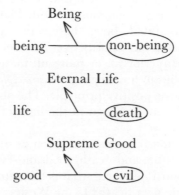

FIGURE 5.2   Since being precedes non-being in ontological validity,
overcoming of the opposition between them necessi-
tates a movement towards Being as the ultimate. The
same thing happens with life and death, good and evil.

II

In the East, people who have identified themselves with the
Confucian tradition, have emphasized human ethics and the intrinsic goodness of the human. Having thus understood positivity and
negativity in a way not unlike Western humanism, their view of
what it means to be genuinely human has a common element with
certain traditions in the West. Taoists and Buddhists, however,
have maintained that the idea of nothingness is ultimate, and in this
sense they have no Western counterpart.

With regard to the Taoist tradition, Lao Tzŭ says in the opening
sentences of the *Tao-tê ching*, 'The Tao which can be expressed in

words is not the eternal Tao: the name which can be uttered is not its eternal name. Without a name, it is the Beginning of Heaven and Earth; with a name, it is the Mother of all things'.[6] He also says 'Heaven and Earth and the ten thousand things are produced from Being: Being is the product of Non-being.'[7] It is clear that, for Lao Tzŭ, the Tao as the basic principle of the universe is completely unnamable, unknowable, and nonexistent, and yet it is all-embracing and unfailing. In this respect Chuang Tzŭ is even more radical. He says, 'If there was a beginning, then there was a time before that beginning. And a time before the time which was before the time of that beginning. If there is existence, there must have been non-existence. And if there was a time when nothing existed, then there must have been a time before that – when even nothing did not exist. Suddenly, when nothing came into existence, could one really say whether it belonged to the category of existence or of non-existence? Even the very words I have just now uttered, – I cannot say whether they have really been uttered or not.'[8]

Here Chuang Tzŭ expresses a realization of the necessity of a thoroughgoing negation in order to reach ultimate Reality, which is completely beyond beginning and end, existence and non-existence, somethingness and nothingness. For Chuang Tzŭ, being and non-being have both sprung from Tao, and thus are two aspects of Tao, which is completely unnameable. On the basis of the Tao, he advocates 'excursions into freedom' as the ideal life. He shares Lao Tzŭ's idea that 'Tao never does, yet through it all things are done.'[9]

In ancient India the significance of negativity is clearly realized even before the rise of Buddhism. Upanishadic Philosophy emphasizes the oneness of *Brahman* and *ātman* (which is expressed only negatively in terms of *neti, neti*) as the seer who cannot be seen, the knower who cannot be known. But *Brahman* and *ātman* are understood as eternal, unchangeable and substantial. Rejecting the substantial nature of *ātman*, Buddhists advocate *anātman* or absence of an eternal self and *anitya* or impermanence. That everything is impermanent, having no eternal selfhood (self-being) and no unchangeable substance, is one of the basic principles of Buddhism. That everything is dependent on something else, that nothing is independent and self-existing, is another basic Buddhist principle. This is termed *pratītya-samutpāda*, which can be translated as dependent origination, relationality, relational origination, or dependent co-arising. The realization that everything is impermanent and dependently originating must be applied to things not only *in* the universe but also *beyond* the universe. Thus Buddhists have maintained that the idea of the one and only God who is the creator and ruler of the universe and the idea of *Brahman* which is the eternal and sustaining power of the cosmos are both ultimately inadequate. For Buddhists, each and every thing is neither the creation of a transcendent God nor something immanent in the imperishable *Brahman*, but rather dependently co-arising without an eternal and substantial selfhood. When one does not fully realize this truth and becomes attached to one's possessions, beloved persons, and oneself as if they were permanent and imperishable, one is in illusion and will inevitably suffer. When one awakens to this truth, however, one realizes ultimate Reality, frees himself or herself from illusion and suffering, and attains *nirvana* in which wisdom and compassion are fully realized and thereby become the basis for one's real life and activity.

Buddhist ideas of *anātman* or absence of an eternal self, the impermanence of all things, and dependent origination, all imply the negation of being, existence, and substantiality. It is Nāgārjuna who established the idea of *Śūnyatā* or Emptiness by clearly realizing the implication of the basic ideas transmitted by the earlier Buddhist tradition. It must be emphasized that Nāgārjuna's idea of Emptiness is not nihilistic. Emptiness which is completely without form is freed from both being and non-being because 'non-being' is still a form as distinguished from 'being'. In fact, Nāgārjuna not only rejected what came to be called the 'eternalist' view, which proclaimed the reality of phenomena as the manifestation of one eternal and unchangeable substance, but additionally denounced its exact counterpart, the so-called 'nihilistic' view, which insisted that true reality is empty and non-existent. He thus opened up a new vista liberated from every illusory point of view concerning affirmation or negation, being or non-being, as the standpoint of Mahayana Emptiness, which he called the Middle Path. Accordingly, Nāgārjuna's idea of the Middle Path does not indicate a midpoint between the two extremes as the Aristotelian idea of *to meson* might suggest. Instead, it refers to the Way which transcends every possible duality including that of being and non-being, affirmation and negation. Therefore, his idea of Emptiness is not a mere emptiness as opposed to fullness. Emptiness as *Śūnyatā* transcends and embraces both emptiness and fullness. It is really formless in the sense that it is liberated from both 'form' and 'formlessness'. Thus, in *Śūnyatā*, Emptiness as it is is Fullness and Fullness as it is is Emptiness; formlessness as it is is form and form as it is is formless. This is why, for Nāgārjuna, true Emptiness is wondrous Being.

This dialectical structure of *Śūnyatā* may be logically explained as follows: since *Śūnyatā* is realized not only by negating the 'eternalist' view but also by negating the 'nihilistic' view, which negates the former, it is not based on a mere negation but on a negation of the negation. This double negation is not a relative negation but an absolute negation. And an absolute negation is nothing but an absolute affirmation, logically speaking, the negation of the negation is affirmation. Yet, it is not a mere and immediate affirmation. It is an affirmation which is realized only through double negation, i.e., absolute negation. Thus we may say that absolute negation is absolute affirmation and absolute affirmation is absolute negation. This paradoxical statement well expresses the dialectical and dynamic structure of *Śūnyatā* in which Emptiness is Fullness and Fullness is Emptiness.

III

This brings us to a crucial point of the discussion. The dynamic structure of *Śūnyatā*, explicated above, would be impossible if, as in the Western intellectual traditions, the positive principle were understood to have ontological priority over the negative principle. Only when the positive and the negative principles have equal force and are mutually negating is the dialectical structure of *Śūnyatā* possible. This is most clearly seen in the Japanese terms, 有 *u* and 無 *mu*. The term 有 *u* stands for being and the term 無 *mu* for non-being. Unlike Western ideas of being and non-being (*to on* and *me on*, *être* and *non-être*, *Sein* and *Nichtsein*), *u* and *mu* are of completely equal force in relation to one another. They are entirely relative, complementary, and reciprocal, one being impossible without the other. In other words, *mu* is not one-sidedly derived through negation of *u*. *Mu* is the negation of *u* and *vice versa*. One has no logical or ontological priority to the other. Being the complete counter-concept to *u*, *mu* is more than privation of *u*, a stronger form of negativity than 'non-being' as understood in the West. Further, *u* and *mu* are completely antagonistic principles and therefore inseparable from one another, and thus constitute an antinomy, a self-contradiction. The Buddhist idea of *Śūnyatā* shows the standpoint realized through overcoming that antinomic, self-contradictory oneness of *u* and *mu*.[10]

In the West, since being is considered ontologically prior to non-being, the ultimate, beyond the opposition of being and non-being, is Being with a capital 'B', which can be indicated by a line slanted in the direction of Being (see Figure 5.2). By contrast, in Buddhism, *Śūnyatā*, as the ultimate, is realized by directly transcending the very duality of *u* and *mu*, which stand on equal footing and are completely reciprocal, as represented by Figure 5.3.

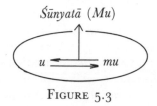

Śūnyatā (*Mu*)

FIGURE 5.3

Accordingly, the ultimate for Buddhists is not 'Being' itself but formless 'Emptiness' which is neither *u* nor *mu* and which is often referred to as absolute *Mu* as distinguished from relative *mu*.

Strictly speaking, however, if Emptiness or absolute *Mu* is a third category which simply transcends and stands somewhat outside of the duality of *u* and *mu* (as Figure 5.3), it cannot be called true Emptiness or true absolute *Mu*, for Emptiness or *Mu* thus understood is only *something* named 'Emptiness' or '*Mu*', i.e.,'nothingness', and not true Emptiness or true Nothingness (*Mu*). In other words, it still stands in a dualistic relation to *u* and *mu*. It is only by overcoming this kind of duality as well that true Emptiness or true absolute *Mu* is realized. Although the realization of Emptiness is essential, one should not cling to Emptiness as Emptiness. This is why Mahayana Buddhism, which is based on the idea of Emptiness, has throughout its long history rigorously rejected the attachment to Emptiness as a 'confused understanding of Emptiness', a 'rigid view of nothingness', or a 'view of annihilatory nothingness'. In order to attain true Emptiness, Emptiness must 'empty' itself; Emptiness must become non-Emptiness. Thus true Emptiness is wondrous Being, absolute *U*, the fullness and suchness of everything, or *tathatā*; it is ultimate Reality which, being beyond *u* and *mu*, lets both *u* and *mu* stand and work just as they are in their reciprocal relationship. Figure 5.4 indicates the dynamic structure of *Śūnyatā* which, being formless (illustrated by a dotted line), is beyond both *u* and *mu* and yet makes them and their reciprocal relationship possible.

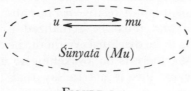

FIGURE 5.4

The erroneous understanding of and attachment to Emptiness is a result of conceptualising it. The Buddhist idea of Emptiness can be properly realized not conceptually, but only holistically, Subjectively, or existentially through the realization and subsequent breakthrough of one's own existence as a self-contradictory oneness of being and non-being, that is, of *u* and *mu*.

This existential realization that true Emptiness 'empties' itself indicates that it is not a static state which is objectively observable but a dynamic activity of *emptying* in which everyone and everything are involved. Indeed, there exists nothing whatsoever outside of this dynamic whole of *emptying*. In true Emptiness, on the one hand, *u* is not *u* but becomes *mu*; *mu* is not *mu* but becomes *u*, because both are being emptied. Thus, reciprocal movements from *u* to *mu* and from *mu* to *u* are fully realized. On the other hand, *u* is always *u*, and *mu* is always *mu*, because in true Emptiness the above 'emptying' is also 'emptied'. Accordingly, self-identical movements from *u* to *u* and from *mu* to *mu* are also fully realized.[11]

In sum, both (1) the reciprocal movements between *u* and *mu* and (2) the self-identical movements between *u* and *u* and between *mu* and *mu* are completely, dynamically, and paradoxically realized in true Emptiness. It is really a vast, boundless and infinite sphere which in itself is the dynamic whole of emptying activity. In this realization of true Emptiness as such an infinite dynamic sphere, the two sides of such polarities as affirmation and negation, positivity and negativity, and *u* and *mu* are paradoxically and self-contradictorily identical. Thus any point of the sphere has the same paradoxical nature.

IV

In this connection the following five points must be clarified:

Firstly, to say that in Buddhism the idea of Nothingness is central and primary means that not relative *mu* but absolute *Mu*, i.e., true *Śūnyatā*, is central and must be actualized if ultimate Reality, wondrous Being, is to be disclosed. Without the existential realization of absolute *Mu*, there is no awakening to ultimate Reality.

Secondly, however, this is not to say that the realization of absolute *Mu* is merely a gate through which one reaches the hall of ultimate Reality. Instead, it in itself is the hall of ultimate Reality because absolute *Mu* or true *Śūnyatā* is existentially realized as such through overcoming *Mu* or *Śūnyatā* as a third category standing beyond relative *u* and *mu*, and through returning to and affirming relative *u* and *mu* as they are. True Emptiness and wondrous Being are completely non-dualistic: absolute *Mu* and ultimate Reality are totally identical, although the realization of the former is indispensable for the realization of the latter.

Thirdly, since in Buddhism the realization of absolute *Mu* is essential in order that ultimate Reality, i.e., wondrous Being, be disclosed, the Buddhist idea of wondrous Being is clearly different from the idea of 'Being' understood as ultimate Reality in the West. In the West, 'Being' is neither non-dualistic (unlike absolute Nothingness) nor realized through the realization of Emptiness. It is not considered to be beyond the antinomy of being and non-being but rather gains its ultimate status by virtue of its being ontologically prior to non-being.

Fourthly, the difference between Western intellectual traditions and Buddhism in their respective understanding of 'Being' as the ultimate Reality depends on whether or not the realization of absolute *Mu* is essential for its disclosure and whether or not relative *mu* (non-being) is understood as completely equal and reciprocal to relative *u* (being). The *negativity* of human life is felt more seriously and deeply in Buddhism than among the followers of Western intellectual traditions. This is true to such an extent that it is not considered inferior but equal to positivity.

Fifthly, when positivity (or being) is ontologically prior to negativity (or non-being) it is natural that 'Being' as the quintessence of this ontological priority should be regarded as the ultimate, and as the symbol of liberation. Negativity in this view is no more than something to be overcome by positivity. On the contrary, when positivity (or *u*) and negativity (or *mu*) are equal and reciprocal, it is the antinomic and contradictory tension between positivity and negativity that is to be overcome. Then, as in Buddhism, liberation is realized in Emptiness as the emancipation from this existential antinomy. Finally, and most important, it is necessary and indispensable for true liberation to 'empty' Emptiness as the final step. Here the symbol of liberation is not 'Being' as the quintessence of the ontological priority of being over non-being but the dynamism of 'Emptiness' which is simultaneously Fullness.

V

The difference between Western intellectual traditions and Buddhism in their understanding of *negativity* in human life involves not only an ontological issue but also an existential and soteriological one. And whether negativity, particularly in human existence, is understood as inferior or equal to positivity is, in my view, not an issue of whether an individual or religion is optimistic or pessimistic but rather an issue of whether they are idealistic or realistic. The Western understanding of human negativity as inferior to positivity is based on an attitude which while apparently optimistic is, in fact, idealistic. On the other hand, the Buddhist understanding of man's negativity as equal to positivity is supported by an attitude which while appearing pessimistic is, in fact, radically realistic with regard to human nature.

What has been said about *u* and *mu* can be equally applied to life and death, good and evil, and so forth. In Buddhism, life is not considered as having priority over death. Life and death are antagonistic processes, negating one another, yet inseparably connected with one another. Since the mutually negating process of life and death is beginningless and endless, it is called, in Buddhism, samsara, transmigration, or the wheel of life and death. Those who follow Buddhism are deeply anxious over the endlessness of samsara and seek for emancipation from it. When the endless process of samsara is grasped not conceptually but holistically and existentially, right now, in the present moment of life, the samsaric process is realized as the antinomic, self-contradictory oneness of life and death. The breaking through this antinomy is called, particularly in Zen, the 'Great Death' because it is the total negation of life-and-death and is beyond a realization of death as distinguished from life.

Nirvana, the Buddhist realization of liberation, takes place only through the realization of 'Great Death'. For Buddhists, it is not that one overcomes death with the power of life and attains eternal life in the future; what is essential is to be liberated from the self-contradictory nature of life and death and to awaken to freedom from the wheel of life and death. Since this awakening is a thoroughly existential one, it can take place only where one is, i.e., here and now. In this existential awakening nirvana is not something apart from samsara. In the here and now, samsara as it is is nirvana and nirvana as it is is samsara.

Again, in Buddhism, good is not understood to have priority over evil. Ethically speaking, Buddhists clearly realize that good should conquer evil. However, through the experience of their inner struggle, Buddhists cannot say that good is strong enough to overcome evil. Good and evil are completely antagonistic principles, resisting each other with equal force, yet inseparably connected and displaying an existential antinomy as a whole. However imperative it may be from the ethical point of view, it is, according to Buddhism, illusory to believe it possible to overcome evil with good and to thereby attain the highest good. Since good and evil are mutually negating principles with equal power, an ethical effort to overcome evil with good never succeeds and results in a serious dilemma. Realizing this existential dilemma innate in human existence and characterizing it in terms of original sin, Christians have propounded the necessity of faith in God who delivers man from sin through his redemptive activity. From a Christian perspective, God himself is Good with a capital 'G', as can be noted in the Biblical statement 'no one is good, but God alone' (Mark 10:18, Luke 18:19). Since the law is the expression of God's will, obedience and disobedience to the law constitute man's good and evil. Moreover, it is emphasized, 'Do not be overcome by evil, but overcome evil with good' (Rom. 12:21).

In Buddhism, on the contrary, what is essential for salvation is not to overcome evil with good and to participate in the supreme Good, but to be emancipated from the existential antinomy of good and evil and to awaken to Emptiness prior to the opposition between good and evil. In the existential awakening to Emptiness, one can be master of, rather than enslaved by, good and evil. In this sense, the realization of true Emptiness is the basis for human freedom, creative activity, and ethical life.

VI

To sum up, in the West such positive principles as being, life, and the good have ontological priority over negative principles such as non-being, death, and evil. In this sense, negative principles are always apprehended as something secondary. By contrast, in the East, especially in Taoism and Buddhism, negative principles are not secondary but co-equal to the positive principles and even may be said to be primary and central. This is so in the sense that the realization of negativity is crucial to reveal ultimate Reality, and in the sense that the nameless Tao or Emptiness is realized as the root-source of both positive and negative principles in their relative sense. In short, the ultimate which is beyond the opposition between positive and negative is realized in the East in terms of negativity and in the West in terms of positivity.

However, in connection with the Western tradition, one should not overlook that there are historical instances in which negativity is understood as something positive. Such instances can be found in Christian mysticism, particularly that current of mysticism which is known as *via negativa* and Negative Theology and in the philosophies of Friederich Nietzsche and Martin Heidegger.[12].

In Christian mysticism, which is based on experience of God's uniting directly with the soul, God is not a transcendental, personal being over against the soul, called 'Thou', but the Godhead from which the personal God emerges. As Pseudo-Dionysius the Areopagite wrote in his *Mystical Theology*, the Godhead is undefinable, unnamable, and unknowable, beyond dark and light, true and untrue, affirmation and negation. Only the *via negativa* provides a way to reach the ineffable God. In German mysticism, the Godhead or *Gottheit* is grasped as *Nichts* by Meister Eckhart and as *Ungrund* by Jakob Böhme. Furthermore, in Eckhart and Böhme the essence of God is not the Supreme Good but lies beyond good and evil. This is strikingly similar to the Buddhist understanding of ultimate Reality.

We can also cite Nietzsche and Heidegger. Nietzsche severely attacks Platonism and Christianity as two-world theories which establish the 'true and eternal world' behind this actual and changeable world. In his attempt at a revaluation of all values (*Unwertung aller Werte*), he proclaims the arrival of nihilism in which traditional positive principles are completely negated. He also advocates the over-man (*Übermensch*) as an active nihilist who thoroughly endures nihility without God and accepts eternal recurrence.

Influenced by and yet overcoming Nietzsche, Martin Heidegger takes the issue of 'nothingness' not only with utmost seriousness, but perhaps with the most profundity in Western history. Considering the history of Western metaphysics as the history of the forgetfulness of 'Being' (*Seinsvergessenheit*), he has tried to ask the meaning of Being itself (*Sein selbst*) which is, according to him, different from the Being of beings (*Sein des Seienden*) as conceived in Metaphysics since Aristotle. In Aristotle, although the 'Being' of beings is taken up as a question, Being is grasped from the side of beings. It is looked at as if it stands 'over there' against us. Being is not grasped in itself from its own side. Just in asking about the 'Being' of beings in this objective manner, Aristotle, and Western metaphysics after him, concealed and forgot 'Being' itself. In order to penetrate 'Being' itself, not just the 'Being' of beings, Heidegger insists that nothingness (*das Nichts*) be realized at the bottom of our own existence. To encounter nothingness is to overcome the forgetfulness of Being. Nothingness opens up Being itself. Again, this is strikingly similar to the Buddhist understanding of Emptiness.

Christian mysticism is merely a strand within Christianity. Nietzsche and Heidegger are often regarded with suspicion in the West as traitors to the Western philosophical tradition. We must ask, however, what was the historical and philosophical lack in the Western intellectual tradition which they felt and attempted to fill? Does not their emphasis on negativity or nothingness have a positive significance? Should we simply neglect them as unorthodox? If, however, one should conclude that Heidegger, Nietzsche, and the mystics are to be rejected as unorthodox and unsound, then let me ask again how in the West the priority of being over non-being is philosophically and ontologically justified with regard to things in general and man in particular?

6 Zen and Nietzsche

I

Nietzsche says: 'God is a sacred lie (*eine heilige Lüge*).'[1] He is not saying that 'God is a lie' as many atheists and anti-religionists do. Rather, he affirms that God is 'the sacred'. In that respect, Nietzsche is in agreement with religionists who believe in God. But, Nietzsche does not stop there. He in effect says: 'God is sacred. And yet, God is a lie precisely in being sacred.' Nietzsche's statement should be understood in this fashion.

In what sense has Nietzsche affirmed God to be 'the sacred'? At the beginning of *The Will to Power*, concerning the advantage which the Christian moral hypothesis brought, he argues that Christian morality granted an absolute value to man who is small and accidental within the flux of becoming and passing away; it conceded the character of freedom and perfection to the world filled with suffering and evil, and posited that man has the possibility of knowing this absolute value and perfection. In this way, it prevented man from rebelling against life and despairing of the ability of knowing. 'In sum: [Christian] morality was the great *antidote* against practical and theoretical nihilism'.[2] It may be thought that Nietzsche has recognized God to be 'the sacred', in that it functions as that fundamental source of value which confers transcendent, absolute value in the midst of man's valuelessness and the world's meaninglessness, and as the ground which saves man from his own self-negation and destruction. But *now* this God is dead. For such a 'God' was a 'lie' which man, who could not bear the *nihilum* of the valuelessness of himself and the meaninglessness of the world, fabricated in the depths of his awareness of that *nihilum*. 'Man does not speak of *nihilum*: man speaks instead of the "other-shore"; or "God"; or the "true life"; or nirvana, deliverance, pure bliss.'[3] And Nietzsche regards this as 'a tendency which is antagonistic to life'.[4]

The paradoxical words of Nietzsche who says 'God is a sacred lie' were deeply rooted in an awareness of what he himself calls a

135

'fundamental falsity'.[5] This indicates that Nietzsche's position was based on an acute historical insight, and that he was attempting to recover life and nature from its deepest source.

The artificial construction of a 'God' in the depths of the awareness of *nihilum* is not some arbitrary and casual matter which man could refrain from doing. Nietzsche rather sees it as an inevitable enterprise rising out of the instinct for self-preservation deeply rooted in man's life. Further, he recognizes that it is a disguised and inverted function – indispensable for man's life itself – of a cosmological 'will to power' which transcends man. But even though it is a *fundamental* enterprise for human life, it is an artificial construct, a self-deception.

To speak in historical terms, the empty construct of 'God' was thus fundamental to human life and, therefore, it has functioned efficaciously to the present day as 'the sacred' in the life of man and especially in the lives of the weak and downtrodden. By believing in the existence of a 'true world' behind this world, men could endure the *nihilum* of this world. But when Nietzsche proclaims that 'now God is dead', he personally discerned, prior to all others, that this era has come to an end, and that no matter how fundamental it is, the era which ought to be aware of this deception as a deception, has arrived. This is the reason he preaches the arrival of nihilism.[6]

On the other hand, Nietzsche bitterly censures the instinct of theologians, which fabricates the Kingdom of God on the other-shore of *nihilum*, claiming that such an instinct brings about a spoilation of life and an attitude of anti-naturalness. 'The instinct of theologians is the most widely spread and truly *subterranean* form of falsity on the earth.... Wherever the influence of the theologians extends, *value-judgments* are overturned and the concepts of "true" and "false" are necessarily inverted; what is most prejudicial to life is here called "true", while what most elevates, extols, affirms, justifies and makes life triumphant is called "false".'[7] According to Nietzsche, the essence of life is the instinct for the development and preservation of life, the instinct toward the accumulation of energy, the instinct to power. However, antagonism against life, nature, and the will to live has been proclaimed in the name of God. 'Since the concept of "nature" has been fabricated as the anti-concept to "God", the "natural" could not help becoming the word for "worthy of being rejected", and the total world of that fiction has its root in *hatred* of the natural [of actuality!].'[8] It was Nietzsche's intention to cause the value judgments of 'true' and 'false' which had been inverted in the name of God to be again reversed and thus to recover life and naturalness which had been robbed in the name of God.

To sweep away every empty construct and return to the *will to power* itself – this is a return to life itself; it is a returning to the innocence of becoming (*Unschuld des Werdens*). That was, for Nietzsche, the attainment of *reality*, and at the same time the full realization of *sincerity*. Nietzsche's ideas of the 'Over-man' (*Übermensch*) who can endure the *nihilum* without God, the will to the eternal return which says 'If that be life, so let it be, once again!' and the Dionysian philosophy which is a 'religious affirmation of life', are all grounded herein. Every attempt at a revaluation of all values which tries to expose the hidden source of the concept of 'God' and to restore at their deepest root the life and naturalness which had been robbed by God fails to succeed if it lacks the awareness of deception expressed in the phrase 'God is a sacred lie.'

Precisely the awareness of deception expressed in 'God is a sacred lie', the awareness of what Nietzsche himself calls 'fundamental falsity', is the decisive moment for the establishment of Nietzsche's nihilism and constitutes its core. In that sense Nietzsche's nihilism may be called a *nihilism based on an awareness of falsity*. As has been already made clear, falsity spoken of here is a fundamental self-deception – called 'God' and 'faith' – functioning in the depths of the fundamental *nihilum* of present existence; it is the self-deception perpetrated by the very disguised and inverted will to power itself.

II

In Zen, too, it is said that 'the triple world is a deception'.[9] This is, of course, an insight shared by all Buddhists, and it constitutes the background of Zen. For example, in the *Awakening of Faith in the Mahayana*, it is written that 'the triple world is a deception and merely the creation of the mind. Apart from the mind, there are no objects of the five senses and the mind'.[10] What is here called 'mind' means, in modern terms, the conceptual mind. This is the discriminating mind which distinguishes between subject and object, being and non-being, right and wrong, good and evil, and so forth. We set up the world of objectivity over against the subjectivity of the self, and taking it as the objective world, make various distinctions concerning it; but this is a false and unreal world produced by the discriminating mind, and not the world of true reality. Once one departs from that kind of discriminating mind, the world of discrimination also disappears and the real world manifests itself in its 'suchness'. The *Awakening of Faith*, continuing the above quotation, adds: '. . . since all things are without exception developed from the mind, and produced under the condition of delusions'.[11] It goes on to say 'Every discrimination discriminates the mind of the self; [but] since the mind does not see the mind itself, there is no form to be obtained.'[12] In these citations we find the true meaning of 'the triple world is a deception', and at the same time discover a clue to the standpoint of Zen.

The discriminating mind, which distinguishes the objective world in various ways and which thereby produces a discriminated world, distinguishes its own mind as well. This is an unavoidable activity arising from the very nature of what is termed the discriminating mind. And yet the mind cannot thoroughly discriminate itself. The mind cannot see the mind itself – just as an eye cannot see the eye itself. For the true Mind is that which is entirely indiscriminable, that which can never be seen; or rather, it is the very subject of activity which *discriminates*, the very subject of activity which *sees*. Even if called mind, it is Mind which has 'no form to be obtained'. Zen endeavors to *awaken* to this kind of Mind immediately and directly. In this awakening there is no need for the mediation of theory and doctrine, and so Zen advocates 'directly pointing to man's Mind'. But what is the meaning of 'directly pointing'? What is the true meaning of 'the triple world is a deception'? And what relation do they have to Nietzsche's nihilism?

As we have seen above, the discrimination of the self-mind is an inescapable activity arising from the very nature of mind (the discriminating mind); and yet, the mind cannot ultimately discriminate the mind itself. Therein lies the essential dilemma which the mind possesses. The delusion rooted in this essential dilemna is generally called *avidyā* (ignorance) in Buddhism, and is termed 'non-awakening' in the *Awakening of Faith*. That 'the triple world is a deception' is also nothing different from this ignorance or non-awakening. Accordingly, the realization that 'the triple world is a deception' is not something pertaining merely to the objective world; at the root of this awareness there is contained the realization of the delusory and deceptive nature of the discriminating mind itself, which sets up that kind of objective world and distinguishes between subject and object. Just as the above dilemma is something essential to the discriminating mind, the realization that 'the triple world is a deception' is, with 'ignorance' and 'non-awakening', a matter intrinsic to the mind. On this point we find something congruous with Nietzsche's 'fundamental falsity'.

Again, Buddhism's 'the triple world is a deception' calls to mind the following words of Nietzsche: 'the *value of the world* lies in our interpretation ...; previous interpretations have been perspectival valuations by virtue of which we can survive in life, i.e., in the will to power, for the growth of power.... This idea permeates my writings. The world with which we are concerned is false, i.e., is not a fact'.[13] This idea that the value of the world lies in our *interpretations*, and that there is no world apart from our *value-interpretations*, is not essentially different from Buddhism and the Zen standpoint which holds that everything arises from the *discriminating* mind. For when there is discrimination, value-interpretation is involved. But in Nietzsche's case, value-interpretations concerning the world, all of which are empty constructs and deceptive, have the positive significance of preserving life through a disguised will to power. The world fabricated in terms of value, even though an empty-construct, is something to be affirmed. For it was also one perspective of the will to power. In Buddhism and Zen, on the contrary, the world perceived by the discriminating mind does not possess positive meaning as such. It is the world of ignorance, of deception, which must by absolutely negated. The idea that it is advantageous for the preservation of life is not found therein.

Why is this so? In Zen, the delusory nature of the world is not grasped from the perspective of the will to power, as in Nietzsche's case; but it is grasped from the perspective of the discriminating mind as the problem of *illusion* or as the problem of *ignorance*. In fact, more strictly speaking, it is grasped as the problem of how to rid oneself existentially of the very dilemma inherent in the discriminating mind: 'Even to set upon the quest for awakening is to go contrariwise.'[14] For just as the mind cannot be objectively grasped, similarly, neither illusion nor ignorance nor 'the deception of the triple world' can be objectively realized as such, for in that very instance of attempting to treat them objectively as issues and conquer them objectively, there is illusion, ignorance, and 'the deception of the triple world' in the true sense. Precisely at that time when that fact is existentially realized at the base of our being do we extricate ourselves from illusion and ignorance. But this hardly means to transcend towards an other-shore beyond illusion and ignorance. As expressed in the words 'outside of mind there is no Dharma; this mind is precisely Dharma', and 'this very mind is the Mind of no-mind',[15] there is no true Mind, apart from the mind of discrimination and delusion. Apart from the true realization of ignorance as ignorance, there is no true Awakening. Hence it is said that 'when seeing, hearing, perception, and consciousness are simply abandoned, the paths of the mind are cut off and there is no place to enter Enlightenment; the original Mind is found only in the places of seeing, hearing, perceiving, and consciousness'.[16] For this reason Zen advocates 'directly pointing to man's Mind.' Mind in its immediacy is no-mind, original Mind.

Consequently, even though Nietzsche similarly makes problematic the delusory nature of the world and fundamental deception in some sense, in his case the will to power is affirmatively posited behind them. In Zen, on the contrary, there is nothing at all that can be affirmatively established in the background. That there is nothing at all that can be so posited means that *outside of this mind* there is no Dharma, that this mind is *originally* the true *Mind*, the *Mind of no-mind*.

However, it is not that Nietzsche's phrase, 'fundamental falsity', refers merely to the delusory nature of the *world*; rather it refers to the fabrication of *God* in the depths of the realization of the delusory nature of the world – the inevitable functioning of the instinct for self-preservation. Therein lies the reason for Nietzsche's proclaiming that 'God is a sacred lie.' Yet it is certain that at the root of that proclamation the will to power was affirmatively established. In any event, it must not be overlooked that the *core* of Nietzsche's nihilism does not consist in the awareness of the delusory nature of the world; it lies in the awareness of the delusory nature of 'God' in the aforementioned sense. Such Nietzschean themes as antagonism to life, robbing man of naturalness, the fabrication of a world beyond, and the active nihilist or Over-man who can endure *nihilum*, are all attendant upon his conviction of the delusory nature of God. Since our focus of inquiry is Zen and Nietzsche's nihilism, we must further examine that point.

III

According to Heidegger, the 'God' of which Nietzsche speaks is not merely the Christian God, but also metaphysical principles from the tradition of Platonic philosophy on. In other words, 'God is used as a name for the supra-sensory world in general.'[17] Nietzsche's attempt at an inversion of values was aimed at overthrowing 'God' as the supra-sensible value common to Christianity and Platonism. This is why Nietzsche so bitterly censured Christianity and Platonism. And when he made these censures, his immediate and direct enemies were Paul and Kant.

The confrontation with Christianity is indeed a theme which runs throughout Nietzsche's career. But the objects of Nietzsche's attacks were institutional Christianity and Christian morals, not Jesus Christ himself; Christian *faith*, not Christian *practice*. Nietzsche writes: 'Christianity as an historical reality must not be confused with that one root that is called to mind by this name. The other roots from which historical Christianity has grown up have been far more powerful. It is an unexampled misuse of words when such manifestations of decay and abortions as the "Christian Church", "Christian faith" and "Christian life" label themselves with that holy name. What did Christ *deny*? Everything that is today called Christian.'[18] Or again: 'The word "Christianity" is already a misunderstanding – in essence there was only one Christian, and he died on the cross. The "good tidings" (Gospel, *Evangelium*) *died* on the cross. What has been called the "good tidings" from that moment was already something contrary to what he lived through: an "ill tidings", a *Dysangelium*. It is false to the point of nonsense to find the mark of the Christian in a "faith", for example, in the faith in redemption through Christ. Only Christian *practice*, only a life similar to what he *lived* who died on the cross is Christian ...'.[19]

There could be no sharper dichotomy between Christus and Christendom than this. For Nietzsche then, who was Jesus Christ, and in what sense did Christendom change the $\overline{Evangelium}$ into a *Dysangelium*? 'He [Jesus] demonstrates how one must live in order to feel "deified" ... and how one will not achieve it through repentance and contrition for one's sins: "Sin is of no account" is his central judgment.'[20] Jesus did not have such concepts as rebellion, revenge, sin, retribution, and judgement. 'He *lived* this unity of God and man as his "glad tidings".'[21] That gospel was pure bliss; it was the freedom and realization of the kingdom of God.

In contrast to this, says Nietzsche, it was Paul who grasped the death of Jesus as 'God hung on the cross' and as 'the sacrifice to redeem man's sins'. It was he who fabricated, not a new practice, but a new faith. 'A God who died for our sins, salvation through faith, resurrection after death – all these are counterfeits of true Christianity for which that disastrous wrongheaded fellow [Paul] must be held responsible.'[22] It was precisely Paul, according to Nietzsche, who brought back the Judaic legalistic spirit and resentment over which Jesus had conquered, who set up the concepts of repayment and retribution in the center of the explanation of life, and who established faith in the world beyond and immortality of the individual in order to make this world value-less. In place of natural causality, he set up a 'moral world-order' in which the will of God rules over the behavior of man, and thus in place of human sanctification he robbed man of his naturalness. 'Paul was the greatest among all the apostles of revenge.'[23]

Nietzsche's censure of Paul is aimed at Paul's *faith* in the redemption of sin by Jesus and his resurrection. Moreover, it is aimed at the point that faith, based on a rabbinical sentiment, produced *Christian morality*, which attempts to rob man of his naturalness, belittle aristocratic values so as to render them trivial, and elevate the inferior and vulgar life. It is a well-known fact that Nietzsche severely criticizes Christian morality as a priestly morality and a slave morality in contrast to an artistocratic morality. In *Ecce Homo* he even writes: 'What defines me, what sets me apart from the whole rest of humanity, is that I exposed Christian morality.'[24]

Within Jesus' *practice* Nietzsche sees true life. In contrast to this, within Paul's *faith* and Christendom thereafter, he finds a hostility to life rooted in a legalistic spirit, a decadence of life which extols self-abnegation. These are the issues pertaining to Christian morality. 'Up to now one has always attacked Christianity not only in a modest way but in an erroneous way. As long as one has not felt Christian morality as the capital crime against life, its defenders have had it all their own way. The question of the mere "truth" of Christianity is a matter of secondary importance as long as the value-question of Christian morality is not touched upon.'[25] Nietzsche's criticism of Christianity becomes essentially a criticism of Christian *morality*. The questions of the truth of Christianity, of knowledge of God, and of faith are also reduced to the issue of Christian *morality*. This fact is essentially linked with his position of seeing a fundamental *falsity* in the concept of God, and of his setting up the will to power in the depths of this fundamental falsity. For morality is based on 'will', not cognitive reason, and the 'fundamental falsity' for Nietzsche does not mean falsity in the epistemological sense but in the volitional sense. The 'fundamental falsity' refers to that self-deception in which man fabricates the existence of God in order to endure the nihility of human life. And this fabrication is after all a refractive function of the will to power.

IV

We have seen above that, for Nietzsche, confrontation with Christianity is the greatest task, and that the focal point of his criticism is not Jesus but Paul. However, apart from his confrontation with Kant, the rational philosopher of the modern world, would not Nietzsche's nihilism lose its sharpness? Is not Nietzsche's *nihilism* in a sense a negative inversion of Kant's *moral teleology*? At any rate, it may be thought to be so in one respect.

In the very beginning of *Thus Spoke Zarathustra*, there is a well-known passage describing the three metamorphoses of the spirit into a camel, a lion, and then a child. The camel which hastens over the desert sands as the pious spirit bearing a heavy burden becomes a lion as it endeavors to create freedom as its own. As the lion itself attempts to become lord of the desert, it clashes with a great dragon as his last ruler. 'What is the great dragon which the spirit no longer calls Lord and God? "Thou shalt" is the name of the great dragon. But the spirit of the lion says "I will".'[26] The great dragon on whose each and every scale 'thou shalt' glitters can perhaps be regarded as a symbol of the Judaic-Christian legalism which is represented by the Ten Commandments. But, is it not even more appropriate to see it as a symbol of Kant's transcendental ethics, which clarified the ground of possibility of every moral principle since ancient times and taught the categorical imperative of the unconditional 'Thou shalt', and as a symbol of Kant's moral and historical teleology, which taught not only the postulate of God as the accordance of happiness and virtue but also the realization of a moral community as the people of God which pure rational faith should set up on earth by transcending the faith of the Churches? For Kant's philosophy is not only a modern reconstruction of Platonism but also a product of Protestantism.

That this interpretation of mine is not necessarily inappropriate should be clear if considered in conjunction with the fact that even in *The Antichrist*, written as a criticism of Christianity, Nietzsche often speaks of Kant: 'How could one fail to feel Kant's categorical

imperative as *dangerous to life* ... the instinct of theologians alone
protected it'; 'Kant's success is merely a theologian's success'; 'The
instinct which errs without fail, *anti-nature* as instinct, German
decadence as philosophy – *that is Kant.*'[27] In fact, Nietzsche sees
Kant as 'in the last analysis, a cunning Christian (*ein hinterlistiger
Christ*)'.[28] That words of criticism of Kant appear everywhere in
Nietzsche, as in the following citations, illustrates the intensity of
Nietzsche's confrontation with him. 'Kant: or cant would be a more
intelligible characterization.'[29] 'Kant, in his "morality" falsifies his
interior psychological propensity.'[30] 'Kant as a fanatic of the formal
concept "Thou shalt".'[31]

Nietzsche's active nihilism arises as a means of destroying Kant's
stifling system of moral teleology, which is permeated by that 'Thou
shalt'. The Over-man overturns even Kant's 'Kingdom of Ends',
which had been substituted for the 'Kingdom of God'. In Kant,
who never ceased teaching the primacy of practical reason, both the
problem of knowledge and the questions of religion and history are
ultimately reduced to the problem of *morality*. They are reduced to
the 'Thou shalt.' Nietzsche stands diametrically opposed to Kant in
this matter. And hence it is a natural conclusion for Nietzsche, who
in reference to Paul censures the Christian morality which he
considers rooted in Paul's faith, that the greatest 'enemy against life'
to be confronted in the modern world is Kant. In his confrontation
with Kant, Nietzsche's nihilism becomes even more scathing. The
common element in Paul and Kant is the legalist spirit which stifles
man's natural life. In order to come to the purity of the child who
utters the sacred word 'Yes', the lion had to bravely challenge the
great dragon whose name was 'Thou shalt.'

V

When Nietzsche says that 'God is a sacred lie', he is astutely
countering the deceptive nature of supra-sensory value which
appears in Platonism, Paul (Christianity), and Kant, the most
modern representative of these two. He counters with the claim that
such supra-sensory value is a fundamental falsity fabricated by life
which can not endure *nihilum*, and hence exposes the fact that life
and naturalness were robbed by the empty construct of God
(supra-sensory value). When Nietzsche in this way regards God as a
deception and says that life is robbed by God, he violently attacks

the *legalist spirit*. Accordingly, he reduces all problems, that is, the problems of cognition, religion, and history, to the issue of *morality*. This reduction, in Nietzsche's case, is inseparable from the fact that the *will* to power is always placed at the root of the issue. This has been our interpretation of Nietzsche, as articulated above. The issues of priestly morality (slave morality) versus aristocratic morality, the one who died on the cross versus Dionysius, and his philosophy of the 'Over-man' over against the 'last man' are all developed by taking *morality, the mode of being of the will*, as the pivot.

Now, what meaning does this standpoint of Nietzsche have when we attempt to consider the question of Zen and nihilism? Nietzsche has censured as a fabrication the search for God and the positing of God in the depths of the awareness of *nihilum*. Zen also severely admonishes against seeking for Buddha and setting up Buddha. 'Do not seek for Buddha outside' is a point which Zen always emphasizes, but 'outside' hardly means the spatial outside alone. Even if one seeks Buddha in the interior of the self, in the depths of an inner *nihilum*, the 'seeking' itself already contains the meaning of *outside in respect to the self itself*. Consequently, 'do not seek for Buddha outside' means do not seek Buddha at all, whether inside or outside, for as long as one seeks Buddha, the true Buddha cannot self-awaken. This is the reason that Lin-chi says: 'If you seek a Buddha, you will be seized by a Buddha-devil; if you seek a patriarch, you will be bound by a patriarch-devil; if you seek at all, all is suffering; it is better that there be no-matter ...'.[32] It is the reason he says: 'When the seeking mind ceases, there is no-matter.'[33]

'The seeking mind ceases' does not indicate something negative. It signifies the breaking through of the ego-self. In the true breaking through of the ego-self, the true Self emerges within an unending 'expanse' of Self-Awakening: there is a realization of the true suchness of the world and the Self. The Self-Awakening in which 'the seeking mind ceases', the endless expanse of Self-Awakening which finds the 'Self' in its midst – this is the *Self-fulfiled* world wherein one seeks neither God nor Buddha; it is the world of *Reality* expressed by the phrase: 'The blue mountains are of themselves blue mountains, the white clouds are of themselves white clouds.' The fact of 'no-matter' is also spoken of here. What Zen refers to as 'your Original Face prior to the birth of your father and mother' is nothing other than the infinite 'expanse' of Self-Awakening out of which arises our ordinary discriminating awareness itself, the seeking mind. Hence it is also said: 'The harder you strive after it the further it is away from you. When you no more strive after it, lo, it is right in front of you. Its wondrous voice fills your ear.'[34] The relations between self and others, between self and world, and even the relation between self and God arise therein. Without the Self-Awakening which clearly and endlessly expands in the ten directions, there is no true Self, no true World.

When Nietzsche rejects God, saying that 'God is a sacred lie', God was grasped as a supra-sensory value inimical to natural life. Moreover, that supra-sensory value was not merely something of an ontological character; it has a legal, moralistic character which attempts to regard what extols life as sin and what suppresses life as noble. We have already touched upon the point that Nietzsche sets up the will to power in the depths of the concept of God fabricated as the entity which performs these functions. In this case, God is a '*sacred* lie' which makes the self-preservation of life possible by causing *nihilum* to attain fullness; and at the same time God is a 'sacred *lie*' produced by the instinct of theologians which brings about an inversion of the concepts of 'true' and 'false'. That it is considered as a 'fundamental falsity' is also because God himself was one perspective – historically, at any rate, efficacious – of the will to power. The perspective which was elaborated by the disguised and inverted will to power was God; it was the other-shore after life; it was Christian morality based on them. Nietzsche's active nihilism tears off this disguise of the name 'God', and by overturning from its foundation the mode of being of the inverting will which regards the extollation of life as a sin, returns to the will to power itself which lies at the deepest root of life. To return to the will to power itself, to always stand therein – for Nietzsche, in this was Reality and the innocence of becoming.

For Nietzsche, then, life, *nihilum*, God, and the innocence of becoming were all perspectives of the will to power. The reason for his considering *God* to be 'a sacred lie' and for his censure of Paul's *faith* as giving a ground to a priestly morality is that despite the fact that they were perspectives – seemingly efficacious for life – of the will to power, Nietzsche sees them as ultimately self-deceptive enterprises of the will to power functioning hostilely against life. That cognition, religion, and history are grasped in essence as questions of morality also stems from their being grasped as perspectives of the will to power.

VI

Now, from the perspective of religion, and especially of Zen, at least the following two questions must be asked of this standpoint of Nietzsche:

First, when Nietzsche speaks of God and faith, how is the *problem of death* grasped therein? Nietzsche writes in the following way in the chapter entitled 'On Free Death' in *Thus Spoke Zarathustra*: 'Die at the right time: so teacheth Zarathustra.' For Nietzsche, the ideal death is precisely death not too late, not too early, 'the free death which cometh unto me because *I* want it'. In the same chapter he also writes: 'The consummating death I show unto you, which becometh a stimulus and promise to the living.' How, then, does Nietzsche view the death of Jesus? 'Verily, that Hebrew [Jesus] died too early whom the preachers of slow death honor: and to many hath it proved a calamity that he died too early.'[35] We have seen above that Nietzsche found what is truly Christian not in the faith of Paul but within the practice of Jesus. That practice was one of compassion (*Mitleiden*) and love which, not being hostile even to those who do one violence, prays together with them, suffers with them, loves them. 'This "bringer of glad tidings" died as he had lived, as he had *taught* – not to "redeem men" but to show how one must live. Precisely this *practice* is his legacy to mankind.'[36]

If I may say so, for Nietzsche, death is the consummation of life. Jesus exhibited the evangelical practice of compassion and love, but since he died too early he ended without knowing how to love the great earth and life. Nietzsche interprets this fact as causing Paul and the apostles of the early church to raise the questions, 'Who killed him; who is his real enemy?', to bring about the faith in both his sacrificial death for the sake of the redemption of sin and his resurrection, and to produce the decadence of life, a morality of resentment. Here we see the figure of Nietzsche, the philosopher of life who views *death* from the side of *life* alone, and the anti-moralist who, in grasping morality as the greatest problem, grasps even *faith* exclusively as a *morality* which causes a degeneration of life.

However, is death in fact something exhausted in the consummation of life? Can the true nature of death be grasped by seeing death from the side of life alone? Do not Paul's words 'I die day by day' (I Corinthians 15–31) on the contrary express the true nature of death, and accordingly the true meaning of life? Zen, which self-awakens to the birth-and-death of the moment and grasps birth-and-death itself as the Great Death, on this point differs from Nietzsche and rather is in agreement with Paul. An existential self-realization of death is essential to a great affirmation of life. From this standpoint the fact that Nietzsche focused his attention only upon the legalistic spirit within the Pauline faith and censured faith exclusively from the angle of morality as something which produces a priestly morality that causes a suppression and degeneration of life must be said to miss the true meaning of faith, and in turn, of religion. This fact causes us to recall that Kant's understanding of religion, while taking radical evil as its theme, ultimately did not touch the core of religion and was based on his attempt to grasp religion from the standpoint of practical reason, morality. To Paul, faith does not suppress life; it was the living of a new life which is supported by the realization of death. As he says, we are 'always carrying in the body the death of Jesus, so that the life of Jesus may also be manifested in our bodies' (II Corinthians 4–10) and 'I have been crucified with Christ; it is no longer I who live, but Christ who lives in me; and the life I now live in the flesh I live by faith in the Son of God' (Galatians 2–20). Paul died and rose again with Christ. In that case, needless to say, Christ's death and resurrection is for Paul a spiritual fact which makes his own resurrection through death possible. It is not something merely fabricated in the depths of *nihilum*, rather it is a living reality in which spiritual life becomes real and present in him. Paul's is a standpoint of the ontological self-realization of life which ultimately cannot be reduced to the issue of morality. On this point, Zen, which realizes birth-and-death itself as the Great Death and gains a new Life of rebirth through the realization of the Great Death, does not differ from the standpoint of Paul in essence.

Having taken up the theme of awareness of death in Nietzsche and having stated that the core of religion cannot be touched as long as religion is grasped by reducing it to the problem of morality, as in Nietzsche, we must inquire secondly whether Nietzsche's standpoint of the *will to power* truly expresses the *innocence of becoming*.

As repeatedly said above, when Nietzsche regards God as a sacred lie, Nietzsche himself recognizes the fact that in one aspect it is an enterprise inescapable from the instinct of self-preservation of life which cannot endure *nihilum*. In other words, for Nietzsche, God, too, is one perspective of the will to power. But God is rejected as an empty construct because it is a self-deceptive function of a disguised and inverted will to power. Nietzsche proclaims the arrival of nihilism and emphasizes that one has to live as an active nihilist, i.e., Over-man, who can endure *nihilum* without a God. This is because however much it was for the sake of preservation of life, he rejects that kind of self-deception and lives with utter sincerity by returning to, and taking his stand in, the fundamental will to power itself. For Nietzsche it is precisely therein that the innocence of becoming becomes present and true naturalness shines forth. Nevertheless, is Nietzsche's standpoint of the will to power one in which the innocence of becoming and true naturalness really present themselves? Rephrased from the perspective of Zen, the question would seem to be best put as follows: Is Nietzsche's standpoint of the will to power in fact 'the place where the seeking mind ceases'? Is it truly 'no-matter' in the sense mentioned above (p. 145)? This rephrasing is necessary because in Zen the innocence of becoming and true naturalness are realized only in 'the place where the seeking mind ceases' and in 'no-matter'.

Nietzsche's will to power may perhaps be said to express the innocence of becoming as a cosmological will which regards even God as a perspective of itself and which also restores the naturalness which has been robbed in the name of God. And yet, when seen from a Zen perspective, even if it is cosmological and not at all of the character of a personal God, is not the will to power still the 'seeking mind'? However deeply the will to power is realized as such it is 'something' affirmatively posited in the background of God as 'a sacred lie', but not 'Nothingness'. It is a 'matter', not 'no-matter'. As has been stated previously (pp. 137ff), Zen, like Nietzsche, emphasizes the delusory nature of the world and severely admonishes against seeking for Buddha and setting up Buddha. Unlike Nietzsche, however, Zen does not affirmatively establish anything in the background of either the world or Buddha – Zen establishes 'nothing' in their background. Hence Zen's realization that 'outside of this mind there is no Dharma; this mind is originally the true Mind'. In this Zen realization, the 'seeking mind' completely ceases and 'no-matter' is realized. The innocence of becoming is also truly realized herein. 'The direct pointing to man's Mind' and Self-awakening to the true Mind are possible only through the realization of 'Nothingness' behind God and the world, i.e., the realization of complete non-objectification. On the contrary Nietzsche posits the will to power as the basic principle behind God and the world. However basic it may be, the will to power is not 'Nothingness' but 'something' affirmatively established and thereby not free from objectification. This is the reason I said the will to power is still the 'seeking mind'. Indeed, since the will to power is the driving force of everything in the universe, is it not the most fundamental form of the 'seeking mind' itself? In that limitation, it cannot be called the standpoint of 'having no-matter; that is the noble person.'[37]

The Zen standpoint of 'the place where the seeking mind ceases is precisely no-matter', as touched on above, is the standpoint of a thoroughgoing Self-awakening. In this Awakening, a 'naturalness' or 'being so of itself' (*jinen*), in which everything personal, including a personal God, is broken through, presents itself. It is 'the originally pure', and 'no-matter'. And yet as *Self-awakening*, it is existential through and through. What Lin-chi calls the 'true Man of no rank' also points to 'the Man of no-matter', 'the originally pure Man', as the manifestation of a 'naturalness' which thus transcends everything of a personal character.

In that limitation, this kind of standpoint of Zen has something in common with the standpoint of Nietzsche rather than of Paul. For Paul's standpoint, though congruous with Zen as stated above in the sense that a new life hinges upon a thoroughgoing existential realization of death, is to the end personal and not transpersonal *in its basic structure*. The standpoint of Zen, on the contrary, together with that of Nietzsche, is cosmological, yet at the same time, existential. Therein lay the reason that Nietzsche's standpoint of the will to power restores the naturalness 'robbed' by the personal God and causes the innocence of becoming to appear. That naturalness, that innocence of becoming, however, is not something predicated upon a thoroughgoing realization of death. This means nothing other than that Nietzsche's innocence of becoming is based solely on the standpoint of life, which means finally, on the standpoint of the will to power.

Nietzsche negates and rejects God as a 'sacred lie' and has a keen awareness of profound deception and *nihilum*. But when seen from the Zen perspective, his standpoint, which grasps everything from the perspective of the will to power, and which, lacking a thorough realization of death, considers the problematic of religion from the angle of morality, can still not be squared with 'the place where the seeking mind ceases is precisely no-matter'. The standpoint of the Over-man must still be said to be far from the standpoint of 'the true Man of no rank'. For the 'innocence of becoming' to truly present itself, the *Over-man* must become the *true Man*. How can one progress from the standpoint of the Over-man to the standpoint of the true Man? And what of the existential, practical questions contained therein? Precisely these are the most important existential questions of overcoming Nietzschean nihilism, but these questions are beyond the scope of this essay.

7 Mahayana Buddhism and Whitehead

As many scholars have already pointed out, the modes of thought found in Whitehead's philosophy and Mahayana Buddhism have striking affinities. Because of their great similarity, Whitehead's philosophy and Mahayana Buddhism appear to be contiguous to one another, so much so that one could move from one to the other merely by taking a single step. Nevertheless, we must not overlook the important differences between the two. These differences, although subtle and often inconspicuous, are deeply rooted in the structure of their respective ways of thinking and of understanding reality. In other words, their differences are not of degree, or extent, but rather of quality and structure. This must be clarified and emphasized at the outset of our approach to the subject 'Mahayana Buddhism and Whitehead.'

This clarification of the essential differences between Whitehead's philosophy and Mahayana Buddhism does not, however, exclude the possibility of a dialogue between them. On the contrary, it indicates that in order to develop a creative and productive dialogue between them, it is necessary at the outset to clearly realize the essential differences in their thought structure. It is only after a clear understanding of these structural differences that a productive and fruitful encounter between them can proceed on a solid basis.

To clarify the essential differences between the structures of Buddhist and Whiteheadian thought, the notion of 'God and the World' in the latter may be the best and most crucial point on which to base a comparison.

I

Whitehead's idea of the relatedness of actual entities is surely strkingly similar to the Buddhist idea of *pratītya-samutpāda*, which may be translated as 'dependent co-origination', 'relationality', 'conditioned co-production' or 'dependent co-arising'. Rejecting the Aristotelian idea of 'primary substance', Whitehead emphasizes the interdependence of actual entities by saying:

> The principle of universal relativity directly traverses Aristotle's dictum, "[A substance] is not present in a subject." On the contrary, according to this principle an actual entity *is* present in other actual entities. In fact if we allow for degrees of relevance, and for negligible relevance, we must say that every actual entity is present in every other actual entity. The philosophy of organism is mainly devoted to the task of making clear the notion of "being present in another entity."[1]

It is not hard to see a parallel between Whitehead's principle of universal relativity and the Buddhist idea of 'dependent co-origination'. This basic principle in Buddhism is generally formulated as follows:

> If this is, that comes to be;
> from the arising of this, that arises;
> if this is not, that does not come to be;
> from the ceasing of this, that ceases.

'This' and 'that' are completely dependent upon each other in their arising and ceasing to be. This Buddhist law of dependent co-origination implies at least the following four points:

1. All things in the universe are concomitant, conditioned by each other, and interdependent in their origination.
2. Yet, everything is equally in itself, and of itself, without one being prior to the other. (Otherwise, *inter*dependence is impossible.)
3. This truth of interdependence must be strictly applied to everything whatsoever without exception.
4. There is nothing whatsoever more substantial or more real which grounds the interdependence of everything. (Thus, the apparently contradictory statements of (1) and (2) can be logically joined together.)

In Whitehead's philosophy, too, both (1) and (2) may be said to be clearly realized. Actual entities, as the final real things of which the world is constituted, are interdependent,[2] and yet each actual entity is 'something individual for its own sake,'[3] and *causa sui* with its subjective aim.[4] The subject-superject nature of actual entities in Whitehead's philosophy indicates clearly the compatibility of points (1) and (2) within his system. When Whitehead says, 'God is an actual entity' and emphasizes, 'God is not to be treated as an exception to all metaphysical principles, invoked to save their collapse. He is their chief exemplification',[5] the third connotation of dependent co-origination in Buddhism – that *nothing* is excluded from this interdependent arising and ceasing – seems to be well realized in his thought. However, we must look more carefully to see whether this is really the case. This question is inseparably connected with another question as to whether the idea of point (4), that is, that there is nothing whatsoever that is more real and serves as the foundation for the interdependence of everything, is fully realized in Whitehead.

If I am not mistaken, the *final* answers to both of these questions must be in the negative. I will try to explain the reason for this negative answer by:

(A) a more careful examination of Whitehead's idea of the relation between God and the world.
(B) a further elucidation of the Buddhist idea of dependent co-origination.

II

In Whitehead, 'actual entities' are also termed 'actual occasions'. These two terms are used interchangeably. There is, however, one exception to this: God. In *Process and Reality*, Whitehead remarks that 'the term "actual occasion" will always exclude God from its scope'.[6] This is because the word 'occasion' implies a spatio-temporal location, whereas God is the one non-temporal actual entity.[7] God is non-temporal – partially unaffected by time and process because of his primordial nature which is free, complete, eternal, actually deficient and unconscious. But this does not mean that Whitehead's idea of God is simply timeless, merely beyond time. As he says in the concluding chapter of *Process and Reality*, '. . . analogously to all actual entities, the nature of God is dipolar. He has a primordial nature and a consequent nature'.[8] The consequent nature of God is nothing but 'the realization of the actual world in the unity of his nature'.[9] Derived from physical experiences in the temporal world, the consequent nature of God is determined, incomplete, 'everlasting', fully actual, and conscious. Accordingly, the description of God as non-temporal does not mean that there is no time, no process in God. Because of his dipolar nature, God is temporal and non-temporal at the same time. At this point it should be noticed that the dipolar nature, though common to all actual entities, including God, takes on a unique characteristic in the case of God. This is implied when Whitehead says in the above quotation,'. . . *analogously* to all actual entities, the nature of God is dipolar'. Despite their dipolar nature, all actual entities other than God are not dipolar in the same way God is. Rather, unlike God who is simultaneously temporal and non-temporal, actual entities are by necessity only temporal. This is the reason that for them the terms 'actual entities' and 'actual occasions' are simply inter-changeable. Hence, it is not in the primordial nature of God, but rather in the *dipolar nature peculiar to God* that we can find the uniqueness of Whitehead's idea of God and the reason for the notion that God is not an actual occasion, although he is an actual entity.

In Whitehead, the principle of universal relativity entails the rejection of absolute immanence as well as absolute transcendence. All actual entities including God are dipolar in their nature in the sense that they are both 'subject' and 'superject'. Just as an actual entity (or an actual occasion) in the temporal realm – as a subject – transcends all other actual entities and yet, as a superject, is immanent in them, God as a subject transcends the world and yet God as a superject is immanent in the world. This means that the world and its actual entities as subjects transcend God, and yet the world and its actual entities as superjects are immanent in God. In other words, just as actual entities in the temporal realm are relative to each other, God and the world (and its actual entities) are relative to each other. Here the distinction must be made between two kinds of relativity. One is relativity between actual entities (or actual occasions) in the world, and the other is relativity between God and the world or actual occasions in the world. The former is relativity within the realm of temporality, whereas the latter is relativity referring to non-temporality, that is, relativity between temporality (the World) and the dipolar nature of the temporal –non-temporal (God). These two kinds of relativity should not be mixed up nor understood as being in the same dimension.

The difference between these two kinds of relativity may be shown by the following observations based on William Christian's summary of his analysis of Whitehead's theory of 'God and the World'.[10]

(A) Actual occasions (as subjects) transcend God by virtue of their freedom and their privacy.

(B) Actual occasions (as superjects) are immanent in God objectively, *completely*, and effectively.

(C) God (as superject) is immanent in the world objectively and effectively.

(D) God (as subject) transcends the world by virtue of his freedom and privacy.

(E) God transcends the world also by virtue of his *perfection* – both in being (as subject) and in power (as superject).

The two italicized words indicate that (1) although actual occasions (as superjects) are *completely* immanent in God, God is *not necessarily completely* immanent in the world, and (2) God transcends the world by virtue of *his perfection*, but the world, though transcending God, is *lacking perfection*. In short, this indicates that although there is interaction between the world and God, God *finally* transcends the world. God is more self-creative, more inclusive, and more influential, than any other temporal actual entity. He alone is everlasting. This transcendence signifies, in Whitehead, that God is the principle of limitation which, by transcending all temporal occasions, gives an initial aim to each of them as a form of limitation. Without God as the principle of limitation, there could be no finite and ordered actualities nor values; there would thus inevitably result an 'indiscriminate model pluralism'.

It may be clear now why my answer was in the negative to the question whether, in Whitehead, the principle of interdependence is strictly applied to everything without any exceptions. It may also be clear why the answer was again in the negative to the other question concerning whether or not there is in Whitehead anything more real which acts as a foundation beyond or behind the interdependence of everything in the universe. In this connection I would like now to turn to a further elucidation of the Buddhist doctrine of dependent co-origination.

III

In Buddhism the idea of interdependence is strictly and thoroughly realized, as is made clear in its doctrine of dependent co-origination. This doctrine is inseparably connected with a radical rejection of any divine transcendence such as God. Buddhism is nontheistic in its basic nature. Buddha himself rejected the traditional Vedic idea of *'Brahman'* which is considered to be the sole foundation underlying the universe, and which is identified with *'ātman'*, the eternal self at the core of each individual. The Buddha said that it was merely an imaginary construction to believe in a *Brahman* of which we have no real comprehension, and that to hold such a belief is analogous to trying to climb a ladder which extends into the sky in order to reach a place one knows nothing about, or is like falling in love with a beautiful queen whom no one has ever seen.[11]

The conception of *Brahman*, the Hindu expression for the Absolute, was replaced by the Buddha with the notion of dependent co-origination and its accompanying notions of 'impermanence' (*anitya*) and 'no-self' (*anātman*). The denial of *Brahman* is also the denial of *ātman*.

Thus we may say that the interdependence emphasized in the Buddhist notion of dependent co-origination is realized in the strictest sense by rejecting both transcendence and immanence. Accordingly, there can be nothing whatever that is 'more real', nothing lying behind or beyond the interdependence of everything, whether in the non-temporal or temporal realm.

The Buddha enunciated the principle of dependent co-origination as the 'Middle Way'. This Middle Way however, should not be taken as a middle point between two poles. On the contrary, the Middle Way breaks through dipolarity; it is the overcoming of dipolarity itself. In this sense the Buddhist notion of the Middle Way is quite different from the Aristotelian idea of *mesotēs*. The interdependence which is implied in the Buddhist doctrine of dependent co-origination is neither transcendence nor immanence nor a middle position which is of dipolar nature and in which transcendence and immanence as two poles are *directly* interacting with each other. To realize the Middle Way, even such a middle position must be overcome; because, however dynamic the middle point may be, it is involved in the duality of transcendence and immanence. A complete over-coming of dipolarity, including the middle point which attempts to function as a mediator between the two conflicing poles, is essential for the realization of the Middle Way and dependent co-origination. This leads us to the following three points:

1. In the Buddhist notion of dependent co-origination, there is *nothing* whatsoever 'more real', (for instance, in terms of transcendence, immanence, or 'in-between'), which lies beyond or behind the interdependence of everything in the universe.
2. But this 'nothingness' should not be taken as nothingness which is distinguished from 'somethingness'. If so, we are involved in another duality, a duality between 'nothingness' and 'somethingness'. 'Nothingness' realized behind the interdependence of everything is not 'relative nothingness' in contrast to 'somethingness' but the 'absolute Nothingness' which is beyond the duality of nothingness and somethingness.
3. When one says that there is absolutely nothing 'more real' behind the interdependence of everything, one means that its interdependence is determined and limited *by itself* without any outside principle of determination and limitation.

Only when one's understanding of the principle of interdependence includes these connotations, has one realized its genuine meaning. Accordingly, the realization of 'absolute Nothingness' is the crucial point for the Buddhist doctrine of dependent co-origination and the Middle Way.

In the doctrine of dependent co-origination expounded by the Buddha, the notion of absolute Nothingness was implicit. It was Nāgārjuna who explicitly enunciated this absolute Nothingness in terms of *Śūnyatā*.

IV

It seems to be clear therefore that Whitehead's notion of God is not quite compatible with the Buddhist idea of dependent co-origination. Despite his interaction with the temporal actual entities (actual occasions), God is not an actual occasion but a non-temporal actual entity, and is the principle of limitation upon actual occasions. In this sense, Whitehead understands God to be *somewhat* beyond the interdependence of everything in the temporal world. By this, however, I do not mean that his notion of God is 'something', or something substantial beyond the world. As Whitehead holds that '... in every respect God and the World move conversely in each other in respect to their process',[12] his notion of God is not substantial or static but dynamic, always interacting with and interpenetrating the world at every point of the process of creativity. In this sense we can say with justification that, in Whitehead, there is *nothing* behind the interdependence of actual entities (or actual occasions) in the universe because God is not 'something'. However, is not this 'nothingness' a relative kind of nothingness as distinguished from 'somethingness', rather than the absolute Nothingness which overcomes the duality of nothingness and somethingness? Stated otherwise, can we say with full justification that in Whitehead there is *absolutely nothing* behind the interdependence of actual occasions in the universe?

This is a crucial question. My answer is 'No'. Despite his close interaction with the world, God alone is not an actual occasion but a non-temporal entity which, as the principle of limitation, performs the function of providing the limitations that make concretions possible. In this respect, Whitehead is lacking the realization of absolute Nothingness or 'Emptiness', a realization which is essential to the Buddhist notion of the interdependence of all things in the universe.

As stated above, it was Nāgārjuna who explicitly developed the notion of 'Emptiness' implicit in the Buddha's doctrine of dependent co-origination. He set forth the theory of dependent co-origination in terms of the Eightfold Negation – neither origination nor cessation; neither permanence nor impermanence; neither unity nor diversity; neither coming nor going. Nāgārjuna not only repudiated the eternalist view, which takes phenomena to be real just as they are and essentially unchangeable; he also rejected as illusory the opposite nihilistic view which emphasizes emptiness and non-being as the true reality. This double negation in terms of 'neither ... nor' is the pivotal point for the realization of Mahayana Emptiness which is never a sheer emptiness but rather Fullness. For 'neither ... nor' is the pivotal point for the realization of Mahayana Emptiness which is never a sheer emptiness but rather Fullness. For 'neither ... nor' *in this case* refers to the two opposing and conversion from the absolute negation (negation of both affirmation and negation, that is, 'Emptiness') into the absolute affirmation (affirmation of both affirmation and negation, that is, 'Fullness').

V

In this connection we must notice the following five points:

1. Nāgārjuna's negation of negation in terms of 'neither ... nor' is not a flat negation of the two parallel items existing on the same plane, but a breaking-through the plane itself by overcoming the contradiction or antinomy between the two opposing poles. For in this negation of negation, affirmation and negation, positivity and negativity are inseparably connected and yet, at the same time, they negate each other. Thus, they constitute an antinomic whole.

2. However, Nāgārjuna's negation of negation is not merely a logical process but an existential and religious issue. The antinomy between 'being' and 'nonbeing', or affirmation and negation, is inherent in human beings, and existentially it is precisely what is called 'human suffering'. It is not that man *has* such an antinomy, but that man *is* this antinomy. Accordingly, the negation of negation does not signify a logical development of negation in an objective or external manner, but a serious inner struggle and an eventual break-through of the existential antinomy innate in the person. In this 'break-through' one is completely emancipated from delusions and sufferings, and thus awakens to Reality. Otherwise stated, one's ego-self dies and no-self is realized as the true Self. This is the realization of one's true and deepest Subjectivity which can be attained only through the negation of negation. With this realization of no-self, *Śūnyatā* is opened up.

3. Through the realization of this 'negation of negation' and of 'Emptiness', the ground of human subjectivity is transformed from mere self to the 'no-self', which is another term for the true Self. Emptiness is thus realized at the deepest core or at the bottomless depth of one's Subjectivity. It is deeper and more profound than one's own self. However, if Emptiness is realized somewhat *outside of* 'myself', it cannot be called the true Emptiness, but is rather an object that is something external to me as Subject, a something merely named 'nothing' or 'emptiness'. As soon as one conceptualizes or objectifies Emptiness he misses it. True Emptiness can never be outside but 'inside' of 'myself', and yet it is deeper than my 'self'. Accordingly, it must be said that 'I am in Emptiness', and yet at the same time that 'Emptiness is in me'. In this connection, it must also be said

that 'I am Empty', and yet that 'Emptiness is me.' As there is
no self, 'I am in Emptiness', or 'I am Empty'. Since 'no-self' is
not a nihilistic idea but is simply another term for the 'true
Self', 'Emptiness is *me*', or, 'Emptiness is in *me*.' I, as the true
Self, am dynamically one with Emptiness itself.

4. Emptiness is boundless and limitless. It is expanding endlessly
into all directions throughout the universe. Nothing can be
outside of this endless and all-dimensional 'expanse' of Emptiness. Although it is opened up through 'my' Subjective realization of no-self it extends endlessly and objectively beyond 'me'.
It is the unrestricted dynamic whole, in which you, I, and
everything else in the universe is included and realized equally
just as it is in its suchness. And yet everything in the universe
retains its individuality because each thing is neither supported
nor limited by any 'something' whatsoever. Rather, each thing
is absolute Nothingness, or *Śūnyata*. Thus everything, including
you and me, interpenetrates every other; yet, each limits every
other and is in turn limited by every other. This dynamic
structure of interaction among all things, without entailing the
loss of individuality by any thing, is fully realized simply
because it takes place in the realization of absolute Nothingness. The latter is not, of course, a particular principle of
limitation. Thus one can say with full justification that 'everything is in Emptiness', and yet 'Emptiness is in everything'; or
'everything is Empty', and 'Emptiness is everything'. Accordingly, Emptiness is not only the deepest ground of one's
subjectivity but also the deepest ground of the universe.

5. Everything in the universe, including you and me, is Empty
and is in Emptiness. There is no underlying principle of
limitation whatever. This means that everything is respectively
and equally limited or determined *by itself*. In other words,
everything is respectively and equally realized *in its suchness*.
However, we should not overlook the fact that this self-
limitation (suchness) or self-determination (freedom) is inseparably connected with the realization of Emptiness. It is
self-limitation or self-determination by means of the realization
of *Śūnyatā*. It is a limitation without a limiter and a determination without a determiner. This explains the Buddhist idea of
the 'law of no law', that is, 'no law is the law', or the 'order of no
order', that is, 'no order is the order'. In this realization of
Emptiness, everything is fully realized as it is in its self-

limitation and is absolutely affirmed in its suchness. However, this should not be taken as an *objectively observable state* nor as a *goal* to be reached. It is the *ground* of one's Subjectivity and of the universe and it is neither objectifiable nor conceptualizable. 'Suchness' is not a static or fixed state but a dynamic and living basis from which the individual, and everything else in mutual interpenetration, begins its activity anew at every moment of the process. This is the activity of self-determination (freedom) based on the realization of *Śūnyatā*. *Prajñā* (wisdom) and *karunā* (compassion) are the two aspects of this free activity of *Śūnyatā*.

VI

It is clear that Whitehead's notion of God as the principle of limitation is not something apart from the universe or an underlying principle essentially distinct from the universe. Toward the end of *Process and Reality*, Whitehead beautifully and impressively elucidates the relatedness of God and the World as follows:

It is as true to say that the World is immanent in God, as that God is immanent in the World.

It is as true to say that God transcends the World, as that the World transcends God.

It is as true to say that God creates the World, as that the World creates God.[13]

The conceptions of the interpenetration, relativity, and the mutual embodiment of God and the world are so conspicuous that we may point them out as the most important characteristics of Whitehead's philosophy with its uniqueness among the philosophical interpretations of God in the West.

Yet in Whitehead, this notion of relativity is not thoroughly carried out in his understanding of the relationship between God and the world. For just like everything in the world, God is an actual entity, but unlike everything in the world, God is not an actual occasion. God alone is always the actual entity that is not an actual occasion. In this connection, as I mentioned earlier, we must distinguish two kinds of relativity – the relativity among things of the world and that between God and the world. The former is the relativity within the temporal realm, and the latter, the relativity referring to the non-temporal realm (that is, the relativity between the temporal realm, namely, the world, and the dipolar nature of temporality and non-temporality, God). But are there justifiable reasons for distinguishing the two kinds of relativity? Can the latter form of relativity be possible logically and existentially? Is the dipolar nature of God in Whitehead completely free from the dualism which Whitehead intends to overcome in principle?

If Whitehead were to carry out thoroughly the denial of dualism that, in my opinion, is absolutely necessary in order to realize the ultimate Reality, he would have to say as follows:

> It is as true to say that God is non-temporal, as that the world is non-temporal.
> It is as true to say that God is temporal, as that the world is temporal.
> It is as true to say that God is an actual occasion as that every real thing in the world is an actual occasion.

According to Whitehead's definition, 'actual occasion' has a spatio-temporal nature. It is extensive in terms of both spatiality and temporality. However, God alone is non-temporal, chiefly because of his primordial nature and, to some extent, because of his consequent nature, especially because of his 'everlastingness'. Through his primordial nature, God acts upon the World as the principle of concretion, and in his consequent nature, God is determined by the physical experiences derived from the temporal world as the world reacting upon God. In this sense, God is interpenetrating fully with the world and as such he, too, in the final analysis, must be said to be spatio-temporal. At the same time, however, God is non-temporal as well as non-spatial in both his primordial and consequent natures. Viewed as primordial, God is 'the unlimited conceptual realization of the absolute wealth of potentiality' and 'deficiently actual'.[14] Viewed as consequent nature, God is 'infinite' in his patience and 'everlasting' in his creative advance and retention of mutual immediacy. In these two senses God is beyond temporality. Here temporality and non-temporality are not completely interrelated.

Thus, although Whitehead emphasizes the mutual embodiment of God and the world, the mutuality does not seem to be complete. This is also discerned in the following quotation from *Process and Reality*:

'In God's nature, permanence is primordial and flux is derivative from the World; in the World's nature, flux is primordial and permanence is derivative from God.'[15]

It seems after all that God includes the world, but not vice versa, because God is primordial in terms of permanence which is complete and eternal, whereas the world is primordial only in terms of flux which is incomplete and changing. As far as permanence is concerned, God is primordial but the World is derivative. Despite their close mutual embodiment, God is all inclusive, whereas the World is, in the last analysis, 'the included'.

If this is the case, we notice a kind of double structure of God and the world in Whitehead's philosophy of organism. By the 'double structure of God and the world' I mean that in Whitehead, God and the world are sometimes understood as completely interdependent and interactive with each other, and yet at other times, God is, especially in his primordial nature, understood as somewhat beyond the spatio-temporal world – because in Whitehead, God is the only actual entity which is *not* an actual occasion. In his philosophy of organism, a trace of dualism still remains. However, I am not saying that in Whitehead, God and the world constitute a double structure in terms of *substance*, but rather in terms of *nature* and *activity* (prehension). Just in this sense his system, therefore, is not completely free from dualism.

VII

Mahayana Buddhists emphasize that to realize ultimate Reality one must overcome all forms of duality, including even the duality between 'duality' and 'non-duality'. When one speaks of duality, one must, consciously or unconsciously, stand somewhat outside of the two poles which constitute the duality. For it is impossible to speak of duality properly by taking as one's standpoint either one of the two poles of that duality or a certain point between them. One can legitimately talk about duality only by taking a *third position* outside that duality itself, and by looking at that duality somewhat from without. In this case, however, the third position is merely one conceptually established – an unreal position. Naturally, the reality which is grasped in terms of duality is a conceptualized or objectified reality and cannot be ultimate Reality. This is why duality must be overcome in order to be completely free from conceptualization, objectification, delusion and attachment. Only in this way can one awaken to ultimate Reality or true Subjectivity.

In order to awaken to ultimate Reality, one must overcome the final duality, that is, the dichotomization of 'duality' and 'non-duality'. To reach the position that is fully beyond any conceptualization and to attain genuine Subjectivity, the most vital and indispensable requirement is the radical 'reversion' or 'turning over' which takes place through transcending every possible conceptualization and objectification. This is signified by the 'death' of one's ego and by the awakening to 'no-self'; the stubborn innate tendency toward duality in the human ego is so strong that the radical 'reversion' is possible only through this 'death' of the ego.

Clearly, Whitehead's notion of dipolarity is not duality in the ordinary sense. It is so dynamic and full of contrast that it is, in a way, beyond duality. However, the dipolar nature of God and the dipolar nature of actual occasions in the world are not the same. Strictly speaking, we must distinguish these two kinds of dipolar nature just as we distinguished earlier two kinds of relativity. As mentioned above, a trace of dualism still remains in Whitehead owing to the double structure of God and the world in terms of their nature and activity. Does not Whitehead unconsciously conceptualize or objectify the relationship between God and the world by taking a third position outside the very relationship itself? Such a third, 'outsider's' position is not acceptable to religion, which is based on existential commitment. Even in philosophy this kind of third position is questionable as a means of reaching ultimate Reality.

In Buddhism temporality and non-temporality are completely non-dualistic. Hence samsara as it is is nirvana; nirvana as it is is samsara. Mahayana Buddhists take samsara (endless transmigration of living and dying) in itself as 'Death' in its authentic sense. Death in its authentic sense is not death as distinguished from life, just as the real Nothingness is not the nothingness as distinguished from somethingness. If we grasp the process of transmigration, not from the outside (objectively), but from within (Subjectively or existentially), then we are always living and yet always dying at every moment. Without living, there is no dying; without dying, there is no living. Living and dying are non-dualistically one in our existential realization. Since living and dying are two opposing principles, this antinomic oneness of living and dying itself is the greatest suffering: Death. In this existential realization, the endless transmigration of living-dying as such is realized as the Great Death.

This implies that the process of transmigration, insofar as it can be said to be a continuity, must be grasped as a continuity of endless living–dying in which each and every moment of living from the past toward the future is radically severed by a dying both from what went before and what comes after. It is a dynamic continuity which is marked by discontinuity at each point. Since this dynamic 'continuity of discontinuity' of the process of living-dying is endless, it is realized as the Great Death. However, with this realization of the Great Death as a turning point, the endless process of living –dying is re-grasped in an entirely new light. It is no longer a negative 'continuity of *discontinuity*' (samsara), but rather a positive '*continuity* of discontinuity' (nirvana). This 'turning over' takes place through the radical reversion at the depth of our existential realization. Through the realization of the Great Death, the realization of the Great Life opens up.

As the above discussion implies, the realization of Great Death has a double connotation: negative and positive. On the one hand, the realization of Great Death is negative in that it realizes the antinomic oneness of living and dying as the greatest suffering – the most serious existential problem which must be solved to attain emancipation. On the other hand, the realization of Great Death is positive in that it entails the resolution to the problem of suffering and the realization of the Great Life. This double connotation and the accompanying shift from the negative to the positive connotation are possible because the realization of Great Death is a total, holistic, and existential realization of the endlessness of living–dying in which one becomes identical with the Great Death and thereby overcomes the endlessness of living–dying. Once we come to this existential realization, we can say with justification that *samsara* and *nirvana* are identical. Thus the realization of the Great Death is the crucial point for the seemingly paradoxical Mahayana doctrines. This is simply another expression for the above statement that the realization of absolute Nothingness is indispensable for attaining the Mahayana notion of Emptiness which is no other than Fullness.

Process and Reality has almost no reference to death even in the mandane sense, let alone to anything like the Great Death. Although the perpetual perishing of actual entities is much talked about, in Whitehead it is not thoroughly, but only partially, realized as the following quotation shows: 'actual entities perpetually perish subjectively, but are immortal objectively. Actuality in perishing acquires objectively, while it loses subjective immediacy'.[16] Again, in *Process and Reality*, the continuum or the conjunction seems to be more emphasized than the disjunction. The result is that Whitehead's philosophy is that of organism and in it God is treated as the principle of creativity, limitation, and judgement. Against the Western metaphysical tradition – which had generally put stress on being, substance, transcendence, and duality – Whitehead emphasizes becoming, process, immanence and relatedness. He established an extraordinary system of organic metaphysics. But, his failure to realize absolute Nothingness and Death in the deepest sense prevented him from breaking through the framework of dualism. Nevertheless, within the context of dualism, he has expounded and developed the notion of the relatedness of everything to its limit. Duality is minimized but not overcome in Whitehead.

On the other hand, Mahayana Buddhism is based on non-duality by rejecting all possible dualisms. Thus it is not mechanistic, or organic, or substantial. Although 'becoming' rather than 'being', 'process' rather than 'substance', 'flux' rather than unchanging 'permanence' are stressed in Mahayana Buddhism, they are at every point supported in one's existential realization by the realization of the absolute Nothingness. Becoming, process, and flux are beginningless and endless in every possible sense, whether these notions are understood in terms of immanence or transcendence, substance or activity. They are thoroughly realized existentially from within. They are grasped through the realization of Emptiness which opens up endlessly. This is the reason that becoming, process, and flux have no teleological implication in Mahayana Buddhism. Thus, becoming is not simply becoming but Being in any moment; process is not merely process but always the beginning and the end at the same time; flux is not just flux but permanance at any point. This is the basis on which Mahayana teleology might be established.

In short, in Mahayana Buddhism Emptiness replaces God, including Whitehead's notion of God. Hence the problem of God and the world does not arise in Mahayana Buddhism. The Buddhist equivalent to the problem of God and the world may be the problem of self and the world. For there is absolutely nothing behind the world or the universe, the fact of which is to be realized by one's self. Both self and the world are thoroughly spatio-temporal. However, only with the realization of there being absolutely nothing behind the spatio-temporality of self and the world is the pivotal point of the radical reversion to the non-spatial and non-temporal nature, which at the same time is non-dualistically identical with the spatio-temporal nature, realized. The Self is the sphere that is open to this realization. The Mahayana idea of *nirvana* means precisely this non-dualistic realization of the unique identity of the spatio-temporal nature and the non-spatial and non-temporal nature.

VIII

In the above, I have tried to clarify the difference between the thought structure in Mahayana Buddhism and in Whitehead. However, as I said in the beginning of this article, the clarification of the differences between the two systems does not exclude the possibility of dialogue between them. On the contrary, it provides a realistic foundation for a fruitful and productive encounter. For without a clear realization of the differences between their thought structures, the dialogue may be unrealistic and hence, barren. In my view, Mahayana Buddhism and Whitehead's philosophy of organism are strikingly similar because the latter minimizes duality and stands almost on the verge of overcoming duality. However, we cannot easily bridge the two, unless the structural differences in their systems are somehow overcome. There are at least two possible ways of overcoming this difficulty. One is the approach from the side of Whitehead's philosophy, and the other is from the side of Mahayana Buddhism.

In order to construct a bridge from the side of Whitehead's philosophy, the limitation inherent in dualism must be *completely* overcome and broken through. This means that God must be understood as an actual occasion as well as an actual entity and that the principle of relativity must be strictly and thoroughly realized throughout the *whole* relation between God and the world, including the problem of temporality and non-temporality. This is possible only through the realization of the Great Death and the conjunction of disjunction. This realization constitutes a radical turning over by overcoming every possible objectification which takes place in one's self. This idea entails the denial of Whitehead's notion of God with its non-temporal nature. In this way, however, God would be interpreted anew as the dynamic function of complete interaction in and throughout the open and limitless universe of spatio-temporal nature without the slightest trace of a double structure. In this new interpretation, God is no longer the principle of limitation. Instead, 'no principle of limitation' is 'God'.

This is the idea underlying this discussion. For herein I have tried to clarify the differences of the thought structures of the two systems by using the conceptions of Mahayana Buddhism as the standard and by trying to see how closely Whitehead's philosophy approaches Mahayana Buddhism. I took this way simply because it is easier for me at present than to approach the problem from the side of Whitehead. Therefore, I do not, of course, exclude the opposite approach of using Whitehead's philosophy as the standard and then taking a look as to how close Mahayana Buddhism comes to it. This would be the second way of overcoming the difference between their thought structures. There arises from this latter method the realization that at least two aspects of Whitehead's philosophy: (1) the dipolar nature of God with his principle of limitation, and (2) the dynamic structure of the interactions among the things in the universe, must be introduced into Buddhism. Point (1), Whitehead's idea of dipolar nature of God, holds great significance for Buddhism because the Mahayana ideas of Emptiness and Suchness always run the risk of being taken negatively just because of their complete denial of duality. As soon as these ideas are understood as an object or a goal, that is, objectively rather than existentially as the ground or the root source of one's Subjectivity, they immediately turn into a dead Emptiness and a very shallow and cheap Suchness. The history of Mahayana Buddhism provides many such examples. The result is nihilism, pessimism, moral anarchy, and indifferent and uncritical acceptance or affirmation of social conditions. Whitehead's idea of the dipolar nature of God with his principle of limitation may be reinterpreted in the Mahayana context as an aid in combating the recurrent negative misunderstandings of the ideas of Emptiness and Suchness. In addition, point (2), Whitehead's idea of the dynamic structure of the interaction among things in the universe should be introduced into Mahayana Buddhism because Buddhism, putting a strong emphasis on the necessity of awakening to the *ground* of one's Subjectivity, that is, to no-self, is thereby generally weak in developing and embodying concretely the no-self in the world. Nishida's philosophy has already developed the Mahayana idea of Emptiness or no-self in a constructive way in connection with society and history, especially through his use of and confrontation with Western science and philosophy. Whitehead's philosophy is certainly another excellent example, in this respect, from which Mahayana Buddhist thinkers have a great deal to learn.

I have, in this section, merely made a few suggestions which may be of help in establishing a positive dialogue between Whitehead and Mahayana Buddhism once the critical structural differences in their thinking have been clearly realized. With these differences and above suggestions in mind, let us begin a creative and a constructive dialogue between them.

8 Tillich from a Buddhist Point of View

All mankind is now facing a global age. This does not simply mean that the whole world is now totally integrated by the rapidly advancing technology, such as jet airplanes and various methods of immediate communication. It also means that the people of the world, as individuals and as nations, interact politically and economically as one group. Almost no part of the globe is free from involvement in the world-wide waves of unity and opposition, tension and conflict. I think, however, what is most significant and decisive for the destiny of mankind in this regard is the encounter of the world religions which is, on a scale and depth never experienced before, taking place 'beneath' (even while entangled with) the complex processes of the political, economic and social integration of the world. Given the intensity of the present situation, the openness and profundity with which the encounter or dialogue among the world religions is carried out in the search for a new spiritual horizon is vital to the future of mankind. The global age will produce dissension as well as unity, will both elevate as well as endanger mankind. As a real basis of the global age, a new spiritual horizon is needed which can open up the innermost depth of human religiosity, and upon which all nations can display their spiritual and cultural creativity without being dehumanized and deindividualized by the world's sociological complexity or by technological uniformity.

At this critical point in history, the appearance of Paul Tillich's book, *Christianity and the Encounter of the World Religions*,[1] is most welcome and highly significant, for the book can be taken as the result of a frontal inquiry into the above-mentioned problem by one of the most outstanding Christian theologians and philosophers of religion of the twentieth century. In this book the inquiry into the problem has been made from the Christian point of view, but with the discerning insight that 'the main characteristic of the present encounter of the world religions is their encounter with the quasi-religions of our time' (p. 5). In this context the author presents penetrating observations, a dynamic point of view, and a new insight for the task of religion. Thus he expects, as expressed in the preface of the book, 'critical thought not only with respect to the relation of Christianity to the world religions but also with respect to its own nature'. The following is intended not simply as a review of his book but rather as a response to the ideas presented therein by a Buddhist who, while critical of as well as sympathetic to his approach, not only has the same concern as the author about this matter, but also is committed to promoting a dialogue between Christianity and Buddhism from the side of Buddhism.

I   TILLICH'S POSITION AND HIS CHARACTERIZATION OF THE PRESENT RELIGIOUS SITUATION

In the first chapter 'A View of the Present Situation: Religions, Quasi-Religions, and Their Encounter', the author first defines his own position in dealing with the present religious situation as an 'observing participant', a position fusing the standpoint of an outside observer and of an inside participant. Next, in the light of his now well-known definition of religion, that is, 'the state of being grasped by an ultimate concern', he describes the main characteristic of the present encounter of the world religions as 'their encounter with the quasi-religions of our time'. His position as an 'observing participant' and his characterization of the present encounter of the world religions are, I think, closely connected with each other in his inner thinking.

   It is a necessary and invaluable insight to find the main characteristic of the present encounter of the world religions not merely in the nature of their mutual encounter but in their encounter with the quasi-religions of today. Tillich rightly says, 'Even the mutual relations of the religions proper are decisively influenced by the encounter of each of them with secularism and one or more of the quasi-religions which are based upon secularism.' (p. 5) I, too, have pointed out that the problem of the encounter of the world religions should be taken in the context of the issue between religion and irreligion.[2] With Tillich, I believe that such a broad perspective, one which includes secularism or the so-called irreligious forces is now absolutely necessary for a proper understanding of the present-day encounter of the world religions. However, where Tillich and I differ is that whereas Tillich emphasizes the quasi-religions,[3] I emphasize the *anti-religious forces* as the other part of that encounter of the world religions apart from which their mutual relations cannot properly and adequately be understood. It is true that my so-called anti-religious forces are not always other than Tillich's so-called quasi-religions. My point is, however, that in a thorough-going study of the encounter among religions proper, it is essential that secularism be taken into account, and that some of its forms be grasped in terms of their anti-religious rather than their quasi-religious character. In so far as we follow Tillich's definition of religion, it is to be recognized that all anti-religious forces are at once quasi-religions because they also elevate a preliminary concern to an ultimate one. Hence, by the term 'anti-religious', I particular-ly mean any form of quasi-religion which, besides elevating a preliminary concern to ultimacy, negates, in principle, religion proper. It is this religion-negating aspect which is most crucial in the encounter between religion and secularism. The conspicuous examples of quasi-religions today are, in Tillich's view, nationalism (and its Fascist radicalization), socialism (and its Communist radicalization) and liberal humanism. In these quasi-religions, especially in their radical forms, nation, social order and humanity, though finite and transitory, are elevated to an ultimate concern. In giving such a panorama of the present religious situation, Tillich seems to take the encounter of the world religions with the quasi-religions today as an historic-cultural religious event and not necessarily as an existential encounter at the risk of his own faith.

This may be a natural consequence of his position as an 'observing participant'. I believe, however, that in the present religious situation, if any religious person takes the matter existen-tially that person cannot remain an observing participant. Rather, he or she should be, or cannot help being, a self-staking participant, for the most acute and serious character of the encounter of the world religions is to be found in their encounter with the anti-religious forces of our time rather than with the quasi-religions of our time. A follower of religion today is now exposed to the attack of the anti-religious forces which, unlike the quasi-religions, con-sciously deny the *raison d'être* of religion from some philosophical base. Scientism, Marxism, and nihilism in Nietzsche's sense may be mentioned as conspicuous examples.[4] In Tillich's view, scientism as the technological invasion of traditional cultures and religions, and Marxism in the form of Communism are taken into account. However, insofar as they are considered as quasi-religions with secularism as their base, their religion-negating aspect (negating religion via a philosophical principle) is overlooked. There can be found no reference to nihilism which, in my view, constitutes the most radical form of a religion-negating standpoint, the overcoming of which is the *sine qua non* for the establishment of the *raison d'être* of religion today. It is, of course, important to characterize the present encounter of the world religions as their encounter with the quasi-religions of our time, taking Fascism, Communism, and liberal humanism as the most conspicuous examples. We should, however, notice that some forms of secularism have taken on the character of anti-religions rather than quasi-religions. While liberal humanism, though rightly regarded as a quasi-religion, cannot be considered as anti-religious, scientism and Marxism are clear examples of anti-religions. When such forms of secularism as scientism and Marxism are taken merely as quasi-religions, there is a possibility of taking the encounter between religion proper and these forms of secularisms not as an existential problem, but rather as a historic–cultural phenomenon. However, when these forms of secularism are taken as anti-religious forces (as they are in reality) their encounter with religion proper becomes, for religious people, an existential problem, a problem upon which one must stake one's faith not knowing whether it will stand or fall. When the religion-negating forms of secularism are understood solely as quasi-religions, the true significance of the present encounter between religions, i.e., the encounter in the face of the attack of anti-religious forces, is not understood internally enough. Only through the awareness of the attack by contemporary anti-religious forces on religion as such, can the *total* experience of the holy be opened up and the *raison d'être* of religion thereby demonstrated beyond anti-religious principles. The present situation demands, in my view, that the dialogue between religions proper be carried out with unceasing reference to the anti-religious forces and their religion-negating principles. Thus, we today cannot and should not be observing participants but deeply existential self-risking participants.

II THE KINGDOM OF GOD AND NIRVANA

In his approach to a dialogue between Christianity and Buddhism, Tillich is much fairer and more perceptive than any other Christian theologian, past or present. He clearly denies that Christianity is the absolute religion, and duly considers Buddhism as a living religion which stands in polar tension to Christianity. The method which he adopts in this regard is a dynamic typology. In the method of dynamic typology the places of both Christianity and Buddhism are determined as the contrasting poles within the whole of man's religious existence or man's experience of the holy. The polar element of Christianity is, in Tillich's view, the social-ethical element or the experience of the holy as it ought to be, while the polar element of Buddhism is the mystical element or the experience of the holy as being (p. 58). From this position, Tillich develops a dialogue between Christianity and Buddhism by contrasting the *Kingdom of God* and *Nirvana* in terms of their telos or controlling symbols. He considers the ontological principles behind these symbols to be *participation* and *identity*, the ethical consequences deriving from these ontological principles to be *agape* and *compassion* and, finally, their resultant attitudes toward history to be on the one hand *revolutionary* and, on the other, *detached*. His approach is penetrating and quite provocative. However, his characterization of Nirvana in terms of identity, compassion, and detachment as Buddhist principles in contrast with their Christian equivalents is not entirely free from a Christian colouration.

As for the formulation of the telos of the two religions as the starting point of the discussion, Tillich uses the following telos-formulas: 'in Christianity the telos of every*one* and everything united in the Kingdom of God; in Buddhism the telos of every*thing* and everyone fulfilled in the Nirvana' (p. 64). In the telos-formula of Christianity, 'every*one*' precedes 'everything', and in the telos-formula of Buddhism 'every*thing*' precedes 'everyone'. And every*one* in Christianity and every*thing* in Buddhism are italicized. This seems to imply that in the Christian symbol of the Kingdom of God humans are taken as superior to things in their unity, and thus the symbol is personal; while in the Buddhist idea of Nirvana, things hold priority to humans in their fulfilment, therefore, the symbol is transpersonal. This supposed implication seems to be supported by Tillich's discussion on participation versus identity, agape versus compassion and so forth. If I am not wrong in this respect, I should say that Tillich misses the important aspect of the dialectical character of Nirvana.

It is true that, as seen in such well-known phrases of Buddhist scripture as, 'All sentient beings without exception have the Buddha-nature' or 'All the trees, herbs and lands attain Buddha-hood', Buddhism often emphasizes the fulfilment of *things* without mentioning humans. Again, it is true in a sense that Buddhism does not give a special or superior position to humans over against other living and non-living things with regard to their nature and salvation; while Christianity, as the Genesis story shows, assigns humans the task of ruling over all other creatures and ascribes to them alone the *imago dei* through which they, unlike other creatures, can directly respond to the word of God. But how is the fulfilment of things understood to take place in Buddhism? Does it take place as a mere objective happening which occurs apart from human realization? No. The fulfilment of things may take place only when, and at the same moment, the fulfilment of humans takes place. Without the fulfilment of the persons and his or her realization of that fulfilment, the fulfilment of things is simply out of the question. Therefore, Nirvana, in which everything and everyone are fulfiled, is not a *state* objectively observable – Tillich calls Nirvana 'the state of transtemporal blessedness' (p. 68) – but is *Enlightenment* or the Subjective *realization* in which everything and everyone are respectively realized as they are. In other words, Nirvana is nothing but a person's realization of the existential true Self as the ultimate ground of both the ordinary self and the world related to it. Nirvana obtains only through a person's realization, the realization of No-Self. In this sense, Buddhism, too, ascribes to humans priority over other things. Accordingly, Nirvana is not simply transp rsonal but also, at once, personal. But if this is the case, why does the Buddhist emphasize the fulfilment of everything?

In Buddhism, samsara, i.e., birth–death transmigration, understood to be the fundamental human problem, is understood to be fully eliminated only when it is resolved as a problem of a more universal nature than that of birth and death. It can only be resolved as a part of the problem of generation and extinction which is common to all living beings, or, more fundamentally, as a part of the problem of being–non-being, (the problem of transiency which is common to all beings, living or non-living). This means that in Buddhism the human problem of birth–death, though fundamental, is wrestled with and eliminated, not only as the problem of birth–death on the human dimension, but also as the problem of generation–extinction or, in the last analysis, as the problem of being–non-being on the ontological dimension. Unless the transiency which is common to *all* beings is overcome at the root of human existence, the particular problem of human birth and death cannot be properly solved. This is why Buddhism emphasizes the fulfilment of every*thing* in Nirvana. However, the being–non-being problem, the problem of transiency, though common to all beings, including humans, is realized as such and sought to be eliminated *only by humans*, whose being alone has self-consciousness. Thus, even though one may transmigrate through other forms of .life, Buddhism emphasizes the necessity of practise and enlightenment while one exists as a human being.[5]

In short, Buddhist Nirvana is the realization of the human existential true Self in which, and in which alone, everything and everyone, including oneself, are respectively and equally fulfilled in its particularity. This involves the following two points: first, in Nirvana everything and everyone are equal and returns, through human realization, to oneness as the ontological ground prior to their differentiation; second, in Nirvana everything and everyone are respectively and distinctively fulfiled, and are more clearly distinguished from every other than before. This dialectical character of Nirvana is possible because Nirvana is not an objectively observable state but is human realization of the ultimate ground of both subject and object, of both self and world.

Mahayana Buddhism severely criticizes a oneness of everything without discrimination as a false equality or a false sameness. Mere equality as the negation of differentiation cannot then be called true equality. Equality in oneness as the ultimate ground, e.g., *to hen*, God, *esse ipsum*, or whatever it may be named, if it is *substantial*, can never be real equality, because even equality in this sense is still involved with, and thereby limited by, a differentiation, the differentiation between the substantial oneness and the things which participate in that substance. On the contrary, in oneness which is non-substantial things do not *participate* in oneness, but are *thoroughly fulfiled* through dynamic identity with that non-substantial oneness. Therein, without eliminating its particularity and differentiation, everything is realized in itself. Only in this non-substantial oneness can real equality take place. This real and dynamic equality is, in Buddhism, usually expressed as 'Differentiation as it is is equality; equality as it is is differentiation.' This is nothing but the living structure of Nirvana as the realization of oneness. It is non-substantial and is the negation of substantial oneness as the negation of differentiation. This dialectical structure of equality can obtain existentially in terms of Nirvana because Nirvana is not a static 'state' but is dynamic realization of the non-substantial oneness of samsara and Nirvana.

This leads us to another emphasis of Mahayana Buddhism concerning Nirvana. Throughout its long history, Mahayana Buddhism has always emphasized 'Do not abide in Nirvana' as well as 'Do not abide in samsara.' If one abides in so-called Nirvana by transcending samsara, it must be said that one is not yet free from attachment, attachment to Nirvana, and is confined by the discrimination between Nirvana and samsara. It must also be said that one is still selfishly concerned with his own salvation, forgetting the suffering of others in samsara. On the basis of the idea of the Bodhisattva, Mahayana Buddhism thus criticizes and rejects Nirvana as the transcendence of samsara and teaches true Nirvana to be the returning to samsara by negating or transcending 'Nirvana as the transcendence of samsara.' Therefore, Nirvana in the Mahayana sense, while transcending samsara, is nothing but the realization of samsara as samsara, no more, no less, through the complete returning to samsara itself. This is why, in Mahayana Buddhism, it is often said of true Nirvana that, 'samsara-as-it-is is Nirvana.' This paradoxical statement is again based on the dialectical character of true Nirvana which is, logically speaking, the negation of negation (that is, absolute affirmation) or the transcendence of transcendence (that is, absolute immanence). True Nirvana is, according to Mahayana Buddhism, the real source of both *prajñā* (wisdom) and *karunā* (compassion). It is the source of *prajñā* because it is entirely free from the discriminating mind and thus is able to see everything in its uniqueness and distinctiveness without any sense of attachment. It is the source of *karunā* because it is unselfishly concerned with the salvation of all others in samsara through one's own returning to samsara.

The above elucidation of the meaning of Nirvana is necessary for an adequate critique of the 'Christian–Buddhist Conversation' section of Tillich's book. It is also necessary if we are to promote and give proper focus and direction to a dialogue between the two religions. In Mahayana Buddhism, criticism against the oneness of everything beyond differentiation as a false equality and the rejection of Nirvana as simply the transcendence of samsara are key points by which Mahayana Buddhism distinguishes itself from Theravada Buddhism. These points have, however, often been overlooked by Western scholars. In the light of the meaning of Nirvana as briefly elucidated above, the reader may come to see that Tillich's discussion of Nirvana, identity, compassion, and detachment in Buddhism somewhat distorts their true meaning and thus does not get to the core of the Christian–Buddhist dialogue. Nevertheless his undertaking should be highly appreciated.

III PERSONAL AND TRANSPERSONAL; PARTICIPATION AND IDENTITY

I will confine myself to taking up the following several points of his 'Christian-Buddhist Conversation'. 1. Referring to Kingdom of God and Nirvana, Tillich says, 'The Ultimate in Christianity is symbolized in personal categories, the Ultimate in Buddhism in transpersonal categories, for example, "absolute non-being"' (p. 65 f). This is a view based on the Christian category of the 'personal' or 'personality'. Nirvana or absolute non-being as the Ultimate in Buddhism is certainly not personal but transpersonal. However, it is transpersonal not in the sense of 'non-personal' as the counter concept of 'personal' but in the sense that, being beyond the distinction between man and nature, the personal and the non-personal, it is able to make both the personal and the non-personal fulfil their respective natures. Even the *esse ipsum*, Being itself, of the classical Christian doctrine of God, though transpersonal, is not so in the same sense as the Buddhist Nirvana. God as Being itself is beyond the contrast of essential and existential being, of finitude and infinity,[6] and, in a sense, of being and non-being. God as Being itself, however, unlike Nirvana as absolute *Mu*,[7] does not thoroughly transcend the duality of being and non-being to the extent that by this transcendence both being and non-being are totally accepted as equally meaningful expressions of human life. God as Being itself does not truly embody the dialectical function of the dual character described by Tillich himself as 'creative' and 'abysmal',[8] a character innate in all beings. Further, *esse ipsum* as the transpersonal does not allow nature (the non-personal) as well as man (the personal) to equally fulfil their respective natures.

In this connection, it is necessary to raise the following questions:

When the Ultimate, which is beyond the contrast of essential and existential being, of finitude and infinity, and of being and non-being, is understood not as absolute *Mu* (Nothingness) but as Being itself or *esse ipsum* is not the Ultimate still somewhat objectified – in that it is not completely free from duality? Is not this Ultimate founded on an unconsciously posited, hidden, last presupposition? Is not priority finally given to the positive pole of every duality? If so, is it not that the Ultimate in Tillich's sense is not the true Ultimate?

2. As the ontological principles lying behind the symbols of the Kingdom of God and Nirvana, Tillich speaks of 'participation' as the ontological principle underlying the symbol of the Kingdom of God, and of 'identity' as the ontological principle underlying the symbol of Nirvana. In this view, he says, 'One participates, as an individual being, in the Kingdom of God. One is identical with everything that is in Nirvana' (p. 68). For Tillich, individualization and participation are interdependent in a polar tension. 'No individual exists without participation, and no personal being exists without communal being.'[9] In the Kingdom of God both individualization and participation reach their ultimate form in this polarity. This is the basis of Biblical personalism and Christian ethics.

However, is not the real polar element of individualization not participation but identity? Participation, however dialectical its character may be, cannot be essentially relieved of its 'partial' or 'relative' nature because the one who participates still remains somewhat outside of that in which he participates. Insofar as this is the case, individualization is not completely realized. It is indeed true that without an encounter with and participation in another individual, no individual can realize itself as an individual. Individualization through participation, however, cannot be *complete* individualization because of the 'partial' or 'relative' nature of *participation*,[10] although such a fundamental relation of the person as communion can well be established by individualization through participation. In Christianity, according to Tillich, 'God is the principle of participation as well as the principle of individualization.'[11] Participation as the polar principle of individualization is necessary in Christianity because God is substantial 'Being-itself', and not non-substantial 'absolute *Mu*' (non-being or nothingness). However, the principle of individualization cannot be completely and thoroughly fulfiled through the principle of participation as

'Being itself' but through the principle of identity as 'absolute *Mu*' – Nirvana. Identity as an ontological principle of absolute *Mu* is neither identity as the mere negation of individuality nor identity in oneness as the ultimate, *substantial* ground such as God, *esse ipsum*, *substantia* (Spinoza) or Indifference (Schelling) – just as equality in Nirvana is neither equality as the mere negation of differentiation nor equality in oneness as the ultimate, *substantial* ground. Identity as an ontological principle of Nirvana is, accordingly, not identity with oneness which is substantial, but identity with absolute Nothingness. Thus, identity in this sense involves in itself total differentiation, and this through individualization, while in identity with substantial oneness, because of the elimination of differentiation, individualization cannot completely be fulfiled. This may be well understood if you recall that Nirvana is, as discussed before, not an objectively observable state but one's realization in which everything and everyone, including oneself, are respectively and equally realized as they are. In Nirvana identity itself is individualization.

In his talk with a Buddhist priest, Tillich said, '*Only* if each person has a substance of his own is community possible, for community presupposes separation. You, Buddhist friends, have identity, but no community' (p. 75). In this connection I am compelled to raise the following questions: are not both community and separation in Christian understanding incomplete insofar as the self as well as God are understood as substantial? Is not the dialectical nature of the Christian understanding of community and separation really not dialectical, thus not reaching the core of ultimate Reality? Buddhist community takes place precisely when there is the *communion* of the 'realizer of Nirvana' with everything and everyone in the topos of absolute Mu in which everything and everyone are *absolute in their particularity* and thus *absolutely relative*.

3. Let me, in this connection, refer to the Buddhist rock garden which Tillich speaks of as 'a quite conspicuous expression of the principle of identity' but, unfortunately, with some misunderstanding. He describes a statement he heard concerning the rock garden as follows: 'These expressively arranged rocks are both here and, at the same time, everywhere in the universe in a kind of mystical omnipresence, and their particular existence here and now is not significant' (p. 70). Buddhists more correctly would say that 'these expressively arranged rocks are both here and, at the same time, everywhere in the universe' not in a kind of mystical omnipresence

but in *Śūnyatā* (Emptiness) which is another expression for Nirvana. The empty garden covered by white sand expresses *Śūnyatā*, identity with absolute *Mu*. True *Śūnyatā*, however, just like true Nirvana, is by no means mere emptiness, i.e., emptiness as the privation or negation of things which are. True *Śūnyatā*, as the negation of emptiness and fulness in the relative sense, is an active and creative Emptiness which, precisely in being empty, makes everything and everyone be and work in their particularity. It may be helpful here to mention that *Śūnyatā*, just like Nirvana, is not a state but 'realization.' The several rocks with different shapes and characters which are placed here and there on the white sand are nothing but the self-expression of the true *Śūnyatā* which makes everything stand as it is and function freely. Each rock is not simply something with a particular form but is *equally* and *uniquely*, the self-expression, through the taking of form, of the true Self which is beyond every form. It can properly be said that 'these expressively arranged rocks are both here and, at the same time, everywhere in the universe' because they are just here and now in the empty garden both as they are and, at the same time, as the self-expression of true *Śūnyatā* which is beyond time and space. If 'their particular existence here and now [were] not significant', the white sand garden would express a dead emptiness, which Mahayana Buddhism, especially Zen, severely rejects as a false equality or annihilatory nothingness. The very existence of these rocks in the empty garden, equally and uniquely, shows the real profoundness, the creative profoundness of the true Self which embraces, as the realization of absolute *Mu*, everything and everyone in their identity and individualization.

In short, the Buddhist rock garden is not a product of nature mysticism, to say nothing of theistic mysticism, but the product of the creative expression of the realization of *Śūnyatā* as one's true Self. A visitor may be strongly impressed by it, for in looking at it, one is drawn into that *Śūnyatā* which is expressed in, and as, a rock garden, a *Śūnyatā* which, even though not yet consciously realized by the visitor, is nevertheless the root-source of existence, ie., the true Self.

IV   AGAPE AND COMPASSION, AND OTHERS

4. In his 'Christian-Buddhist Conversation', Tillich, along the basic line of his understanding as mentioned above, further discusses the

matter of *agape* and *compassion*, one as the Christian, the other as the Buddhist ethical principle of human relations in society. He also discusses the matter of the *revolutionary* nature of Christianity and the *detached* character of Buddhism in their attitudes toward history. It may be, I now hope, understood without a detailed discussion that his understanding of Buddhist compassion and the Buddhist 'detached' attitude toward history does not quite hit the mark. In this regard, let me raise several questions to which I shall add some short comments.

Is the will to transform the individual as well as the social structure absolutely necessary in the religious attitude to man, to society and to history? Is the prophetic quest for justice an indispensable element in religious activity as regards the human situation? Can a religion justify itself in its response to the human socio-historical reality only by basing itself on the will to transform with a revolutionary force? Does not, and did not, the very will to transform or the very prophetic quest for justice, even while based on *agape*, cause, after all, and against its original intention, a new and incessant struggle in human history, thereby falling into a 'false endlessness' (in Japanese, *aku mugen*; in German, *schlechte Unendlichkeit*)? Is there not an optical illusion in Christian eschatology? Does not the Christian will to transform, however much it may spring from *agape*, in the last analysis approach and try to transform the other or the social and historic structure not from within but somewhat from outside, insofar as *agape* is, by its very nature, a movement from higher to lower? And thereby does it not produce inevitably a new conflict as well as an improvement?

In Tillich's understanding, Buddhist 'compassion' is 'a state in which he who does not suffer under his own conditions may suffer by identification with another who suffers. He neither accepts the other one in terms of "in spite of", nor does he try to transform him, but he suffers his suffering through identification' (p. 71). In contrast to this understanding, in genuine Buddhist *mahākaruṇā* (great compassion), even though one may be deep in the midst of suffering one 'does not suffer' because one has become identical with absolute *Mu* through the death of the ego. However, this does not mean that the person is insensitive to suffering. On the contrary, one is now able to truly 'suffer with' others – this is the meaning of 'com-passion' – for the first time. Thus, however deeply one may actually suffer, through the realization of the emptiness or nonsubstantiality of 'suffering', one remains undisturbed by that suffering. On the other hand, one can suffer with another who suffers, through the fundamental identification with the other on the basis of the awakening to absolute *Mu* or Nirvana, which the other must also, in his or her original nature, return to and realize. One does not, in one sense, accept the other insofar as the other, in egoistic attachment, does not yet return to and realize absolute *Mu*. At the same time, however, on the basis of the realization of absolute *Mu* as the principle of 'differentiation as it is is equality' he totally accepts the other *just because* the other, in his egoistic attachment, does not yet return to and realize absolute *Mu*. In Buddhist compassion one accepts the other not 'in spite of' but 'just because of' his selfishness, thereby deepening and transcending the 'in spite of' position through one's realization of absolute *Mu* in which everyone, including oneself, as well as everything, are equally and respectively enables to work in perfect freedom from the very ground of their existence.

It may well be said that the 'in spite of' character of the Christian faith by means of prophetic criticism and the 'will to transform' based upon divine justice, functions as an active force (as expressed by the terms 'church militant' and 'church triumphant') in the realm of human society and history, whereas the 'just because of' nature of Buddhist realization, by dissolving and regenerating personal and collective *karma*, functions as a stabilizing element running beneath all social and historical levels. And yet the 'in spite of' character of the Christian faith is apt, I am afraid, to increase as well as decrease tension among people, to cause new dissension even as it strengthens unity, thus falling into a false endlessness (*schlechte Unendlichkeit*). On the other hand, in the 'just because of' nature of Buddhist realization which accepts everything indiscriminately, even social and historic evil, there is always the risk that one's attitude towards the world will be, because of having fallen into a false sameness, indifferent.

As Tillich points out, it is notable that 'prophetic' religions such as Judaism, Christianity, and especially Islam, for the most part resisted and are resisting the invasion of Communism in the West while such Eastern 'mystical' religions as Hinduism, Buddhism and Taoism allow the invasion of Communism in a great part of the Orient without displaying sufficient resistance. The encounter of religion with Communism is unquestionably an important problem of today. The Communist infiltration of China and other parts of the East is no doubt partly due to the corruption of the various

Oriental religions, especially Buddhism with its 'just because of' nature.

As a more fundamental religious question, however, I believe it must be asked if the only legitimate way for a religion to react to secularism is for it to directly resist attacks and challenges on the *same level* that secularism works. Simply because they lack the form of resistance taken by Christianity should Buddhism and other Eastern religions be immediately judged as totally powerless to transform the sociological and psychological structure of man in any way? What, after all, should religion's attitude be toward secularism as such? This question leads us to a final point in the review of Tillich's 'Christian–Buddhist Conversation', that is, the matter of the understanding of the nature of the 'Holy' in these two religions. This problem is also closely connected with the last chapter of the book now being reviewed, 'Christianity Judging Itself in the Light of Its Encounter with the World Religions,' especially its essential point: the Christian criteria for judging Christianity and religion in general. This issue I will take up at another time.

9 Self-Awakening and Faith – Zen and Christianity[1]

The dialogue between Zen and Christianity has been becoming more serious and important during the past decade or so. Those of us involved in it are pleased with this development because we maintain that such a dialogue is necessary for the development of mutual understanding between East and West.

To make this sort of dialogue effective and fruitful, we have to be very frank and open, as well as sincere. To be frank, I find it necessary to clarify the difference rather than the affinity between Christianity and Zen. Of course it is necessary for such a dialogue to elucidate both affinities and differences between the two religions. It is rather easy to point out the affinity between Christianity and Zen, because both of them are equally, in their essence, religions. So, naturally there are some kinds of similarity. However, the emphasis on similarity, although important, does not necessarily create something new. On the other hand, an attempt to disclose the differences, if properly and relevantly done, promotes and stimulates mutual understanding and inspires both religions to seek further inner development of themselves. I hope my emphasis on differences in this talk is not understood as a rejection or exclusion of Christianity from a Zen point of view, or as a presumption of the superiority of Zen to Christianity. My point is to reach a real and creative mutual understanding. My understanding of Christianity is, however, insufficient and limited, so I hope you will correct me later, my discussion being completely open to your criticism.

To simplify the point to be discussed in connection with the theme, 'Self-Awakening and Faith – Zen and Christianity', I will try to contrast some central motives in Christianity and Zen:

| Christianity: | God | Faith | Salvation |
| Zen: | Nothingness | Enlightenment | Self-Awakening |

The difference between Christianity and Zen could be formulated in the contrasts of God–Nothingness, Faith–Enlightenment, Salvation–Self-Awakening.

A Zen master once said, 'There is one word I do not like to hear, that is "Buddha".' Rinzai, a Chinese Zen master of the T'ang dynasty said, 'Encountering a Buddha, kill the Buddha. Encountering a patriarch, kill the patriarch.... Only thus does one attain liberation and detachment from all things, thereby becoming completely unfettered and free.' As you can understand from these words, Zen rejects or denies the idea of Buddha and emphasizes the idea of no-Buddha or non-Buddha. So, in that sense Zen is not theistic, but atheistic.

One of the well-known utterances of Zen is this: 'When all things are reduced to the one, where is that one to be reduced?' Zen does not end with that one, which is beyond any particular and transcends any form of duality. Rather, Zen starts with the question: Where is that one to be reduced? It emphasizes the necessity of abandoning even the one. Zen transcends not only dualism, but also monism and monotheism. It is essential 'not to maintain even the one'. To go beyond the absolute one means to go to Nothingness. The absolute oneness must be turned into absolute Nothingness.

This realization of absolute Nothingness is in Zen the realization of one's true Self. For the realization of absolute Nothingness opens up the deepest ground of one's Subjectivity which is beyond every form of subject–object duality, including the so-called divine–human relationship. Enlightenment takes place only through the realization of absolute Nothingness which is beyond every form of duality. This is not faith in the divine mercy nor salvation by a divine, other power, but Self-Awakening – the Self-Awakening of true Self. In the realization of absolute Nothingness, the true Self awakens to itself. This Self-Awakening is not something to be sought for sometime in the future or somewhere outside yourself, but it is originally and already realized in yourself, here and now. If enlightenment is something to be sought for somewhere outside yourself or in the future, that so-called enlightenment will not be true. It is not absolute Nothingness, but rather a sort of something-ness which would be realized beyond the present *now* and outside the *here*. So Zen always emphasizes that you are originally in enlightenment. You are already inseparable from Self-Awakening.

On the other hand, if I am not wrong, the affirmation of the absolute oneness of God is taken for granted in Christian thinking. When a scribe wanted to know if Jesus was in agreement with the Biblical tradition, he tempted him by asking about the greatest commandment in the Law. Jesus answered by quoting the Old Testament passage about loving God with all the heart, soul and mind, mentioning the classical Biblical confession: 'Hear, O, Israel, the Lord our God, the Lord is one' (Mark, 12: 29). The scribe then said to him, 'You are right, teacher, you have truly said that he is one, and there is no other but he.' (Mark, 12: 32). In Christianity God is the one and only living God. He is father, creator, judge and ruler of the universe and of history.

Why does Zen not accept the only and absolute one and instead emphasize Nothingness? What is the doctrinal background for Zen's emphasis of *Mu*, absolute Nothingness? As you know, one of the most basic ideas of Buddhism is expressed in the Sanskrit term *pratītya-samutpāda*, which we call *engi* in Japanese. It is translated in various ways, as 'dependent co-origination', 'relationality', 'relativity', 'dependent co-arising', 'interdependent causation', etc. The Buddhist idea of *engi*, dependent origination, indicates that everything without exception is dependent on something else. Nothing whatsoever is independent or self-existing. This idea is generally expressed by the formulation, 'When this exists, that comes to be. When this does not exist, that does not exist. When this is destroyed, that is destroyed.' In this formulation 'this' and 'that' are completely interchangeable and are mutually dependent on each other. This idea must be applied to things not only in the universe, but also beyond the universe. It applies also to the relation between immanence and transcendence, between the human and the divine.

Christianity teaches that all men are equal before God. So they should all be relative and interdependent. But God is not dependent upon man, while man definitely is dependent upon God. We can therefore say with full justification that when God exists, the world comes into existence. When God does not exist, the world will not exist. However, is it possible to say that when the world exists, God comes into being? Or, when the world does not exist, God does not exist? At least the last statement is impossible in Christian thinking. The world cannot exist without God, but God can exist without the world. Because God is the self-existing deity, God can or does exist by himself without depending on anything else.

Against this basic Christian standpoint Zen may raise the

question: How is God's self-existence possible? What is the *ground* of God's self-existence? God said to Moses, 'I am that I am.' Theologians like Dr T. Boman and Dr T. Ariga have said that the Hebrew word *hāyāh*, which is the root of *éhyeh* (I am), does not simply mean to *be*, but to *become*, to *work* and to *happen*. So in God, his being is his action and vice versa. This dynamic character of God's being stresses his independence. His being is not to be understood in terms of dependent co-origination.

From a Buddhist point of view this idea of a self-sustaining God is ultimately inadequate, for Buddhists cannot see the ontological ground of this one and self-sustaining God. This is the reason why the Buddha rejected the traditional Upanishadic view of Brahman as the ultimate power of the universe and proclaimed that everything without exception is transitory and perishable, nothing being unchangeable and eternal. The idea that everything is transitory is inseparably connected to the idea of interdependent co-origination. So again, from this point of view we have to ask: What is the *ground* of the one God? How can we accept the one God as the ruler of the universe and history? The Christian might answer this question by stressing the importance of faith in God, this faith being nothing but the 'assurance of things hoped for, the conviction of things not seen' (Heb, 11: 1).

Before discussing the concept of faith, however, I must return to the Christian concept of God. If I am not wrong, the truth that God is a *living* God is more evident in Christianity than that he is the *one* true God. Being a living and personal God, he calls men through his word, and man must respond to his word. Hence the I–thou relationship between man and God.

In Jesus Christ, this I–thou relationship is most deeply and significantly actualized. Jesus is the mediator between man and God. He has the nature of *homooūsios*, consubstantiality, in which the immanence and transcendence are paradoxically one. Thus, Jesus Christ may be said to be a symbol of the Buddhist idea of relationality or interdependent causation. With full justification, Buddhists regard Jesus as a Buddha or as an Awakened one. The new life through death is clearly realized in him.

However, the Christian idea of the I–thou relationship in terms of faith, although interdependent and relational, is not completely reciprocal. Having faith in Jesus Christ, the Christian believes that if we die with him, we shall also live with him. So the Christian *participates* in the death and resurrection of Jesus Christ. He is the saviour and we are the saved; he is the redeemer and we are the redeemed, not vice versa.

In faith, Jesus Christ and I are, ultimately speaking, not in the relationship of interdependent causation. This is the case because man's finitude, that is his sinfulness, is deeply and keenly realized in Christianity. The faith in Jesus Christ is inseparably connected to the realization of man's sinfulness. Death is for the Christian nothing but 'the wage of sin'. From this Christian point of view, I am afraid that the Zen expression, 'Encountering a Buddha, kill the Buddha.... Only thus does one attain liberation', may sound blasphemous. The Zen saying that man is originally a Buddha and an Enlightened one, may sound arrogant or self-deceptive. And the Buddhist realization of man's finitude merely in terms of transiency may appear quite insufficient.

Frankly speaking, however, from the Zen point of view, the Christian realization of man's finitude in terms of sinfulness, and consequently, the idea of salvation through Jesus Christ does not seem thoroughgoing enough to reach the ultimate Reality. Can man's finitude in terms of sinfulness be fully overcome through faith? What is the ground of this faith and hope in which our death and sin can be redeemed? Is man's finitude the kind of finitude which can be overcome by faith? These questions imply that for Zen, man's finitude is so deep and so radical that it cannot even be overcome by faith, not even through the work of the divine other power. Hence the need for the realization of absolute Nothingness.

Let me develop this question by considering the question of good and evil. In Buddhism in general, and Zen in particular, good and evil are, like every other thing, interdependently originated. There is no good without evil and vice versa. How is it possible that good can stand without evil? Good and evil are in Buddhism entirely interdependently originated. There is no priority of one over the other.

> *Question from the audience*: If you are born in enlightenment, is not
> that in itself a priority of good over evil?
> *Answer*: Enlightenment is not something good in the relative
> sense, as distinguished from evil. Enlightenment is the realiza-
> tion of my being prior to the duality of good and evil.
> *Question*: But that realization in itself is good, or are we talking in
> different terms?
> *Answer*: When you say that realization in itself is good, from which

point of view are you so doing? I am afraid you are from the outset talking about good and evil from the dualistic point of view. Good has no priority over evil. The priority of good over evil is an ethical imperative but not an actual human situation. In human beings good and evil have equal power: I cannot say that my good is stronger than my evil although I should try to overcome my evil by my good. The Buddhist shares the Pauline thought that the more we try to do good, the more we become aware of evil in ourselves. This dilemma between good and evil in our being is so deep that it cannot be solved by the power of good. In faith in God as the Supreme Good, the dilemma is believed to be solved in the future in the form of hope. This is not, however, a complete solution of the dilemma *at the present*, but a pushing away of the solution into the eternal future. The dilemma of good and evil is so radical that there is no way for us to escape it even in the future. It is not that I *have* a dilemma between good and evil, but that I *am* that dilemma. It is not that I *have* an aporia, but that I *am* an aporia in this sense. In the final and deepest realization of the dilemma between good and evil, the structure of my ego collapses and I come to the realization that I am not simply good, or simply bad. I am neither good nor bad. I am nothing whatsoever. However, this realization is not negative but positive, because in the full realization of Nothingness we are liberated from the dichotomy of good and evil, life and death. At that point we awaken to our true nature prior to dualistic consciousness. That is the reason why Zen often asks us to see our 'original face' as it is prior to any distinction between good and evil. Enlightenment is precisely to see one's 'original face'.

To return to my discussion, practically speaking, I have no way to overcome evil by the power of good. This applies to not only the non-religious humanistic dimension, but also to the transcendental religious dimension. The reason that the dilemma between good and evil is so deep and thoroughgoing is because good and evil are interdependently originated, negating each other with equal power. Therefore, it cannot be overcome even through faith in God who is absolutely good. If God is absolutely good, what is the origin of the evil in man and in the world?

Tillich said, 'In God evil is conquered not by being annihilated, but by not being actualized. It is actualized in the finite world, but not in the infinite ground of being, i.e., God.'[2] This means that the actuality of evil is never in God, but evil is left as a potentiality in God. I think this is to be regarded as a sort of theodicy regarding the origin of evil. God created everything but he is not responsible for the actuality of evil. Thus, the dichotomy between good and evil can be solved in Christianity by saying that in eternity evil is conquered by being reduced to mere potentiality. I am afraid this Christian view may be that of a false endlessness. The problem of evil is moved from actuality to potentiality, from time to eternity but without a definitive solution.

The point in which you are not limited by the duality of good and evil can be realized in yourself, *right here* and *right now*, through the realization that you *are* the dilemma of good and evil. Once you thoroughly realize that you *are* the dilemma of good and evil you can break through the dilemma and come to a standpoint which is neither good nor evil. Thus, from the Zen point of view, the essential point is not faith in God, but realization of Nothingness and awakening to one's true nature. This is the inevitable conclusion of the Buddhist idea of dependent co-origination. Not only good and evil, but life and death, God and man, are interdependent. Therefore Buddha, when understood as something beyond man, must be killed to realize our own true nature and to attain Self-Awakening.

Though contrasting Zen and Christianity, I want to stress that it is an oversimplification to say that Zen is based on Nothingness, while Christianity is based on God as Being, in contrast to non-being. If this were the case, Zen and Christianity would be entirely without any correspondence.

According to my understanding, when Christianity emphasizes the one God who is the ruler of the universe and of history, who is the absolute good and eternal life, who can overcome death and evil, etc., this is not simply an ontological issue, but rather an *axiological* issue. In Christianity the most significant point is not the issue of being and non-being, but the question of what I as a human being ought to do. The idea of righteousness is very important, although righteousness must be fulfiled as an aspect of love. The Christian idea of love always includes the idea of justice. Without justice, there is no real love. In that sense the 'ought' or 'divine imperative' is important. When Christians confess God as the one, self-existing God, it is not primarily because He is the only divine Being, but because He is the personal God who rules the whole universe and calls for man's response to His commandments. The idea of justice represented by the 'ought' is rather lacking, or at least very weak in Buddhism, particularly in Zen, while the idea of being and non-being, life and death, is very strong.

The Christian idea of the one God should not be understood merely ontologically, but also axiologically. The Christian faith in the one God is more concerned with justice and love than the ontological questions of God's being. In that sense Zen's criticism of the Christian view of the one God, based upon the Buddhist idea of dependent co-origination, does not necessarily hit the core of, or do justice to, the essence of Christianity.

Both in Zen and Christianity ontological and axiological aspects are inseparably connected. But in Zen the ontological aspect, the question of being and non-being, life and death, is much more central than the issue of good and evil. On the other hand, in Christianity the issue of good and evil is much more strongly emphasized than the question of being and non-being.

So we may try to draw the lines from Zen and its ontological understanding of Nothingness to the Christian faith with its axiological emphasis on God's 'ought' and find the crossing point. See Figure 9.1

Zen   Christianity

Nothingness   God

FIGURE 9.1

The strength in Zen is the weakness in Christianity and vice versa. Based on this recognition of these mutual strengths and weaknesses, we must enter into dialogue.

Discussion

Ms Bray: I have a very practical question: What does Zen do with the innate sense of guilt within people and the evident need for redemption or forgiveness?

Prof. Abe: Buddhism may not have the same sense of guilt as Christianity, rather a sense of suffering and karma. Human life is suffering, that is the basic realization in Buddhism and in Zen.

Prof. Doi: Could it be said that guilt is included in the sense of suffering and karma?

Prof. Abe: Yes, you may say so. The different forms of suffering are in Buddhism understood as birth, sickness, old age and death. Basically this is an ontological issue of man. Guilt seems to be more concerned with the ethical relationship between men. In Buddhism this is not so crucial, even if it is not excluded.

Ms Bray: In the three topics of the three lectures of this seminar, the word 'Zen' has been used, but 'Buddhism' has not been in any of the titles of the lectures. What is the relationship of *Zen* and *Zen Buddhism*? You are the first one to even mention Buddhism.

Prof. Abe: It is often asked whether Zen is a form of Buddhism or not. My answer is *yes*, and at the same time *no*. Historically speaking, Zen is one form of Buddhism; it was established in China and further developed alongside of other forms of Buddhism throughout China, Korea and Japan. So Zen could be said to be a form of Buddhism, Zen Buddhism. However, Zen is somewhat beyond Buddhism because it is not based on any Buddhist scripture, but directly returns to the root and source of all forms of Buddhism, i.e., enlightenment. It is one of the basic characteristics of Zen to be a special transmission outside doctrinal teachings. In that, Zen stands somewhat outside so-called traditional Buddhism.

Prof. Doi: There are so many sects of Buddhism in Japan. When you compare Zen with Jōdo Buddhism (Pure Land Buddhism), you might find the distance between them to be as far as the distance between Unitarians and Pentecostals in the Christian tradition.

Father De Weirdt: In my reading and study of Buddhism, what has always puzzled me and still puzzles me is the concept of Nothingness. As you said in your lecture, 'The realization of one's Nothingness is the realization of one's true Self', and 'I am nothing whatsoever.' If that is true, both in the ontological and in the actual sphere of life, what is the use of talking? What are we doing in this life if we are absolutely nothing? And how can we do something to improve the society which is also nothing?

Prof. Abe: Do you think that the self is something?

Father De Weirdt: We have to realize the absolute nothingness in order to realize our own true Self, as you said. That means that I am absolutely nothing. If that is true, what are we doing here in this world, both in the ontological and actual spheres of life?

What is the meaning of our life personally, – if we *are* persons? What can we do for society, – *if* society exists?

Prof. Abe: My counterquestion is this: do you think that the human self is something?

Father De Weirdt: I think so, Professor, I do!

Prof. Abe: What is it who thinks of yourself as something?

Father De Weirdt: My consciousness of being something, a somebody. And I believe that people around me are real people, that this house is a real thing, that the universe is a real thing. I am conscious of that in my mind. '

Prof. Abe: What is it that has such a consciousness?

Father De Weirdt: The human being.

Prof. Abe: Human being in general?

Father De Weirdt: Each human being! It is difficult to say if it is up here in the head or in the heart – I don't know. But as a human being I have that consciousness.

Prof. Abe: Who is talking about 'I' as a human being – what has that consciousness?

Father De Weirdt: Many people are talking about themselves. Each individual being talks about himself and others.

Prof. Abe: What is it that is talking about yourself and other people in that way?

Father De Weirdt: Well, this lady here, that gentleman there. Each one of us does. The personality of each person is thinking about himself or herself and is talking about himself or herself to other people.

Prof. Abe: My question is: *what is it* that is talking about yourself and other selves?

Father De Weirdt: My own consciousness of myself and of the relationship to others.

Prof. Abe: May I ask you again, what is it that is talking about your own consciousness of yourself?

Father De Weirdt: I would say that it is my personality.

Prof. Abe: I am afraid, Father De Weirdt, you always objectify yourself when you talk about yourself or your own consciousness. Whenever I ask you 'What is it that is so talking?' you say that it is your consciousness, it is your own consciousness of yourself, your personality or so on. Thus you objectify your own consciousness, your own existence, your own self, and in that way *you yourself* move back step by step. When you answered my questions in that way, you were always regressing, trying to present something more inner including your 'self'. However, your *true* 'Self' can never be presented in that way because it is always standing 'behind' your presentation, 'behind' your regression.

You may, of course, objectify your 'self'. An objectified self, however, is not the *true* Self. The true Self must be the true Subjectivity which is beyond objectification. The 'Self' is the unobjectifiable. As soon as the self is objectified it becomes 'something'. However, the true Self, as the unobjectifiable, is not 'anything' whatsoever, but 'nothing' in the sense that it is beyond objectification. And 'Nothingness' in this sense is not simply negative but rather positive, because it indicates one's true Subjectivity as the root source of one's activity of objectification.

Prof. Doi: Is this what Dr Nishitani called the immediate experience of the Self in totality?

Prof. Abe: Yes, it is. It is the immediate realization of the self as the Self – it is the Self-Awakening to the Self. In our thinking, we objectify everything including ourself and, in objectifying, we always regress, taking a step backwards. Of course, we can think of our self, and think also of our self which is thinking of our self. However, in doing this, we step back in an endless regression. In such an endless regression we always miss our true Self, our true Subjectivity. In this case, therefore, our understanding of the self and its relation to everything in the world does not indicate the totality. It becomes partial and does not reach the ultimate Reality. Through our thinking we can understand the self and its relation to the world *only so far as they are objectfied*. In order to reach ultimate Reality or the total understanding of Reality, we must go beyond thinking and objectification. That is the non-conceptualized, immediate realization of the Self. So the crucial question is: How can we grasp our Self immediately without stepping back?

Let me speak a little more concretely to clarify the point. I am standing here, and there must be a ground on which I am now standing. If you ask me to show the ground on which I am standing, I may show it by stepping back and pointing to the ground with a finger. However, that is not the ground on which I *am standing now* but the ground where I *was standing before.* To show the ground on which I *am standing now,* I may again step back and point to it. Again, however, it is only the ground where I was standing before. How can I show *the ground on which I am standing now?* This ground cannot be shown objectively by regression. The ground you are now standing on is not 'something' to be pointed out in an objective way. It is *not anything whatsoever to be objectified.* It is *the unobjectifiable.* Therefore it is called 'Nothingness'. (Nothingness) But it is not simply nothing as distinguished from something. Nothing as distinguished from something is still a kind of 'something' merely called 'nothing'. So, *true* Nothingness is beyond a mere nothingness, i.e., a *negative* nothingness, as distinguished from somethingness. It is neither something nor nothing. This real Nothingness, i.e., *positive* nothingness, is neither nothingness nor somethingness, but includes both. It is not mere emptiness, but fullness as the root and source of both being and non-being. Being and non-being appear out of that Nothingness. Thus, the unobjectifiable is positive, because it is the *ground* of your *present being.* It indicates the true Self, true Subjectivity – which can never be objectified, the root of your existence, your life, your activity in society and history.

To speak figuratively, the ground on which you are standing now can be shown, not by regression but by progressing, in the act of walking forward, because the ground is nothing but the point of departure of your activity.

A few moments ago Father De Weirdt asked 'What can we do for society?' As you see, 'Nothingness' as the unobjectifiable is the true Subject or true Self. It is the root-source of not only being and non-being, but also self and others, self and society. Through the realization of true Self one can properly and effectively work in the social relations between self and others. Of course, to do so one needs objective knowledge of the social environment and historical change. But the realization of true Self is essential as the ground on which our social relationships can be properly established.

Prof. Tucker: I think that when we objectify the self, we are not really objectifying it. We are rather making a conceptual abstraction that we can think about, just as when we say the numbers 2, 3, 4, we are making abstractions which have no existence. Two apples have an existence, but the number 2 has no existence. If we have these abstractions in our speech, we can make ourselves understood. If we cannot use the abstractions, we cannot philosophize or talk about religion. We need these to think and to communicate. These concepts are not objects, but concepts and abstractions. And I think you are wrong to say that we are objectifying. We are not. The self, we believe, is a selfhood which exists because it is created by God. When I speak as a person or look upon myself, it is not my conscious mind that looks upon myself as an object. It is rather a part of the dynamic process of the self going through its living process of reflecting on itself and reflecting about God. It is not right to say that we objectify ourselves. We are making a conceptual abstraction which we can then talk about and think about.

Prof. Abe: Even if you prefer 'conceptualize' to 'objectify' the situation does not change. The conceptualized self is not the real, active Self. To awaken to the real Self which is active we must go beyond conceptualization.

Ms Kuhlman: To me the self in this sense is not object, but ultimate subjectivity. Maybe this is what you were saying. But to me that is the opposite of nothingness . . .

Rev. Thelle: When Professor Abe and other Buddhists talk about nothingness, many Westerners tend to understand this in nihilistic terms or as a nothingness that is a sort of mere non-existence.

Prof. Abe: I am painfully aware that the English translation 'Nothingness' is rather misleading in a Western context. In Japanese we say *mu*, nothingness, or *kū*, emptiness. In Buddhist contexts *mu* and *kū* have used and emphasized as key terms. These are often misunderstood also by Japanese, but still Nothingness must be emphasized to indicate the necessity of going beyond any conceptualization and objectification. As Rev. Thelle suggested it is not mere non-existence, not the absence of being. It is neither existence nor non-existence. It is beyond being and non-being. Without the realization of this absolute Nothingness, there is no true realization of the Self.

Prof. Lloyd: Can we say that the concept of Nothingness is in some way positive?

Prof. Abe: Yes, the Buddhist idea of Nothingness is a positive and dynamic idea. It is *neither* somethingness *nor* nothingness, yet it includes both. It is the dynamic whole which attaches itself to neither. There is nothing outside Nothingness. You and I and everything else are included without losing our particularity in the dynamic structure of this *positive* Nothingness.

Sr. Parachini: You keep saying that Buddhism emphasizes that you are *already* inseparable from Self-Awakening, which in my understanding is the experience of Nothingness. If that is true, and if I understand correctly, I do not understand why people are practising *zazen*. If we are already experiencing this as a part of our original being, what is the purpose of *zazen*?

Prof. Abe: I had another question in the coffee break which is related to your question: 'The Buddha attained enlightenment at a certain point of his life. So before that was he not unenlightened?' *Zazen* is often thought of in this way as a process leading towards enlightenment. Through practice we approach the goal of enlightenment. This understanding is quite natural, but thinking along these lines, will we ever be able to reach enlightenment? We may come closer and closer to the end but will never reach it. For the goal is a projection from the side of ourselves as being on the way. We are in the unenlightened state and enlightenment becomes a projection from this state of unenlightenment. Thus, there will be an essential gap between the so-called delusion and the so-called enlightenment, between practice and attainment, a gap which can never be bridged.

The more we try to reach out towards enlightenment as a projection, the clearer we see that there is a gap. And finally we come to realize the delusory nature of this approach as such. Not only our present state of unenlightenment, but also the 'enlightenment' which is projected by us as a distant goal are delusions. With the realization of these delusions, the whole approach must collapse, and then you may realize that enlightenment is not over there. It is present *right here under your feet* and can be realized at any point of the process.

In a sense we must say that we are in the process of practice, without which enlightenment is impossible, but this does not mean that we are simply on the way towards enlightenment; if this were the case, then we would always be on the way without attaining enlightenment. When we realize the limitations of this very approach, we realize that we are not simply on the way towards enlightenment but have *originally* been *in* enlightenment. There is a dynamic unity of being on the way and having reached the goal. *Zazen* has no purpose. True *zazen* in itself is true enlightenment.

Sr. Parachini: Can I make a parallel with Christianity to see if I am understanding what you say? In Christianity we believe that salvation is not completely in the future, but that the Kingdom has already come in the presence of Jesus. We are in a sense working within it, but it is not completely fulfilled. Is that part of what you are saying?

Prof. Abe: Exactly, Jesus said that the Kingdom of God is present among you. It is not far away.

Prof. Doi: Professor Abe seems to understand Christianity in terms of *theism*. God becomes a theistic God. But even Karl Barth said in one of his latest articles that we can no longer speak about God himself as isolated theology. We can only speak about theoanthropology. Where there is no man, there can be no God. So man and God are correlative. So Professor Abe's understanding of Christianity is somewhat outdated.

Prof. Abe: I am sorry. Can you, however, say in a Christian context that God is me and I am God. If man and God are really correlative, this should be possible.

Prof. Doi: God is *with* me, but I myself am not God. You cannot say that you yourself are a Buddha, but a Buddha-to-be.

Prof. Abe: I did not say that I am a Buddha, but that I am Nothingness; Nothingness is me. That is the Self-Awakening which may be called the realization of Buddhahood.

Prof. Doi: The term Nothingness could be replaced by freedom: you are free from yourself.

Prof. Abe: Not 'free from'. If you are free *from* something, there is still duality.

Prof. Doi: In Christianity we could talk about this freedom as a total openness.

Prof. Abe: That might be a better word. Man is completely open. So he is empty. Not something, but Nothing. That Nothing is not outside me. I am Nothing and Nothing is me.

Rev. Evjedal: Is Nothingness the ultimate in the same way as we talk about God as the ultimate? This seems to be founded on a sort of belief. How can you say that there is not an equivalent some-thingness related to Nothingness, just as in the relation between good and evil? Why is Nothingness unrelated?

Prof. Abe: Good and evil are completely interdependent. There is no good without evil and vice versa. There is no nothingness without somethingness and vice versa. Yet good and evil, nothingness and somethingness are principles contrary to one another. They are negating one another and yet are inseparably connected with one another. At the extreme limit of opposition they turn into a single mass, becoming a serious contradiction. This is the most critical issue for man. As I said: It is not that I *have* a dilemma, but I *am* a dilemma. When we come to the point of *total* realization of this existential dilemma, it is overcome from within. And I come to the point where there is neither good nor evil, neither life nor death, neither nothingness nor somethingness. This is the root and source for good and evil, life and death, etc. This is the existential ground for life and activity, in which we can work without being limited by any kind of duality. This is freedom. Nothingness related to somethingness does not indicate freedom or openness just as good related to evil does not. Freedom is fully realized by going beyond the duality of somethingness and nothingness, good and evil, and so forth. This is why the Buddhist Nothingness is beyond both somethingness and nothingness.

Prof. Augustine: I would like to comment on what seems to be happening here as in most discussions. Professor Abe said that Christianity has *faith*: man's meeting God in his salvation from sin. And you posed Zen as *realization* of the Self. What I see happening is that you are opposing your Zen system to the Christian understanding saying: Christianity simply blindly be-lieves in God, and if they believe . . .

Prof. Abe: Not 'blindly'!

Prof. Augustine: Well, your point is that Zen is based on realization as an experience and not as a concept. But I believe that Christians would simply reverse it and say, 'Primarily we have a realization in God. This can be expressed in concepts, but basically we *realize* God. You have *faith* in enlightenment'

Last night Professor Nishimura said that 99.9 per cent of all Zen priests and monks were not deeply enlightened. But they all have a deep faith that they will be enlightened. So here we have people who are working towards enlightenment. Having some enlightenment experience and having a whole system by which they understand reality, they find another system to be inadequate for different reasons.

My question is: why can't we see that we both have systems and that we both are aiming at an encounter with a transcendent reality? If we cannot see that, if we cannot realize that we will never agree upon the symbols of these systems – that we are grappling to find symbols and committing ourselves to systems, then we can simply talk *at* one another, but we cannot co-operate in the work we both are trying to do for ourselves and for other people. Why can't we see that we are both in the same thing and are just arguing about one another's systems ... They are both good; they are both working towards this realization that is beyond the normal rational activity.

Prof. Abe: In the beginning of my lecture I said that the emphasis on similarity of the two religions, though necessary, is not sufficient to develop a creative dialogue. My emphasis on difference does not intend to judge which one is better. I would like to reach a deeper and a more creative understanding beyond the essential differences. So we should not overlook even subtle differences. Speaking from the Zen point of view, Zen must raise the question: What is the ground of the one God; what is the ground of faith in God? This Zen question will not destroy but rather deepen the Christian faith in God. However it is more ontologically oriented than the Christian action-oriented understanding of God's Being. Christianity is justified in its idea of the one God in the sense that He is the living personal God with ethical character who justifies man in spite of his sinfulness through unconditional love. Zen must learn more about this ground of the Christian faith in God.

Part III
Three Problems in Buddhism

10 Buddhist Nirvana – Its Significance in Contemporary Thought and Life

I

Nirvana is generally regarded as the goal of the Buddhist life, in that it is essential for Buddhists to enter nirvana. Nirvana has been compared with the Christian notion of the Kingdom of God. In the West, however, it is often misunderstood as something negative. This misunderstanding even occurs in the Buddhist world, for the literal meaning of nirvana is the extinction or annihilation of passion, often compared to the extinguishing of a fire. But is nirvana negative? What is the real meaning of entering nirvana?

The Four Noble Truths, the fundamental teaching of Gautama the Buddha, run as follows: that existence is suffering; that the cause of suffering is craving or thirst; that by the extinction of craving, nirvana may be attained; that the means for the attainment of nirvana is the practice of the Eightfold Noble Path: right view, right intention, right speech, right conduct, right livelihood, right effort, right mindfulness, and right concentration.

When Gautama the Buddha says 'existence is (characterized by) suffering', he does not mean that human life is simply full of suffering without any pleasure at all. It is obvious that there is pleasure as well as suffering in human life. In daily life we distinguish between pleasure and suffering, seeking for and clinging to pleasure while avoiding and detesting suffering. This is an inclination inherent in human nature. According to Buddhism, real suffering (henceforth referred to as 'Suffering') lies precisely in this very inclination. Pleasure and suffering are in reality inseparable and intertwined – one is never found without the other. Hence the position that they are rigidly separable is abstract and unreal. The more we try to cling to pleasure and avoid suffering, the more entangled we become in the duality of pleasure and suffering. It is this whole process which constitutes Suffering. When Gautama the Buddha says 'existence is (characterized by) suffering', he is referring to this Suffering and not to suffering as opposed to pleasure. It is the reality of this non-relative Suffering which person must realize in his or her existential depths. Since life and death are the fundamental sources of pleasure and suffering, and human existence is entangled in attachment to life and detestation of death, human existence is understood in Buddhism to be irrevocably bound to samsara, the cycle of birth and death.

Accordingly, when Gautama the Buddha says 'the cause of suffering is craving', he means by craving not simply the attachment to pleasure but a deeper and more fundamental attachment that is rooted in human existence, that of loving pleasure and hating suffering, with its accompanying phenomenon of making a distinction between the two. According to Gautama's teaching, this fundamental attachment originates in an illusory view of life in the world which is the result of the basic ignorance innate in human nature. Craving is a human passion linked to man's entanglement in the duality of pleasure and suffering, and deeply rooted in the ego. It is by extinguishing this craving that nirvana can be attained. Thus nirvana is not a negative or *lifeless state* such as the mere annihilation of human passion would suggest, but an existential awakening to egolessness, *anattā* or *anātman*, attained through liberation from craving, the attachment to the dualistic view which distinguishes between pleasure as something to be sought after and suffering as something to be avoided (see Figure 10.1).

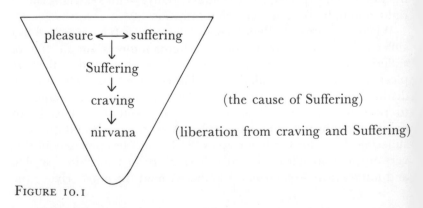

FIGURE 10.1

The position of the Buddha clearly emerges in his first sermon after his enlightenment:

> Monks, these two extremes should not be followed by one who has gone forth as a wanderer. What two?
> Devotion to the pleasure of sense, a low practice of villagers, a practice unworthy, unprofitable, the way of the world [on the one hand]; and [on the other] devotion to self-mortification, which is painful, unworthy and unprofitable.
> By avoiding these two extremes the *Tathāgata* [the Buddha] has gained knowledge of that Middle Path which giveth vision, which giveth knowledge, which causes calm, special knowledge, enlightenment, nirvana.[1]

In this connection, the following four points are to be noted:

1.   Gautama the Buddha takes the Middle Way, transcending both hedonism and asceticism. Accordingly, he does not negate human desire as such, but, in avoiding these two extremes, relegates it to its proper position in human life. The Middle Way is not simply a midpoint between pleasure and suffering, but rather is the Way which *transcends* the very duality of pleasure and suffering. Thus, living the Middle Way is none other than being in nirvana.

2.   For Buddhism, the Middle Way or nirvana is not an objectively observable state or something which can be considered merely a goal of life, but rather an existential ground from which human life can properly begin without becoming entangled in the duality of pleasure and suffering. By living the Middle Way, in nirvana, we can be master of, and not enslaved to, pleasure and suffering. In this sense, nirvana is the source of human freedom and creative activity.

3.   In his awakening to egolessness, Gautama overcame duality itself by transcending the particular duality of pleasure and suffering. In other words, he could awaken to egolessness only when he became free from duality itself. This he achieved by breaking through the particular duality which impinged upon him most as a burning existential dilemma – the duality of pleasure and suffering. Accordingly, nirvana as the existential awakening to egolessness is beyond any kind of duality, including that of good and evil, right and wrong, life and death, man and nature, and even that of man and God. To attain nirvana in

this sense is, for Buddhism, salvation. Nirvana as the awakening to egolessness is most clearly realized in Mahayana Buddhism. In that tradition, to enter nirvana is not to die one's physical death, but to die the death of the ego and thereby to live a new Life – to live the life of the true Self.

4. Although nirvana, or the Middle Way, is beyond duality, it is not characterized by a monistic view. Monism is not yet free from duality, for it is still opposed to dualism or pluralism. Being beyond duality, the view of one who has attained nirvana is not monistic but rather non-dualistic. This is why Buddhism does not proclaim the one God, but speaks of *Śūnyatā* (Emptiness). Emptiness is realized by going beyond the one God and thus is not the relative emptiness of a mere vacuum. That is, being beyond the one God, Emptiness is identical to, or, more strictly speaking, 'non-dualistic' with respect to individual things, making them truly individual. Indeed, in Emptiness, everything is itself in the sense that everything is as it is, and yet *at the same time*, everything is equal in its as-it-is-ness. The following *mondō* (question-and-answer) between a monk and Chao-cho (Ja: Jōshū, 778–897) illustrates the point. The monk asked Jōshū, 'All things are reduced to the one; where is this one to be reduced to?' Jōshū replied, 'When I was in the province of Tsin I had a monk's robe made that weighed seven pounds.'[2] That which is ultimate or universal is not the one to which all things are reducible but a particular thing, absolutely irreplaceable, such as a monk's robe, which has a particular weight and is made in a particular place at a particular time. The universal and a particular thing are paradoxically one in the realization of Emptiness, which goes beyond the understanding which sees all things as reducible to the one.

Oneness as a universal principle, if substantial and self-existing, must be overcome; otherwise we as particulars lose our individuality and cannot possibly awaken to Reality. From the Buddhist point of view, this is true even for God, the "only One". On the other hand, if all particular things are respectively self-identical, there is no equality between them and everything is self-centred. Both Emptiness, the negation of oneness, and egolessness, the negation of everything's self-centredness, are necessary for Awakening. In the realization of Emptiness, which is another term for nirvana, all particular things are respectively just as they are and yet equal in their suchness.

This is expressed in Mahayana Buddhism as 'difference as it is, is sameness; sameness (of things in their suchness) as it is, is difference'. This very realization is the source of wisdom and compassion in which both ignorance and self-centredness are overcome. Just because nirvana is in itself empty, it is full of particular things functioning freely, which neither lose their particularity nor impede one another.

II

What significance does Buddhist nirvana hold for us today, East and West, with regard to contemporary thought and life, especially as it pertains to the problems of understanding ultimate Reality, nihilism, the relation of man to nature, the irrational in human existence, the achieving of true community, and the understanding of the meaning of history? I would like to deal with these problems from the standpoint of Mahayana Buddhism, a form of Buddhism developed in northern Asia, especially in China and Japan, and based on a dynamic interpretation of Gautama's teaching.

First of all, nirvana has relevance to the human understanding of ultimate or universal Reality in that it overcomes the major objection to monistic absolutism, the objection which was mentioned earlier in Section I (point 4, p. 208). The concept of the one God who is essentially transcendent, self-existing apart from everything relative, is illusory to Buddhism in that God cannot be spoken of without a knower. In Buddhism, mutual relativity or interdependency is the ultimate truth, and doctrines of absolute truth which exclude other views of truth as false are similarly considered illusory. In nirvana, nothing is independent, self-existing, or permanent; having no permanent selfhood, everything is mutually related to each and every other thing. This is not a fixed relativism simply rejecting absolutes and resulting in a form of scepticism or nihilism, but a dynamic relativism in which even the absolute and the relative, the holy and the secular, the divine and the human, are all totally interrelated. This idea of the total interrelatedness of each and every thing at every moment is also termed 'dependent co-origination' in Buddhism, the realization of which is none other than nirvana. Dynamic relativism, beyond the opposition between relativism and absolutism, is at once dynamic absolutism. This paradoxical truth can be realized not through speculation but only through existential practice. Hence, the practice of the Eightfold Noble Path and sitting meditation have been emphasized.

The position of Buddhism toward other faiths is often called 'tolerant' by Western scholars. It may, however, be that the term 'tolerant' has been applied according to Western, especially Christian, standards, and is misleading in that it does not get to the heart of Buddhism. The Buddhist position, founded in nirvana, is a 'positionless position' in the sense that, being itself empty, it lets every other position stand and work just as it is. Naturally, Buddhism does not exclude other faiths as false, but recognizes the relative truths which they contain. This recognition, however, is a starting point, not an end, for Buddhist life. Properly speaking, Buddhism starts to work critically and creatively *through* this basic recognition of the relative truths contained in other positions, hoping for productive dialogue and cooperation with other faiths.

The Buddhist position as realized in nirvana may prove effective in a contemporary world which is witnessing, as the world becomes more and more closely united, a remarkable rise of a sense of the diversity of values. The dynamic relativism of nirvana may provide a spiritual foundation for the formation of the rapidly approaching One World in which the co-existence of a variety of contrasting value systems, ways of life, and ways of thinking will be indispensable.

Second, nirvana offers a freedom beyond nihilism. One of the serious problems in the world today is the permeation of the nihilism proclaimed by Friedrich Nietzsche and others. The collapse of traditional value systems and the cry that 'God is dead' are somewhat universal phenomena in industrialized societies. A loss of the sense of the holy and despair with regard to the corruption and impotence of the established forms of religion prevail in the world today. As a consequence of the pervasion of the scientific way of thinking, it has become increasingly difficult for modern people to believe in 'God'; nevertheless, people today are searching seriously for something to fill the vacuum which has been created in their spiritual lives. In this respect, Nietzsche is a touchstone for religion, for he advocated as a prototype of future humanity, the active nihilist who, grounded in the will to power, courageously faces emptiness without God. It is, however, unlikely that Nietzsche's active nihilism can successfully serve as a substitute for religion. It would seem that what is needed today and in the future is a religion beyond active nihilism, i.e., a religion beyond 'emptiness without

God'. Buddhism, which is based on nirvana, is precisely a religion of this sort. Negating the existence of the one God, Buddhism advocates *Śūnyatā* (Emptiness), which is not a nihilistic emptiness but rather a fullness of particular things and individual persons functioning in their full capacity and without mutual impediment. In Emptiness, everything is realized as it *is*, in its total dynamic reality. This radical realism involves not only liberation from 'God', but also the overcoming of an active nihilism such as that advocated by Nietzsche.[3] Thus, nirvana is a realization of great freedom, both from theistic pietism with its dependence on God and from nihilism in a Nietzchean sense with its dependence on the will to power, making possible genuine self-determination by removing the illusion of a determinator.

Third, nirvana has relevance to our understanding of the relation of mankind to nature. Christian scholars often contend that Buddhist nirvana is impersonal. Christian personalism, if I am not mistaken, is based on human responsibility to the word of God. Unlike other creatures, humans are created in God's image and can respond to the calling of God. Nature is ruled by God through humans whom God gave 'dominion over' other creatures. In this sense, Christian personalism is connected with anthropocentrism among creatures. Buddhist nirvana, on the contrary, is based on egolessness and is not anthropocentric but rather cosmological. In Buddhism, humans and the things of nature are equally subject to change, i.e., transitory and transmigratory. A person cannot achieve emancipation from the cycle of birth and death until he or she can eliminate a more universal problem – the transience common to all things in the universe. Here we see that the *basis* for Buddhist salvation is cosmological, not personalistic as in an I–Thou relationship with God, and thus impersonal and trans-anthropocentric. However, it is only humans with self-consciousness and free will who can go beyond anthropocentrism and reach an awareness that transience is not limited to humans but is common to all things. Furthermore, it is noteworthy that Buddhist salvation is primarily concerned with individual persons, and is not simply concerned with mankind in general, for as is written in a sutra, 'One is born alone, dies alone, comes alone, and goes alone.'[4] In this sense Buddhism may also be said to be personalistic and existentialistic. Yet this does not mean that the human is understood in Buddhism in terms of a divine-human encounter in which nature is excluded, but rather that the human is grasped as a being with self-consciousness and free will on a cosmological basis which includes all of nature. Without the realization of transience and selflessness on such a cosmological basis, a human being cannot become an 'awakened one'.[5]

Thus the following two aspects of Buddhist salvation must be noted: (1) Buddhism is primarily concerned with salvation of a human as a person who, unlike other living beings, has self-consciousness and free will and thereby alone has the potential to become aware of and emancipated from the transience common to all things in the universe. This is the existentialistic and personalistic aspect of Buddhism. However, (2) a cosmological dimension is the necessary *basis* for this Buddhist salvation, because in Buddhism salvation is not from sin as rebellion against God, but emancipation from the cycle of birth and death which is part of the transience of the universe. This is the cosmological aspect of Buddhism. These two aspects are inseparable – the more cosmological the basis of salvation, the more existentially thoroughgoing the salvation.[6] In this sense, the Buddhist cosmology which is the basis of nirvana is an existential cosmology, and Buddhist existentialism or personalism may be called 'cosmo-existentialism' or 'cosmo-personalism'.[7]

The Buddhist position with regard to the relation of mankind and nature may contribute a spiritual foundation out of which could arise a solution to one of the most pressing problems with which man is today faced – the destruction of the environment. This problem is inextricably connected with human estrangement from nature. It results from anthropocentrism whereby a person regards nature merely as a means or obstacle to the realization of selfish goals, and thus continually finds ways to utilize and conquer it. The cosmological view which is the basis of Buddhist nirvana does not see nature as something subordinate to humans, but sees them as subordinate to nature, more precisely as a part of nature from the standpoint of 'cosmos'. Thus the cosmological view both allows humans to overcome estrangement from nature and to live harmoniously with nature without losing their individuality.

Fourth, let us consider what significance Buddhist nirvana may have in dealing with the irrational in human existence. Interest in mythology and primitive cultures as well as an irresistible demand to satisfy instinctive, especially sexual, desire is on the upsurge in highly industrialized societies. This phenomenon may be regarded as a reaction to the emphasis on human rationality and science which grew up in modern European culture and formed the basis for industrialization. Western thinkers such as Schopenhauer, Marx, Freud, and Jung, and more recently, Camus, Marcuse, and others, have emphasized the importance of the irrational aspects of human existence. Most critically, modern European culture has completely neglected the problem of death, a problem which has plagued humanity since time immemorial and is for modern people the supreme irrationality.

In short, modern European culture with its scientific orientation, pervasive as it is in highly industrialized societies, is based on human rationality and a preoccupation with life, while neglecting to deal with the irrational elements in human existence, especially death. It is not wise, however, for us simply to accept and follow present reactionary tendencies which try to counteract, by means of an influx of irrationality, this emphasis on rationalism. What is necessary today in order to deal successfully with this problem is a profound basis upon which the conflicts between the rational and the irrational, reason and desire, and life and death can be resolved. Buddhist nirvana, or the Middle Way, in which people overcome duality and extinguish the 'craving' deeply rooted in human existence, can provide such a basis.

Fifth, let us consider what significance Buddhist nirvana may have in the understanding and achieving of true community. It is the realization of nirvana described previously as 'difference as it is, is sameness; sameness as it is, is difference' which, for Buddhism, provides an existential ground for true community. We find ourselves equal, not as children of the one God, but in the common realization of egolessness or Emptiness, which is at the same time the realization of true Self. Realization of egolessness is not something negative, like losing one's self-identity, but rather is positive in that through this realization one overcomes one's ego-centredness and awakens to Reality, that is, to one's own true Self as well as the true Self of others. It is in this awakening that one can live with others in true community, sharing the realization of true Self. In nirvana, the loss of ego-self is the gain of true Self, and the sameness among individuals in their egolessness and the difference between individuals in their true Self-ness are paradoxically one.

Accordingly, in the realization of nirvana, I am not I because I am egoless, and yet I am absolutely I because I am my true Self. Likewise, you are not you because you are egoless, and yet you are absolutely you because you are your true Self. Moreover, since I am not I, I am you, and since you are not you, you are I. Each person remains just as he or she is, yet each person is equal in that each is his or her true Self. This dynamic interrelationship occurs in the realization of egolessness and Emptiness which is possible and in fact necessary for each human existence. This realization provides the Buddhist foundation for humans in true community. Furthermore, this realization applies not only to human relationship to other humans, but also to all things in nature, from dogs to mountains.

Sixth and finally, what significance does nirvana have in regard to understanding the meaning of history? Since there is no God in Buddhism, there is no creation or last judgement, but rather Emptiness. Thus, for Buddhism, history has neither beginning nor end. This view of history derives from the deep realization of the *karma* of human beings. *Karma* is the universal law of act and its consequence which is self-operating in making the self transmigrate unceasingly from one life to another and making the world a process of perpetual becoming. Thus, it is the driving force behind all action which produces various effects according to the nature of the action and which binds people to the wheel of birth and death. Unlike the Hindu concept of *karma*, however, *karma* in Buddhism is not deterministic since there is in Buddhism no idea of God who is the controller of *karma*; rather Buddhism takes *karma* as moral power, emphasizing the possibility of final release from the round of transmigration through a free decision of the will. Accordingly, on the one hand, we are bound by our own *karma* which shares in and is inseparably linked to *karma* operating in the universe but, on the other hand, we, as beings with self-consciousness and free will, have the opportunity to be liberated from *karma* through our own free act performed by our personal choice, an act which is based on the total realization within oneself of the beginningless and endless process of *karma*, i.e., *karma* operating in the universe beyond oneself. In this total realization of *karma*, personal and universal, past, present, and future, one is liberated from *karma* and awakens to nirvana.

At the very moment we truly realize the beginninglessness and endlessness of history, we transcend its boundlessness and find the whole process of history from beginningless beginning to endless end intensively concentrated within the here and now. Apart from the realization of the here and now, there is no history. We realize our true life and true Self at this moment in which beginning and end, time and eternity, and one and many are not seen in duality but in dynamic oneness. This is nothing other than the realization of nirvana.

Universal *karma* can be realized not objectively but only Subjectively, i.e., in and through the existential realization of personal and individual *karma* – and personal *karma* can be truly transcended only when universal *karma* is Subjectively overcome within oneself. Thus (1) *to one who has attained nirvana* through the total realization of *karma*, the whole universe discloses itself in its reality, and history as the endless process of operating *karma* ceases, eternity manifesting itself. In this sense history ends in nirvana. This is the universal salvation of nirvana realized by an awakened one, and constitutes the wisdom aspect of nirvana. At the same time, however, (2) for the *awakened one* history begins in nirvana because those who, despite *the fact of* universal salvation realized by an awakened one, *think themselves* to be 'unsaved', remain innumerably in the world and will appear endlessly in the future. Thus, history takes on new significance for an awakened one – it is an endless process in which he or she must try to actualize universal salvation in regard to those 'unsaved'. This constitutes the compassion aspect of nirvana. Since the wisdom and compassion aspects are inseparable in nirvana, history begins and ends at each and every moment in the realization of nirvana.

In short, for an awakened one who is living in nirvana, universal salvation is completely realized in the here and now, and yet it is to be realized endlessly in the process of history for those who *think themselves* to be 'unsaved'. These two aspects are dynamically united in nirvana. Accordingly, at each and every moment of history a development toward the endless future is *at once* the total return to the root and source of history, that is, eternity, and conversely, the total return to the root and source of history, that is, eternity, is *at once* a development toward the endless future. The process of history is a succession of such moments whose dynamic structure consists of an advance which is simultaneously a return, a return which is simultaneously an advance. This Buddhist view of history leads us to a double realization: in the light of wisdom, eternity manifests itself in the here and now, and life at this moment is not a means to a future end, but is the end itself, while in the light of compassion, life is an endless activity of saving others, an instrument for universal salvation.

The six points discussed above are central to understanding the significance of Buddhist nirvana for contemporary society.

11 The Idea of Purity in Mahayana Buddhism

My task in this essay is not to discuss the various forms of rites of purification in Mahayana Buddhism nor to present the view of purity in a particular Buddhist sutra or school, but rather to clarify the religious meaning of what I consider to be the fundamental idea of purity underlying Mahayana Buddhism.

In Mahayana Buddhism, there are two well-known phrases from the *Mahāyāna-samgraha*[1] concerning purity which are usually quoted in connection with one another. The first, *prakṛti-śuddhi, honshō shōjō* in Japanese, can be translated as 'Original Purity', or 'everything is essentially pure in itself'. The second, *vaimalya-śuddhi, riku shōjō* in Japanese, can be rendered 'the purity of ridding one's self of defilement', or 'purity by virtue of what may be called "disdefilement"'. The latter expression thus has the connotation of '*becoming* pure by ridding oneself of defilement or impurity'

In general, we do not consider ourselves to be pure. We see ourselves as having evil passions, gross bodily desires, egoistic attachments, and so forth. In other words, we know that emotionally, morally, and spiritually we are impure. We therefore try in various ways to cleanse ourselves by removing our impurity and defilement. Such perceptions about our impurity and the consequent attempt at purification are quite natural and almost inevitable, and account for the origin of all rites of purification.

In recognizing our own present situation as impure and in projecting a 'pure' state as the primary goal to be reached beyond the present state, we endeavour to proceed from our present 'impurity' to some hoped-for state of 'purity' in which we will have rid ourselves of our defilement. However, this very attitude, even though its aim is none other than the attainment of purity, is regarded in Mahayana Buddhism as essentially defiled and impure in that it is based on the discrimination between impure and pure and seeks for the pure as a state to be reached *outside* of one's present condition.

Why should the attitude of seeking for the pure be regarded as impure? Because in distinguishing impure from pure and thereby trying to arrive at a purity considered to be beyond and devoid of the impure, one is necessarily captured and bound by the very distinction itself. Mahayana Buddhism maintains that in distinguishing *anything* we objectify it. We thereby clarify in a sense the thing we objectify and yet in so doing we centre the world around ourselves. Hence to objectify something and to centre the world around ourselves are two aspects of one and the same act of distinguishing one thing from another.

In this dual process, a bondage arises which theoretically can be divided into two kinds, but which in reality is one. That is, when we distinguish one thing from another by objectifying it, on the one hand we are limited or determined *by that* which we objectify; that is, we are restricted by the discrimination. In conjunction with this, things which are distinguished and thereby in a sense clarified are understood only in so far as they are objectified and *not* as they are *in themselves*. On the other hand, in distinguishing something by objectifying it, we centralize all significance in ourselves; we are thus caught and bound *by ourselves* – 'self-bound' so to speak. This state of being self-bound, combined with one's being limited by discriminated things, is fundamentally no other than true 'defilement'. Therefore, even if the 'pure' is sought after, so long as the pure is sought for as an object and, thereby, is distinguished from the impure, this attitude itself must be recognized as impure and done away with. In this sense, we should be free from rites of purification.

The standpoint – and by 'standpoint' I mean existential rather than any mere logical standpoint – in which the discrimination of impure and pure is completely eliminated is, according to Mahayana Buddhism, the truly pure one. This is a standpoint 'prior to' the discrimination between impure and pure. Here, 'prior to' does not mean 'temporally' but 'essentially' prior to. Nor does doing away with the discrimination of impure and pure mean a mere negation through which we become indifferent to values. Rather it means that by breaking through the discrimination of impure and pure and penetrating to the very root-source of the discrimination process, we free ourselves from all such discriminations and yet can respond and act freely within the world of discrimination. This root-source (the true or self-less Self) prior to the discrimination of impure and pure is itself the truly pure because, in its being free from discrimination, it is neither captured by the *process* of discrimination nor disturbed by feelings of impurity or purity about itself. Thus in the return to this root-source everything, whether impure or pure in its relative sense, is disclosed as pure in its original nature. This is the meaning of the phrase *honshō shōjō*, 'Original Purity'.

What has been said about impurity and purity applies as well to delusion and enlightenment. We usually think of ourselves as being in a state of delusion rather than enlightenment. Hence we try to attain enlightenment by removing delusion. Taking 'enlightenment' as the end, we try by various means to go *from* delusion *to* enlightenment. This very attitude, however, is itself nothing but a delusion. In other words, to take enlightenment as an end to be reached beyond the present deluded state, that is, to distinguish delusion and enlightenment from each other, is itself delusion. It is real delusion – not in a relative but in an absolute sense. To truly realize this very point with one's whole being, to penetrate to the very root-source of the discrimination between delusion and enlightenment, is itself genuine enlightenment.

However, the realization that the attempt to overcome delusion and gain enlightenment is itself delusory in no way obviates the necessity of practice. The ability to abandon one's practice on the basis of such a realization indicates only that from the outset the desire for enlightenment was rather superficial and lacking in zeal. On the contrary, even if a serious practitioner with zealous desire, realizes that the enlightenment-seeking approach is delusory, he or she can never simply give it up. For it is the only possible way for the person. Thus, as one continues to practice, one finally falls into an even deeper form of the dilemma wherein one 'must seek for' and yet 'should not seek for' enlightenment. The delusory nature of the enlightenment-seeking approach is realized only when such a dilemma is existentially broken through. Only then is enlightenment attained.

To realize the very attempt to go from delusion to enlightenment as *real* delusion is to attain *real* enlightenment. *Real* enlightenment, therefore, is none other than to totally awaken to *real* delusion in its quality of real delusiveness. So, in genuine enlightenment one becomes free from both so-called delusion and so-called enlightenment, and thereby comes clearly to realize as well in what way they are distinct from one another. This realization D. T. Suzuki has called the discrimination of non-discrimination.

When, under the supposition that we are *now* defiled or deluded, we take purity or enlightenment as an end to be reached, we consider ourselves to be 'on the way' to an end. We therefore assume that if we can reach our goal, we shall be able to grasp the true starting point for life. By means of that discrimination process, however, we will never be able to reach the end and thereby appropriate the true starting point. We may indeed endlessly move toward the 'true starting point' but we will never reach it: we can never overcome 'being on the way'.

For in this approach, while we view ourselves as standing in impurity or delusion, we look forward to purity or enlightenment at the end *beyond* the impure or delusory. We thus take the relation between the impure and pure, delusion and enlightenment as a *process* moving from the former to the latter. But in taking the relation as a process, we never really do find ourselves.

When we take our present position as one of 'impurity', that is, as being in the impure realm while in the process toward purity, it is impossible to *truly* grasp the *total* relation between the two poles (impurity and purity) in terms of *process*. For it is not possible to fix oneself at some point in the impure realm while simultaneously going beyond it so as to grasp the total moving process between the two poles. And needless to say, while we are looking toward purity or enlightenment as a goal, our existence *is not* based on the purity or enlightenment considered to be the *end*. Accordingly, in taking the relation between impurity and purity, delusion and enlightenment as a process, our existence has a basis neither in our present state nor in our desired goal. In distinguishing impurity from purity, delusion from enlightenment, one must have already been situated in a *third* position outside of the two – one built on mere conception – and be looking down on the whole movement from impure to pure, from delusion to enlightenment as a 'process'.

But in taking such a third position above and outside the process, we objectify and conceptualize not only purity (enlightenment) as an end, but even impurity (delusion) as our actual present state. Thus the whole attitude underlying this third position must be said to be itself a delusive, conceptual construction. This is the reason we never come to the real starting point of life so long as we base our efforts on such an attitude.

However, when and only when we come to realize this sort of attitude or approach as *fundamentally delusory* do we find ourselves at a genuine starting point for life. When the enlightenment-seeking approach collapses, we find ourselves in *enlightenment*. Not somewhere beyond or separated from the present, but directly 'under' or within the present – *only here* can *enlightenment*, i.e., the real starting point for life, be found. This means that here and now, and only in the here and now, can we arrive at the real starting point for life. If we do not find the point of departure for life in the here and now, where and when can we find it? We must know that at *any* moment we always stand on the real starting point. Without realizing this basic fact we usually look forward to finding it somewhere outside the here and sometime in the future, and regard ourselves as being presently 'on the way'. In marked contrast to this future-oriented approach, however, we are, according to Mahayana Buddhism, *originally* and *essentially* enlightened.

Thus 'purity' or 'enlightenment' should not be taken as an end to be reached sometime or somewhere in the future. It is the *ground*, not the aim, of our existence and activity. Only when one is existentially grounded in this original Reality do everything and everyone *actually* manifest themselves in their Original Purity. This is the reason it is often said in Mahayana Buddhism, 'Mountains and rivers and the earth itself all disclose their *dharma-kāya* [truth-body].' Here Original Purity is the real starting point for everything and everyone.

This is *Śūnyatā* (Emptiness) or *bhūtatathatā* (true suchness) in the Mahayana sense. Original Purity can be equated with Emptiness because Original Purity is not a counter-concept to impurity in some relative sense, but rather is purity in the absolute sense 'prior to' the conceptual opposition between impurity and purity. That everything and everyone are as they are means nothing other than *honshō shōjō*, that is, 'everything is pure in itself'.

Honshō shōjō can therefore stand without the support of *riku shōjō*, that is, 'becoming pure by ridding oneself of defilement or impurity'. From the standpoint of the former, that is, 'being pure', the latter, which entails 'becoming pure', is entirely delusory. Prior to 'becoming pure' we are originally and essentially 'being pure'. Original Purity, however, is not a state which is objectively observable, but is *realization*, that is, one's *ex*-istential realization which must be Subjectively realized through the collapse of self-centredness. It is one's living and active realization which spontaneously develops itself as the starting point of life in the process of the 'becoming' of the world. As the active and creative realization, Original Purity unfolds itself and serves to purify the world. If the realization of 'being pure' does not develop itself in this manner, it is nothing but a dead realization. Whether it is truly 'being pure' depends upon whether it is involved in the process of 'becoming pure'.

In this sense then, we may say that there is no 'being pure' apart from 'becoming pure'. However, this 'becoming pure' must be understood here in a new light. It no longer means to move from the impure to the pure, but rather to make the world, self and other included, become pure on the basis of Original Purity. Only here can rites of purification have a *truly* religious significance. Otherwise such rites will never be more than a means to, and never become an expression of, Original Purity.

The statement that there is no 'being pure' apart from 'becoming pure' actually contains a dual meaning – one negative, one positive. In its negative connotation this statement means that *'being* pure' realizes itself only through the *negation* of *'becoming* pure'. As stated above, only when we genuinely realize with our whole being that our usual attitude of looking for purity or enlightenment ahead of us is, as such, fundamentally delusory do we come to find ourselves in Original Purity. This realization of fundamental delusion constitutes the *prajñā* or wisdom aspect of Original Purity in which 'becoming pure', grasped as delusive, is done away with.

In its positive sense, however, this statement means that 'being pure' realizes itself through the *affirmation* of *'becoming* pure'. Insofar as we find ourselves to be in Original Purity, 'being pure' thus becomes the real starting point for ourselves to purify the world at every moment. 'Being pure' or Original Purity does not remain apart from the actual affairs and problems of our existence in the world. It manifests itself through ourselves in the form of 'becoming pure', for ourselves and for others. This is the active and creative mode of 'becoming pure' manifested in the *karuṇā* or compassion aspect of Original Purity. 'Becoming pure' in this positive sense can purify others, as well as ourselves, from their very ground. The Bodhisattva is a symbol of 'becoming pure' in this positive sense.

Dōgen, the initiator of Japanese Sōtō Zen tradition, emphasizes the universality and ever-presence of the Buddha-nature, which is another term for Original Purity. Yet he emphasizes the simultaneity of practice and attainment. In *Shōbōgenzō* 'Busshō' fascicle, Dōgen says, 'as for the truth of the Buddha-nature, the Buddha-nature is not incorporated prior to attaining Buddhahood; it is incorporated upon the attainment of Buddhahood. Buddhahood is always manifested simultaneously with the attainment of Buddhahood'.[2] He also says in 'Bendōwa,' 'This Dharma [an equivalent

of Original Purity] is amply present in every person, but unless
one practices, it is not manifested, unless there is realization, it is
not attained.'[3] 'In the Buddha Dharma, practice and realization are
identical. Because one's present practice is practice in realization,
one's initial negotiation of the Way in itself is the whole of original
realization. Thus, even while one is directed to practice, he is told
not to anticipate realization apart from practice, because practice
points directly to original realization. As it is already realization in
practice, realization is endless; as it is practice in realization,
practice is beginningless.'[4]

Practice ('becoming pure') and realization ('being pure') are
inseparable and dynamically one. Both of them are necessary. But
we must know that practice is necessary as the *condition* for attainment whereas realization is necessary as the *ground* for attainment.

As already stated, we can say in the double sense that apart from
'being pure', there is no 'becoming pure'. As the ground 'being
pure', Original Purity, can stand without 'becoming pure'. On the
other hand, 'being pure' does not realize itself apart from 'becoming
pure' in both its negative and positive senses. In the negative sense,
'becoming pure' must be overcome as delusive to awaken to
Original Purity. In the positive sense, 'becoming pure' must be
fulfilled in order to unfold Original Purity. 'Becoming pure' thus
serves as both the negative and positive condition in its relation to
'being pure' as the ground. This is the dynamism involved in
Original Purity. This living dialectic is possible for Original Purity
because it is nothing but the living realization of *Śūnyatā* or
Emptiness. Original Purity as the realization of *Śūnyatā* is the
root-source of *prajñā* and *karuṇā*, that is, the primordial essence of
wisdom as well as of compassion.

12 Emptiness is Suchness

Buddhists emphasize 'Emptiness' and say that everything is empty. Although this is a very important point for Buddhism in general and for Zen in particular, I am afraid that it is quite misleading, or at least very difficult to understand, particularly for the Western mind. So I think that 'everything is empty' may be more adequately rendered in this way: 'Everything is just as it is.' A pine tree is a pine tree; a bamboo is a bamboo; a dog is a dog; a cat is a cat; you are you; I am I; she is she. Everything is different from everything else. And yet, while everything and everyone retain their uniqueness and particularity, they are free from conflict because they have no self-nature. This is the meaning of the saying that everything is empty.

A pine tree has no sense of superiority over bamboo; bamboo has no sense of inferiority to a pine tree. A dog has no sense of superiority over a cat, a cat no sense of inferiority to a dog. We human beings may think that plants and animals entertain such thoughts, but this is merely a projection of human capacities onto the non-human dimension. In fact, plants and animals do not have such a mode of consciousness; they just live naturally, without any sense of evaluation. But human beings are different; we often think of ourselves in comparison to others. Why is he so intelligent? Why am I not as gifted? Why is she so beautiful? Why am I not as beautiful? Some feel superior to others while some feel inferior.

This is because, unlike plants and animals, we human beings have self-consciousness. Because we are self-conscious we look at ourselves from the outside, through comparison with others. Although we are 'self', we are not really 'self' because it is from the outside that we look at ourselves. In our daily life, there are moments when we are 'here' with ourselves – moments in which we feel a vague sense of unity. But at other moments we find ourselves 'there' – looking at ourselves from the outside.

We fluctuate between here and there from moment to moment: homeless, without any place to settle. Within ourselves there is always a gap. On the other hand, plants and animals are just as they are because they have no self-consciousness; they cannot look at themselves from the outside. This is the essential difference between human beings and other living beings.

This characteristic of human beings has a positive aspect. Since we have self-consciousness and are always thinking of something, we can plan, reflect, conceive ideals, and can thus create human culture, science, art, and so forth. We are living while thinking how to live, how to develop our lives. This positive aspect, however, is at the same time quite problematic, because, as I mentioned above, through self-consciousness we look at ourselves from the outside. We are thus separated from ourselves. We are here and there, there and here. We are constantly moving between here and there, between inside and outside. This is the reason for our basic restlessness, or fundamental anxiety, which plants and animals do not have. Only human beings are not 'just as they are'.

D. T. Suzuki often talks about 'suchness' or 'as-it-is-ness'. Plants and animals are living in their suchness. But we human beings are separated from our suchness, are never 'just as-we-are'. So far as we are moving between here and there, between inside and outside, looking at ourselves in comparison with others, and looking at ourselves from the outside, we are always restless. This restlessness or anxiety is not accidental to man, that is, peculiar to some individuals and not others. It is not that some have this inner restlessness while others do not. Insofar as one is a human being, he or she cannot escape this basic anxiety. In fact, strictly speaking, it is not that one *has* this anxiety, but rather that one *is* this anxiety.

How can we overcome this fundamental restlessness and return to suchness? To do so is the *raison d'être* and essential task of religion.

According to Genesis, whenever God created something, he saw that it was good. When God created Adam and Eve, he blessed them and saw that they were good. Do you think that the term 'good' in this context is meant in the merely ethical sense? My answer would be no. When God saw that his creation was good, he was not referring to the merely ethical dimension. Rather he was indicating that all of creation is ontologically good, or, to use D. T. Suzuki's term, that all of creation is in 'suchness'.

God created a tree just as a tree, and saw that it was good. It is in suchness as a tree. He created a bird – a bird is really a bird, not a fish. When he created a fish, it is really a fish – very different from a bird. Everything is in its own suchness. He created Adam and Eve, and just like the plants and animals and so forth, Adam is really

Adam, Eve is really Eve. Adam is good. Eve is good. They are just as they are, respectively and equally. They thus symbolize the original (true) nature of human beings.

But according to Genesis, Adam and Eve ate the apple of knowledge – the apple of knowing good and evil. Does this indicate good and evil only in the ethical sense? The story in my opinion illustrates far more than that. The eating of the apple suggests the making of value judgements. You may say, for instance, 'Today we have good weather, though yesterday we had bad weather', or 'This is a good road, but that one is bad'. Here, the terms good and evil can be made to apply to the weather, the road conditions, etc. It is in this broader sense of knowing good and evil that the apple of knowledge symbolizes the ability to make value judgements.

The ability to make value judgments is the unique attribute of self-consciousness. With self-consciousness one can judge 'This is good' or 'That is bad' and so forth. In this way we make a distinction between this and that. We love this and hate that, pursue this and avoid that. Through this capacity for making distinctions, people come to be involved in attachment. Love is a positive attachment. Hate is a negative attachment. By making distinctions, we come to like some things and dislike others. And in this way we become attached to some things and reject others – rejection being the negative form of attachment. We are involved in and confined by our attachment. This is the result of having self-consciousness.

Through self-consciousness, we also make a distinction between our self and others. As a consequence of this distinction, we attach to the self, making ourselves the centre of the world. We become involved in and limited by the distinction between self and others, the duality between love and hate, and so forth. Distinction turns into opposition, conflict, and struggle as soon as the distinction becomes an object of attachment.

But this is not the state of man's original nature. As God saw, Adam is good and Eve is good, just as plants and animals in their original state are good. Fundamentally, everything in the order of original creation is good.

Thus the question is: how can we return to that original goodness, our original suchness? I think Christianity has its own answer to this question. In Christianity self-consciousness as the result of eating the apple of knowledge is regarded as 'sin' because eating the apple constitutes rebellion against the word of God who said, 'Thou shalt not eat.' It is through the reunion of man and God by virtue of Jesus Christ's redemptive love that the human being can return to his or her original suchness. In Buddhism self-consciousness is regarded as 'ignorance' because in self-consciousness we are cut off from the reality of suchness and are limited by our outsider view of things in the universe. As such we view even ourselves from the outside. This outsider view of our self comprises the fundamental ignorance inherent in human existence.

Trying to grasp one's self by one's self from the outside may be compared to the metaphor of a snake swallowing its own tail. When the snake bites its tail, it makes a circle. And the more it tries to swallow its tail, the smaller that circle becomes. When the snake carries this effort to swallow its own tail to its final conclusion, the circle turns into a small dot and finally, it must disappear into emptiness. More concretely, the snake must die through this effort. As long as the human self *tries* to grasp itself through self-consciousness (out of which evolves inferiority or superiority, etc.), the human ego-self falls into an ever-deepening dilemma. At the extreme point of this dilemma, the ego can no longer support itself and must collapse into emptiness. When the attempt of self-consciousness to grasp itself is pressed to its ultimate conclusion, the human ego must die. Through the death of ego-self, no-self is realized. The realization of no-self is a necessity for the human ego. Someone may realize the necessity of confronting this dilemma only on his or her deathbed. But others may existentially *intuit* the need for resolving this dilemma even while quite young, and thus embark on the religious quest. In any event, the realization of no-self is a 'must' for the human ego. We must realize that there is no unchanging, eternal ego-self.

It is essential that one face this dilemma and break through it, in order to realize Emptiness or suchness. This realization of Emptiness is the liberation from that dilemma which is existentially rooted in human consciousness. Awakening to Emptiness, which is disclosed through the death of the ego, you realize your 'suchness'. This is because the realization of suchness is the positive aspect of the realization of Emptiness.

In this realization you are no longer separated from yourself, but are just yourself, no more, no less. There is no gap between you and yourself; you become you. When you realize your own suchness, you realize the suchness of everything at once. A pine tree appears in its suchness. Bamboo manifests itself in its suchness. Dogs and cats appear in their suchness as well. A dog is really a dog. No more, no less. A cat is really a cat. No more, no less. Everything is realized in its distinctiveness.

Then for the first time you come to understand the familiar Zen phrases, 'Willows are green, flowers are red', or 'The eyes are horizontal, the nose vertical.' Trees, birds, fish, dogs or cats – from the beginning they always enjoy their suchness. Only man is cut off from that suchness. One is in ignorance. Therefore one does not know the reality of human life and becomes attached to one's life and fears one's death. But when ignorance is realized for what it is through the realization of no-self, one may awaken to suchness, in which everything is realized in its uniqueness and particularity.

This is, however, not just a goal to be reached. It is rather the point of departure for our life, for our real activity; for suchness is the *ground* of both our self and the world. Not sometime in the future, but here and now we can immediately realize suchness, because we are never separated from suchness even for a moment. Suchness is always here. Without our awakening to it, however, it is not realized as 'suchness'. Once we awaken to it, we clearly realize that suchness is always here and now. It is the ground to which we must return and from which we must start. Without the realization of suchness as our ground or as our point of departure, our life will be restless and groundless. Once we return to that point of suchness, everything is realized in its distinctiveness. The distinctions between self and other, good and evil, life and death, are *regrasped* in the new light of suchness. Accordingly, it becomes the real point of departure for our lives and for our activity. Then, however rich or poor our ability may be, we display that ability in its fullness just as it is, without being entangled by any sense of inferiority or superiority. Whether you have three-power or five-power or eight-power or ten-power ability, you display your own power just as it is, at any moment, according to the given situation and can thus create something new. Without creating conflict with others, you can live your life really and fully so that everyday is a good day. This is what is meant by saying 'everything is empty'.

Part IV
Religion in the Present and the Future

13 Religion Challenged by Modern Thought

I

When religion began is a difficult question to answer. Roughly speaking, we may say that we can trace religion's origin back to the time when the human being came to exist. Since then, throughout human history, hardly anyone has doubted the necessity of religion for human beings. But in the past few centuries, doubts about religion itself have arisen. Questions such as 'Is religion truly indispensable to man?' and 'Cannot human being live his or her life without religion?' and 'Is religion not, perhaps, an obstacle to human progress?' have been raised. It may be said that it was sometime during the nineteenth century that these doubts developed into a radical questioning of the necessity of religion itself. Of course criticism of a particular religion had been made since ancient times. But the fundamental significance of religion as such for man had not always been questioned. In the West, some questions about religion were brought out during the Age of Enlightenment. But religion at that time was not questioned in the same way as it is now. People in the time of the Enlightenment criticized religion for its world-view and its understanding of nature. But, even then they probably did not doubt the significance of religion for the human soul. Now, however, ideologies and philosophical schools exist which deny *in principle* religion itself. These ideologies predominate among many people of the world today. This fact characterizes, I feel, the current challenge of modern thought to religion.

Now, with this in mind, I would like to consider the phenomena of the current situation. In modern society those who are indifferent to religion are increasing in number. They are neither affirmative nor negative towards religion. This phenomenon has been called 'secularization' and has become a characteristic of modern society. But why this indifference has grown is not so easy to explain.

231

I believe that this phenomenon has, in the last analysis, been caused by the fact that modern people have gradually become insensitive to their own hearts and souls, thus becoming spiritually impoverished. We modern people, I am afraid, are losing the ability to either rejoice or grieve with our whole hearts. Modern people are unable to cry or laugh in the depths of their being. On the contrary, primitive or ancient man, though limited in his knowledge of the natural world and of social and historical processes, and while not free from the basic anxiety inherent in all human life, had, I feel, an overall and integrated understanding of his existence in the universe. He had an honest and keen sense of his own soul. Therefore he could rejoice or grieve, laugh or cry in a more genuine sense. Nowadays, with extremely advanced scientific techniques and under the control of intricate political and economic systems, people have become fragmented, cut off from nature. They today have increased their objective knowledge of the world but have lost the basic and overall understanding of their existence in the universe, losing the 'instinctive' feelings of the soul. Man has become analytic and fragmented, losing his integrity with nature and the world. This may be the main reason why modern man has become indifferent to religion.

Various negative viewpoints towards religion have appeared, especially in Europe since the nineteenth century. These criticisms have denied religion, not from an emotional standpoint, but on the basis of a certain philosophical theoretical view. Such criticisms include scientism, psychoanalysis, Marxism, nihilism, etc. These did not explicitly deny the particular truth of a particular religion but far more importantly, denied in principle the validity of religion itself as not serving any useful purpose for human beings. In its stead, these systems of thought developed powerful ideological forces which have had control and influence over a great many people and upon the world as we know it today. It is understandable that traditional religious organizations, challenged by these ideologies, have been barely able to maintain their traditional forms. Some disintegration can be seen in their structure as well as in their teachings. Unless these religious organizations discover new directions, they can neither develop themselves nor even hope to continue to exist.

On the other hand, people are searching for a substitute for religion. Some of these substitutes we can hardly term 'religion'. This search differs in degree and in appearance. In contrast to those traditional relgious establishments mentioned above, this seeking for religion is not bound to the limits of religious organizations. Many people seek a religious type of existence outside the pale of these organizations. For instance, there are many people who are neither baptised nor belong to churches, yet revere Jesus Christ in their hearts. They read the Bible by themselves and live on the basis of the Bible. We can find many such people throughout the world. In Japan, those who admire Shinran or Dōgen are not always members of a Honganji or a Sōtō Zen temple. Thus, we can see that there are many people who find spiritual inspiration in Christ, Shinran or Dōgen, yet remain outside of religious organizations such as churches. We cannot say that they are not true Christians or true Buddhists.

We find two basic types of people among the members of religious orders. One type consists of confirmed devout believers who observe traditional rituals and teachings. These people are indeed confronted with the currents of their times, but their faith is strong enough to remain unmoved by them. The other type is composed of those innocent and naïve believers who, never influenced by current anti-religious ideologies, remain almost completely untouched by our changing world. People comprising both types lead religious lives while remaining within the traditional religious structures. Those people who belong to neither of these groups, however, are today rapidly increasing in number. They are searching for a spiritual home somehow outside of traditional religious limits. 'Religionless Christianity', which is proposed from the theologian's side by Bonhoeffer, means that true Christianity should be unframed by so-called traditional Christianity. This might be considered as one form of groping for non-religious religion.

Something religious is being sought after in literature as well. Much of current literature seems driven not only to depict human conflict but also to perceive a religious element in this human conflict. Art, in its creation and its appreciation, seems also impelled to imply something religious. Current art is quite different from Medieval religious art. Considered from the standpoint of Medieval religious art, we have to admit that current art is not religious at all. However, there is a certain religiosity in modern art that strikes responsive chords and it is true that such works are continually being produced. We can find many young people who are attracted to those social reformation movements which are supported by devotion or pathos. Though these movements appear to be non-religious, we can find something truly religious in them. The hippy movement initiated in America, though not considered to be a religious movement from the conservative point of view, does not turn its back on religion itself. My contention is that it too is one form of the groping for non-religious religion.

In this search for non-religious religion, that element of 'something religious' which is being sought for outside of traditional forms, may be divided into two kinds. The one is only vaguely 'religious', and is somehow connected with sheer secularity. Here is an example: I once visited PL Kyōdan, a new religion of Japan, with some travellers from abroad. At PL Kyōdan, playing golf or amusing oneself with fireworks had a kind of religious significance. Traditional religions have had the inclination to be ascetic and to repress the desire for amusement. Here, however, we can see one way in which religion attempts to meet modern people's needs by taking amusements positively into itself. New approaches to religion of this kind can be seen in the United States, especially in California. Another kind of 'something religious' is purely and directly religious, even though it overlooks all traditional religious organizations, rituals and teachings. It is sought for by returning to the spirit of the founders of each religion prior to the development of a religious establishment within its tradition, or by penetrating inwardly into the root source of one's own self by meditation, prayer or similar ways.

Thus, in the contemporary society, while there are many people indifferent to religion, many are searching for non-religious religion, or for new kinds of religion. Yet though this phenomenon can be analysed in various ways, what is most crucial for religion is the appearance of the religion-negating ideologies mentioned earlier. Ultimately, it was the appearance of the various anti-religious ideologies that caused the above described new phenomena in religion.

II

I will now take these religion-negating ideologies up one by one and consider how they deny religion. First, scientism. We should not confuse the basis on which science stands with the basis on which scientism stands. The standpoint of science does not necessarily contradict that of religion. Of course these two phenomena have some points of essential difference, but they do not mutually exclude one another. Instead, we find at least a chance of compatibility. On the contrary, the standpoint of scientism can never be compatible with that of religion. This is because scientism, by making the standpoint of science absolute, holds the 'scientific' to be the *one* and *only* criterion of truth. Anything non-scientific becomes false. Thus religion, being non-scientific, is considered false according to scientistic thinking. Since science has made remarkable advancements in modern times and since scientific laws have always been proven by experiment to be irrefutable, scientific truth has impressed many people as the absolute truth, although it is only one truth. Eminent scientists rarely espouse scientism. For example, Albert Einstein and Hideki Yukawa[1] admit the standpoint of religion. There are, however, many non-scientists who judge everything in a scientistic way. If the 'scientific' is taken as the only criterion of truth, the denial of religion inevitably follows. Espousers of scientism hold that religion still exists today only because the scientific way of thinking has not yet permeated into the masses. They believe that religion will naturally cease to exist once science has progressed to the extent that the scientific way of thinking is accepted by all. For scientism, the continued existence of religion has nothing to do with the nature or essence of religion, but is merely a problem of time. Thus, religion is denied in principle by scientism. Though the clear and pure realization of such scientism may not be widespread, there are many whose basic viewpoint is ruled by such a belief.

Next psychoanalysis. There are some arguments as to whether or not psychoanalysis contradicts religion. But in fact, psychoanalysis denies religion in certain ways. Sigmund Freud, the founder of psychoanalysis, compared religion with obsessional neurosis observed in childhood, and defined religion as man's collective childhood neurosis. From the psychoanalytical and psychological standpoints, Freud's theory was that theism, or the belief in one God or the Father, is an illusion caused by human desire. He attempted to prove that theism is unrealistic. Carl Jung, who developed many of Freud's essential doctrines in his own manner, observed the existence of a collective unconscious which all human beings share at the deepest level of the individual mind. This collective unconscious is beyond the individual unconscious and is the place where myth and religious symbols are rooted. According to Jung, religion comes from and goes back to this collective unconscious. He is affirmative to religion when compared with

Freud because, rejecting a merely scientific and objective approach, he expounded his theory of the autonomy of the collective unconscious. By virtue of this autonomy, religion is protected against manipulation by science and provided with its *raison d'être*, since the locating of the source of religious symbols in the collective unconscious guarantees religion an unassailable position in human life. It is in this fashion that Jung gave a depth-psychological foundation to religion.

Nevertheless there is an important element lacking here. Jung does not seem to realize the need for a 'spiritual death'. Both St. Paul and the great Buddhists clearly saw this as an essential element of true religion. 'If we have died with Christ, we believe that we shall also live with Him' (Rom., 6:8). Similar are the Buddhist ideas of 'Great Death' (through which one attains 'Great Life') and 'Rebirth in the Pure Land'. Because Jung overlooked the possibility of a 'spiritual death' it must be said that his understanding of religion did not reach the full realization of the essential character of religion. In Jung, authentic religious consciousness is after all replaced by the collective unconscious. Today various psychoanalytical methods of treatment based upon Jung's theory are being applied to many patients. In the United States, those who have mental disturbances go to psychoanalysts instead of seeing their minister. Churches are now attempting to incorporate psychoanalytical theory and practice into their programmes through formal training in Pastoral Counseling. While this phenomenon has an obvious merit, it serves to undermine the genuine religious basis of the various religions if it overlooks the need for 'spiritual death'.

According to Erich Fromm, a neo-Freudian, psychoanalysis does not always deny religion. Fromm classifies religion into two types – authoritarian and humanitarian. According to Fromm, psychoanalysis does not always influence these two types of religion in the same way. Authoritarian religion preaches obedience to the God who transcends and rules over human beings. On the other hand, humanitarian religion, preaching the oneness of everything, teaches that God is a symbol of the ideal being which human beings can also aspire to become. Fromm thinks that it is authoritarian religion which is more seriously threatened by psychoanalysis. He notes that psychiatric patients' modes of behaviour are sometimes surprisingly similar to religious rituals. For instance, some patients obsessed by compulsive ideas attach importance to ritualistic purifications which sometimes extremely resemble purification rituals found in many religions. Such patients compulsively engage in ritualistic activity although it has nothing to do with religion. If we consider such actions to be rites, they would be a very private form of ritual compared to historical and social religious rites. Fromm, however, finds remarkable similarities in the mental mechanisms involved in the two kinds of rituals. It is noteworthy that although Fromm believes that psychoanalysis can clarify the psychological motives involved in a compulsive desire for ritual performance, he nevertheless holds that religious rituals should not be regarded in the same light as the ritualistic behavior of obsessional neuroses.

As we mentioned above, the standpoint of psychoanalysis does not completely deny religion. But psychoanalysis attempts to explain religion through theories such as 'childhood neurosis' and 'projection of a father image'. My contention is that such theories *finally* lead to the denial of religion.

Marxism also, in its radical form, denies genuine religion. As I have already explained, scientism denies religion by maintaining that scientific knowledge is absolute. Psychoanalysis illustrates this point in that it denies religion from the standpoint of a scientific *psychology*. Marxism makes the same denial from the *social scientific* standpoint. According to Karl Marx, human suffering is ultimately rooted in the struggles between the different social strata of a class society. That is, those who belong to the proletariat cannot be fully human because they are continually exploited by the bourgeoisie. Labour, the result of man's creativity, has become a commodity in the capitalist society. In the mechanism of such a society, the capitalist always exploits the laborer, even though he may be a good man in his personal morals. The worker, deprived of the fruits of his work, is robbed of a part of his very humanity. This is due, according to Marxism, not to the innate immorality of the bourgeoisie but to the mechanism of a class society. Here lies the root cause of human suffering. In order to relieve human suffering, Marxism insists on a classless communal society in which all persons are given equal human rights and human labour becomes a fulfilment of one's personality. In this, we can find a hidden denial of religion which is not a subordinate event to the revolution, but is rather an indispensable part of the Marxist revolution. In his book entitled *'Introduction to a Critique of Hegel's Philosophy of Law,'* Marx insists that the criticism of religion is the foundation of all social criticism. According to Marx, in so far as people believe in religious deliverance or salvation, they do not seek the realization of human emancipation in this world, but in another ideal world or heaven. These people interpret the miseries and contradictions of this world as divine providence or trial, or the results of karma, i.e., the accumulation of one's deeds in one's previous existence. According to religious thought, people should obey God's will or seek release from their karma and find spiritual peace in heaven or in enlightenment.

Marx maintains that this is not the true solution to human suffering but a completely misleading attempt to subvert the enthusiasm for socio-political revolution. Thus, religion is the greatest obstacle on the way to revolution, and man must completely deny religion in order to bring about a classless society. Such are the ways in which Marxism denies religion.

Finally we come to nihilism. Here I mean the type of nihilism which Friedrich Nietzsche expounded. Scientism and Marxism deny religion from standpoints outside of religion. Psychoanalysis inquires into the depth of human psyche, but does not include the essence of religion in its exposition. Nietzschean nihilism explicitly denies religion in its essence. Nietzsche states that 'God is dead' and that 'God is a sacred lie.' Here we must recognize that he does not merely say that God does not exist, but that 'God is *dead*.' Those without religious experience may say that 'God does not exist.' But Nietzsche says 'God is dead', meaning God *did live* and *is dead now*. Therefore, Nietzsche must have had some religious experience, or experienced a living God in a certain way. Nietzsche insists that one must be an 'Over-man', or an active nihilist, in order to endure the *nihilum* without God. Thus, Nietzsche denies religion at its very basis.

Nietzsche did not simply not believe in God, he transcended God. Then he asked, 'Where does God come from?' His answer was, 'From the will to power' as the root source of man's fundamental instinct for self-preservation. According to Nietzsche, belief in God as the ruler of the universe does not fulfill human existence. Behind this notion of God, he recognized a cosmological 'will to power'. This is the most fundamental will. God is nothing but an artificial construction which this fundamental will has fabricated in the depths of the *nihilum* of this world in order to preserve man's life. People have lived by believing in the fabricated 'God' as the living God. This was, it is true, meaningful and effective to human life until now. But Nietzsche proclaims that we have entered into a completely new era in which the above way of life becomes of no use. This is the arrival of nihilism. People must now be aware that the God in whom they have believed down to the present day is a self-deception. They must return to the 'will to power' from which 'God' himself has been constructed. One has to transcend oneself and become an 'Over-man', who can endure the *nihilum* without God. Thus Nietzsche denies the principle of religion at its core. His ideas of 'the eternal return', the 'Dionysian philosophy', and *'amor fati'* i.e., love of fate, are all grounded herein. Nietzsche has thus opened a new way for non-religious religion.

III

Scientism, psychoanalysis, Marxism and nihilism deny religion in different ways. From the religious standpoint, these four ways of thought challenge religion.

Religion insists that human reason should be transcended in order to reach a place where human being can find true spirit, true heart and true soul. Further, religion takes as its task the salvation, not only of individual human beings but also the world as a whole. Religion preaches the realization of the Kingdom of God or construction of the Buddha Land, and reformation of this world. In this way religion not only preaches salvation but also challenges the ultimacy of social, political and human institutions and desires. Thus, God or Buddha-nature always constitutes the most fundamental principle and goal for religion.

Religion does not recognize human reason and judgement as something ultimate in the way scientism does. Modern psychoanalysis considers the soul, spirit and heart to lie beyond human reason but sees it as stemming from the unconsciousness, not from God or any transcendent Reality. Marxism advocates a logical and practical methodology for human salvation by realizing an ideal communal society through class struggle, thus denouncing religion, which attempts to save this world through realizing the Kingdom of God or the Buddha Land. Finally nihilism denies God and all transcendent Reality, repudiating them as deceptive fabrications of the will to power. These four standpoints challenge religion at its foundation from various angles based upon certain theoretical and philosophical standpoints. This is the first time in history that religion has been challenged this way. Unless religion can meet the challenge, it may become a fixed, organizationalized profession and finally lose its vitality. Modern people must grapple with these religion-denying standpoints in the depths of their being. Religious bodies themselves also have to make their responses to these challenges clear. Buddhism, for example, must show theoretically and practically its authentic spirituality through its response to these challenges. Otherwise religion cannot be creative or productive in the future. In this sense, these denials might be said to be a great grace for religion.

14 Religion and Science in the Global Age – Their Essential Character and Mutual Relationship

It is almost impossible to deal with a problem of the magnitude of 'Religion and Science in the Global Age' in its full scale and depth. Nevertheless I would like to discuss what I consider essential to the issue and elucidate it from a Buddhist point of view.

Modern science may be said to be a human enterprise through which man and nature are investigated as objectively as possible, that is, without subjective judgement. It is *fundamentally* free from any anthropocentric interest such as value, meaning and purpose. This mode of science was methodologically established by the Cartesian idea of *Mathēsis ūniversālis* and the Baconian method described in *Novum Organum*. It was a complete replacement of the Aristotelian teleological–biological standpoint by an approach based on mathematics and physics. The present form of science is the radical development of this approach.

In the eighteenth and nineteenth centuries in the West, serious conflicts arose between Christianity and science, as epitomized by the controversy surrounding Charles Darwin. It could be argued that Christian theology acted as an important catalyst in the development of modern science, for the idea of God as ruler of the universe made people sympathetic to the idea that God had arranged things in an orderly way and that there were natural laws which could be discovered if one looked hard enough. However, the assertion that science could not have arisen without the stimulus of theological ideas certainly does not demonstrate that those theological ideas have any genuine basis in reality.[1]

In our time it is sometimes said that those who still maintain that there is a conflict between religion and science are rather naïve and old-fashioned, since contemporary theologians, having as a rule abandoned the view that the Holy Scriptures are literally the word of God, are well disposed toward dialogue and mediation between Christianity and science. Simultaneously it is suggested that the peculiar characteristics of twentieth-century science render it far less inimical to religion than was the science of the nineteenth century. I do not think, however, that this is really the case. While on the surface the problem may seem to have diminished, it is clear at a deeper level that science poses a serious threat to religion.

Let us examine the essential character of both science and religion. At the risk of oversimplification, one may say that science is concerned with the answer to the question 'how' whereas religion is concerned with the answer to the question 'why'. As used here, 'how' refers to the process of cause and effect or 'means' while 'why' refers to meaning, purpose, or *raison d'être*. Science can provide an answer to the question of how a flower blooms, or how man comes to exist. It cannot, however, give an answer to the question of why a flower blooms or why man comes to exist. It can explain the cause of a given fact but not the meaning or ground of that fact. It is religion, not science that can offer an answer to the question 'why'.

Pre-modern science, which was based on the Aristotelian teleolo-gical–biological approach, gave a teleogical answer to the question 'how', for everything in the universe was then understood organical-ly, that is, in terms of living entities. And a teleological answer to the question 'how' was not necessarily incompatible with a religious answer to the question 'why'. The teleological view of the world offered by ancient physics was rather harmonious with the theistic view of man and nature as explained in Christianity. With the advent of modern science, however, the situation changed radically. Modern science, which is based on mathematics and physics, gives a non-teleological and mechanistic response to the question 'how', and such a mechanistic answer to the question 'how' is quite incompatible with the religious answer to the question 'why'. This is especially the case with a theistic religion such as Christianity, which is inextricably rooted in the notion of a personal God who is the Creator, Redeemer, and Judge of the universe. The modern scientific mechanistic view of the world is entirely indifferent to human existence. In the mechanistic view, not only physical matter, but also biological life and even the human psyche and spirit are reduced to entirely lifeless mechanistic phenomena. This is evident in contemporary molecular biology, experimental psychology, and genetics.

Unlike the teleological and biological view of nature in pre-modern science, the mechanistic view of the world of modern science grasps everything in the universe as lifeless, that is, in an entirely inhuman and insensitive manner. Such a mechanistic view of the world is not only incompatible with but also inimical to religion, which is concerned with the 'why' question of the final meaning or ultimate ground of human existence in the world. It is inimical to religion because it deprives everything of its meaning, value, aim, and purpose. It may be said that the mechanistic answer to the question 'how' as seen in modern science has 'horizontally' severed the religious answer to the question 'why'. In so saying, I have in mind an image, in which a vertical line, representing religion which seeks for the ultimate ground of human existence, is severed by a horizontal line, representing science which is mainly concerned with the cause and effect of things in the universe. As a result, man is left hanging. It is now a serious task for religion, which is primarily concerned with the ultimate meaning of human life, to find a way to embrace the meaning-negating science which prevails in the modern world.[2]

The modern scientific mechanistic view of the world has created a still more serious problem for religion. It has brought forth atheism and radical nihilism. The mechanistic world view destroyed the 'spiritual' basis on which all the teleological systems in religion hitherto rested, and opened up nihility at the base of the world, leaving no place for God. This abyss of nihility was also opened up at the bottom of human existence. The existentialism developed by Jean Paul Sartre, who insists that one's subjectivity can be established only in the realization of that nihility, is a direct consequence of the awareness of the nihility brought about by modern science. Contemporary atheism is not merely a materialistic atheism, but rather a more radical, existential atheism which tries to take 'nihility without God' as the basis of Subjective freedom. In this regard, we must pay special attention to Friedrich Nietzsche, who proclaimed the arrival of nihilism about a century ago through his sharp insight into the nature of science and human destiny.

In his book, *Beyond Good and Evil*, Nietzsche presents his unique idea of the three stages of human history as follows:

> Once upon a time men sacrificed human beings to their God, and perhaps just those they loved the best ... then, during the moral epoch of mankind, they sacrificed to their God the strongest instincts they possessed, their 'nature'; *this* festal joy

shines in the cruel glances of ascetics and 'anti-natural' fanatics.
Finally, what still remained to be sacrificed? ... Was it not
necessary to sacrifice God himself –? To sacrifice God for
nothingness – this paradoxical mystery of the ultimate cruelty
has been reserved for the rising generation; we all know something of this already.[3]

To the first stage, Nietzsche ascribes the sacrifice of all primitive
religions and also the sacrifice of the Emperor Tiberius in the
Mithra-Grotto of the Island of Capri. It may be said that this first
stage corresponds to the time of the Old Testament which records
the story of this kind of sacrifice in the case, for example, of
Abraham and Isaac. It would also be safe to say that the second
stage represents the time of the New Testament and following
Christian era in which the death and sacrifice of Jesus is seen as the
redemption of original sin inherent in human nature. The third
historic stage in which we 'sacrifice God for nothingness' announces
the advent of nihilism in the Nietzschean sense.[4]

It may be said that we have already arrived at the third historic
stage which Nietzsche described above. As he predicted, we are now
experiencing the 'nihility without God' which has been opened up
by modern science at the base of the traditional notion of God. How
to cope with this 'nihility without God' is the most urgent problem
emerging from the conflict between science and religion.

In this regard, the following two points must be emphasized if
religion is to remain viable in its dialogue and confrontation with
science:

1. It is necessary for each religion to re-examine the basis of its
    world view. For any religion, its world view is not like clothes
    that one can change whenever one pleases. A world view is to
    religion what water is to a fish. It is the indispensable condition
    through which religion can actually come into existence. Water
    is neither the life of the fish as such, nor its body, yet it is
    fundamentally linked to both. For a religion to change its
    world view is a matter no less fatal to it than for a fish to
    change from salt water to fresh.[5]

2. What is even more crucial and important is that each religion
    re-examine and reinterpret that tradition's understanding of
    God or the 'ultimate' and His or its relation to human beings
    and the world. With regard to this second point, Buddhism,

which is fundamentally non-theistic, is in a somewhat different situation from Christianity, which is basically theistic. As I mentioned before, religion provides an answer to the question 'why'. Christianity gives a theistic answer to the question 'why', in terms of the 'will of God', the 'rule of God', and accompanying notions such as creation, incarnation, redemption and last judgement. On the other hand, Buddhism provides a non-theistic answer to the question 'why' through its emphasis on 'dependent co-origination', 'no-self', 'Emptiness', 'suchness' and so forth.

Theistic answers to the question 'why' in Christianity, such as the 'will of God' and the 'rule of God' are incompatible with the modern scientific answer to the question 'how'. This is because the former strongly emphasize the personality of the ultimate while the latter is essentially impersonal. The personal God and his personal relationship to human beings are quite incompatible with the mechanistic view of the world. To overcome this incompatibility, various theological attempts have been made in the realm of Christianity. One of the most remarkable of these attempts is that of Process Theology, as exemplified by the efforts of John Cobb and others.

Process Theology is based on the philosophy of Whitehead, which in turn is based on critical consideration of modern science and mathematics. According to Process Theology, the ultimate is not the personal God, but creativity, which is somewhat impersonal. Both God and the world are equally understood as outcomes of the principle of creativity. God and the world as thus understood are mutually interpenetrating in terms of concrescense in which individual occasions of experience are dynamic acts of becoming. The notion of the ultimate as creativity in Process Theology is certainly less alien to the modern scientific mechanistic view of the world than the traditional Christian notion of a personal God. However, I wonder if it is *really* compatible with modern science. In order for a theology to be completely compatible with modern science, it must be of a thoroughly mechanistic and impersonal nature while fully retaining a teleological and personal nature as well. In other words, a dialectical unity of completely mechanistic – impersonal and completely teleological – personal natures is necessary for such a theology. Although Process Theology includes both mechanistic and teleological aspects by setting forth efficient and final causation, it combines these two aspects somewhat in a parallel manner, not in a dialectical or paradoxical way. That is to say, it is partially mechanistic and partially teleological. And however much the momentariness of events which constitute the process is emphasized, in the basic notion of 'process' the teleological nature takes precedence over the mechanical nature. This is clearly seen when creativity as the ultimate is understood to be realizable only in actual instances of the *many becoming one*,[6] and when creativity is possible only through an open future and closed past, that is, through the irreversibility of unidirectional time. I wonder if Process Theology can legitimately overcome the 'nihility without God' which is opened up at the bottom of contemporary human existence by the modern scientific mechanistic view of the world.

In Buddhism, the non-theistic response to the question 'why', as expressed through the notions of 'dependent co-origination', 'Emptiness' and 'suchness', is compatible with the modern scientific mechanistic answer to the question 'how', because these Buddhist notions, though deeply religious, are somewhat impersonal. To say they are impersonal does not mean Buddhism is indifferent to human affairs. On the contrary, Buddhism as a religion is essentially concerned with human salvation. In this respect, there is no difference between Christianity and Buddhism, for both traditions are equally concerned with salvation. However, the *foundation* on which salvation becomes possible is understood differently. In Christianity that foundation is understood as something personal, that is, as the personal relationship between man and God. On the other hand, in Buddhism, the foundation of salvation is not something personal, but impersonal and common to all beings. Human *salvation* and *its foundation*, though inseparable, must be distinguished. This distinction is important because the present conflict between science and religion is to a great extent related to the foundation of salvation.

The Buddhist notion of 'dependent co-origination' insists that everything is interdependent with every other thing, both in regard to its existence and its ceasing to be. Nothing is self-existent and independent. For instance, bigness and smallness are interdependent; there is no such thing as bigness self-existing apart from smallness or smallness self-existing apart from bigness. Bigness is bigness and smallness is smallness, and yet they are completely interdependent. In the same way, good and evil are interdependent.

It is illusory to think of the good as self-existing apart from evil or to think of evil as self-existing apart from the good. Good is good; evil is evil. There is a distinction. Yet good and evil are completely interdependent. Again, in the same way, the absolute and the relative are interdependent.

It is erroneous to conceive of the absolute as self-existing apart from the relative or to conceive of the relative as self-existing apart from the absolute. The absolute is the absolute and the relative is the relative, and yet the absolute and the relative are completely interdependent. And so, everything is interdependent; nothing is independent. This is the Buddhist notion of dependent co-origination. Accordingly, dependent co-origination or interdependence itself is neither absolute nor relative. Since it is neither absolute nor relative, it is also called 'Emptiness'. This is not, however, a mere emptiness. On the contrary, precisely because they are interdependent, the absolute is really the absolute and the relative is really the relative; good is really good and evil is really evil; bigness is really bigness and smallness is really smallness. Everything is just as it is. The differences between things are clearly realized. And yet their interdependence is realized as well. This is why 'Emptiness' is also called as-it-is-ness or suchness. Emptiness is not a mere emptiness, but rather fullness in which the distinctiveness of everything is realized in a thoroughgoing manner.

I hope it is now clear that 'dependent co-origination', 'Emptiness' and 'suchness' are simply different verbal expressions of one and the same Reality. In Buddhism, the ultimate is not God or creativity but 'dependent co-origination'. Buddhism is a religion which teaches us how to awaken to this truth of dependent co-origination. One who awakens to this truth is called a Buddha.

In 'dependent co-origination', 'Emtpiness' and 'suchness', everything is realized as reciprocal and reversible. There is nothing one-sided or unidirectional. Accordingly, the Buddhist notion of 'dependent co-origination' as the ultimate is completely free from any teleological character. In this respect, it is compatible with modern science. Yet it is not merely mechanistic, for it is an answer to the religious question 'why'. In brief, Buddhism is neither teleological nor mechanistic.

Christianity provides a positive answer to the question 'why' in terms of the will of God. Even when human reason does not understand why something happens in a certain way, faith in God accepts it as a trial or the mercy of God. In contrast, Buddhism, in answer to the question 'why', responds with 'it is so without why' or 'it is just as it is.' 'Without why' as an answer to the question 'why' is quite compatible with the modern scientific mechanistic answer to the question 'how'. But, the Buddhist answer 'without why' does not indicate agnosticism or nihilism. It is not a negative answer in the sense of abandoning inquiry into 'why'. It is rather a positive and affirmative answer which is realized within a thoroughgoing inquiry into 'why' and reached by breaking through the question 'why.' In short, the Buddhist answer 'without why' does not signify agnosticism as the mere absence of a positive answer to the question 'why,' but, rather, indicates a great affirmation of Reality which cannot be analyzed by the question 'why' and hence is beyond it.

The crucial task for Buddhism is this: how can Buddhism on the basis of 'without why' as its ultimate ground, formulate a *positive direction* through which ethics and history can develop? In other words, how can *a new teleology* be established on the ground of 'suchness,' which is neither teleological nor mechanical? Here I must limit myself to suggesting that the Mahayana notion of 'compassion', which is inseparably connected with 'wisdom,' and the idea of the 'Bodhisattva' which is based on 'Emptiness' and 'suchness,' can provide the foundation for such a Buddhist teleology.

Science without religion is dangerous, for it necessarily entails a complete mechanization of humanity. On the other hand, religion without science is powerless in that it lacks an effective means by which to actualize religious meaning in the contemporary world. Science and religion must work together harmoniously. It is an urgent task for us who approach the global age to find a way to integrate the two.

15 Sovereignty Rests with Mankind

All of mankind on this planet has entered into an age
When it must realize that it now is based
On the clear realization of itself as "mankind",
And that it is "living-and-dying"
In the vast reaches of the universe
As a community with a single destiny –
One living self-aware entity.

In order to live this age
Mankind must awaken to its true Self,
And everyone must know that by transcending
The relative differences of self and other,
One exists within the "expanse of Self-awakening"
Wherein both self and other are fulfiled.

The present crisis of the world arises
From the ceaseless conflicts and disputes
Of sovereign nations which do not know self-negation.
What we must establish now
Is not an international confederacy
In the sense of a league of sovereign nations.
Even less should it be a world empire
Based on one great sovereign state
Which has acquired hegemony as a result of a struggle.
Rather, it must be a world of mankind
Wherein sovereignty rests precisely with all mankind
In the sense of one self-aware entity
Which has become profoundly aware of itself
As "mankind".

It must be a human community without nation-states,

Wherein the dignity and freedom of the individual
Are guaranteed
And wherein the multi-colored flowers of races
And cultures may bloom.
The age of nation-states as the bearers of history
Must proclaim its end,
And the age of mankind must begin.

We must not despair of the historical evil
Which has transcended the power of the individual.
We must realize that national egoism is mankind's karma
Deeply rooted in the essential nature of human beings.
We must place mankind within a new cosmology
Which has extricated itself from anthropocentrism.
Is not the boundless "expanse of Self-awakening",
Which gives life to both self and other
As it sets up the distinction between them –
Is not this precisely the foundation of a new human society?

I

"Mankind" is a corporate entity with a single fate, one living,
self-aware unit placed within the vastness of space.

To speak of 'mankind' as a unit is not something historically new.
Especially the modern era, which takes humanism as its basic
principle, has frequently treated the concept of 'mankind' as a
problem. In the contemporary era, wherein the world has rapidly
become one entity – particularly in the past two or three decades,
as we have undertaken space exploration – the word 'mankind' has
even become a kind of jargon term. But, has *mankind itself* been
clearly perceived as a corporate entity with a single fate, as one
living, self-aware entity 'living-and-dying' in the vast reaches of
space? Even in the present day, when we use the term 'mankind', it
is thought of as referring to the aggregate of the various races or
peoples; they together are seen as confronting and involved in the
turbulence of international politics among such super-states as the
United States, China, and the Soviet Union, which compete with
each other using the world as their stage.
   The term may also refer to the totality of human beings who,

through the encounter of Eastern and Western cultures, are deepening their contact, interaction, and influence on each other, and are gradually becoming one entity. Or, even further, the term may refer to human beings who as one biological species live on this planet in this galaxy. This latter concept can be said to have emerged with sending astronuts into space, landing on the surface of the moon, and proving scientifically the possibility of space travel to other planets. This is as yet a vague collective group concept. Even if the clear outlines of the concept of mankind are recognized, its limits have been imposed merely from without. 'Mankind' is still a quantitative concept, not a qualitative one.

What is of paramount importance today is to internalize and grasp 'mankind' as a qualitative concept. We must grasp it as a *single, living, self-aware entity.* For without doing so, we can never overcome the conflicts between nations which we are facing, and we cannot bring true peace to the world. Nor can we build a profound and rich human society which is permeated by individual freedom and the special characteristics of races and cultures wherein all live in harmony with each other.

From what position is it possible to grasp mankind as a single, living, self-aware entity? I believe that the foundation of this position is for *each of us* to awaken to his or her true Self, that is, each individual must break through his or her ego structure, thereby realizing original Self. At the same time that this is a thoroughly individual 'Subjective' matter, it is also a thoroughly universal, objective one. Why is this so? It is so because to overcome the ego is to overcome the very standpoint wherein one distinguishes between self and other. In such a case, the distinction between self and other does not refer only to the distinction between the self and other people but also includes the distinction between the self and all things which are in opposition to the self; that is, the distinctions between the self and things, the self and world, and the self and history. The ego is indeed nothing other than the basic source of all such distinctions and oppositions. If we turn our backs on the world, there can be no investigation of the self; if we avoid our conflicts with history, which often progress beyond human control, there can be no awakening to the true Self. The true investigation of the self is always the investigation of the world and of history.

At the same time that the Self-awakening wherein each of us awakens to his or her original Self is the true 'Subjective' Self-awakening of each of us, it is the Self-awakening of the world itself, and the Self-awakening of history itself. The Self-awakening which one awakens to by breaking through the ego transcends the ego and extends infinitely in every direction. There is nothing whatsoever which stands outside *this expanse of Self-awakening*. The so-called self, others, the myriad phenomena of the world, and the flow of history as well are not exceptions to this. Indeed, the grasp of mankind as a single, living, self-aware entity takes place within this 'expanse of Self-awakening'. It is precisely within this 'expanse of Self-awakening' that all things exist in the true sense and live vibrantly. 'Mankind' also exists vibrantly in this same 'expanse of Self-awakening'.

II

A human society must be built in which present-day sovereign states are negated, and in which it is precisely "mankind" as a living, self-aware entity that has the sovereignty.

If mankind is to be grasped as a single, living, self-aware entity, sovereign states which oppose each other and claim that sovereignty resides with specific races or peoples must be negated. National sovereignty, on behalf of continued existence as a nation-state, ultimately demands the sacrifice of the lives of the individuals composing it; and turning outward, it wages a life-and-death struggle, using military force, with other sovereign nations opposing it. Therein we find no higher authority able to check the operation of this kind of national power. Sovereign states do not know self-negation. They take as their basic principle a position of self-affirmation and self-assertion in which, during a crisis, the position of 'mankind' is overlooked and destroyed. Consequently, even though international cooperative organizations, which are the products of compromises and agreements between sovereign states, become to a certain degree the means of resolving international conflicts, as long as they presuppose sovereign states, they basically can neither check national egoism nor totally eliminate war. Instead, although international organizations can exert some control over smaller nations, I fear that such organizations may be transformed into magnificent edifices of hypocrisy wherein the arrogance of the larger nations possessing great military power cannot help but be tacitly recognized. The plan to establish a world league of nations or a world government cannot be said to be the path that will bring about true world peace so long as the standpoint of sovereign nations is not overcome in principle and sovereignty transfered from the nation-state to mankind seen as a single, living, self-aware entity.

In a human community which takes as its foundation the idea of 'mankind' as a living, self-aware entity, the concept of *sovereignty* must likewise be transformed. It must no longer be a self-affirmative, self-assertive sovereignty wherein the individuals composing the human community are ordered to go to their deaths, or a sovereignty in which the special characteristics of the individual races and cultures are destroyed. On the contrary it must be a sovereignty which always is based in self-negation. It must be a sovereignty which takes wisdom and compassion as its principles rather than authority and justice. That which indeed makes such sovereignty possible is the Self-awakening of the original Self, which, while establishing the distinction between the self and others, makes both self and others come alive completely. In the boundless 'expanse of Self-awakening', wherein *individuals, peoples,* and *mankind* (the three categories of human beings) can make each other come alive completely without alienating each other, *individuals, mankind,* and *the myriad phenomena of the universe* (the three categories of the universe) can also make each other come alive completely without alienating each other. Only when mankind's sovereignty takes this kind of self-negation as its principle and is based upon wisdom and compassion will a single government having all mankind as its basis be possible. At the foundation of all governmental organizations there must be social unity. It is precisely mankind as a self-aware entity which can develop a unified, cooperative human community in the complete sense of the term. Consequently the source of the sovereign authority of mankind lies not in law and justice but rather in true Self-awakening. At the same time that true Self-awakening as 'mankind' is the most internal authority for a human society, it is also the most transcendent authority.

III

The transition from national sovereignty to the new sovereignty of mankind cannot be achieved in a linear manner. For therein, two factors are essential: first, the realization that the sovereign nation is the product of a karma rooted in the basic nature of mankind; and second, the realization that all mankind is jointly responsible for this historical evil which each individual must take as his or her own.

How can the sovereign nation be overcome? How is the transition to the sovereignty of mankind possible? Each nation possesses both the aspect of power in the sense that it is an organ of political control and the aspect of an ethic which represents the moral force of the races or peoples which compose it. The so-called 'rationale of the state' (*Staatsräson*) exists as a unity of this power and ethic, of this force and justice. Therefore, it is incorrect to assume immediately that the state is an evil existence. The ethical or moral force of the state is also often considered to be a higher form of human ethics (*Sittlichkeit*), transcending the birth and death of individual people and preserving the eternal continuation of races and peoples. It is difficult to find an age in human history when states did not exist. In almost the same way that the family is an indispensable ethical form for an individual, so too for tribes and races, and for peoples occupying a certain land, the state has been an indispensable moral form. We must say that the state is not an accidental existence, but is something deeply rooted in the basic nature and experience of the human race.

However, today's problem lies in the fact that the very rationale of the state which is supposed to be the unification of power and justice has begun to assume the character of an evil which must be negated. In the midst of the opposition and struggles of today's super-states in which these structures of power have been enlarged and have achieved a high degree of complexity, the justice of the state can no longer control the power, so that this massive force leaps beyond moral restraints, pursuing its own course pell-mell. We can perceive this situation in the case of the Vietnam War, and in such events as the invasions of Hungary and Czechoslovakia. It appears as if the balance of terror based on nuclear weapons has made total war impossible while rendering meaningless, hypocritical, and corrupt the rationale of the state. How many people today can believe that the moral restraints of the state can check the dynamism of huge national power linked to gigantic technical systems and structures of production? Moved by a blatant national egoism, the power of the state is now developing a demonic character as it destroys the balance of moral restraint and controlling power, which should be visible in the rationale of the state. As it moves on its reckless course, this imbalance must finally lead to a destructive, full-scale war or into the whirlpools of various latent and blatant power struggles intermingled with periods of false peace. Destruction? One world empire? Confused anarchy? The future of the world is not a bright one.

In this situation we cannot but perceive historical evil and awaken to mankind's karma. This is historical evil in the sense of an evil which has indeed gone beyond the individual's moral power; it is the karma, hard to eradicate, which people bear as something deeply rooted in the basic experience and character of mankind. However, this does not mean that we should despair of overcoming this historical evil. We must not simply view this karma of mankind from the sidelines. It is certainly true that the nation-state is now being transformed into an historical evil and that its control exceeds our individual power. And yet we must recognize that the source of this historical evil is rooted very deeply *within ourselves*. We ought not to criticize national egoism merely as an external force, but rather we ought to awaken to it as a collective responsibility deriving its reality from the human karma of each of us. To criticize this admonition by saying that this is the subjectifying and conceptualizing of an objective situation, or a kind of defeatism, is possible only from the viewpoint of one who does not know what sort of a thing 'Subjective' Self-awakening is.

Apart from the investigation of the world and of history, there is no true investigation of the original nature of the Self. The investigation of what the world or history is is fundamentally linked with the investigation of what the true Self is. Apart from the investigation of the original nature of the Self, there is no true investigation of the world or history; the true 'Subjective' Self-awakening is the Self-awakening to the source of world evil and historical evil within one's self. In awakening to the true Self, one breaks through the ego and simultaneously overcomes the source of world evil and historical evil, thereby manifesting and opening up the true path which enlivens both the self and others. Moreover, this is not our point of arrival but our point of departure. Unless we stand in that place, we cannot advance toward the true overcoming of all world evil and historical evil, for only there can we find the true starting point.

Historical evil cannot be resolved simply within history. For it has roots in the radical evil latent at the foundation of history itself. To believe blindly, in spite of this, that one can resolve historical

evil within history, and to act accordingly, only rapidly increases
the historical evil and finally gives rise to a demonic historical evil.
For historical evil can only be resolved from a standpoint transcending history. It can be resolved only by taking the Self-awakening of
the original Self as the basic foundation.

IV

What is necessary for the present day is not a new humanism but
a new cosmology. We must overcome anthropocentrism and
build such a new cosmology. The world of mankind's sovereignty
will also be built therein.

Although we assert that sovereignty resides in mankind, this
does not mean anthropocentrism. Through the realization of the
sovereign state as a product of karma rooted deeply within basic
human nature, and through the realization of the solidarity of this
karma at the depths of individual human existence the 'expanse of
Self-awakening' opens up. It extends into all directions embracing
everything in the universe beyond human beings. Accordingly it
truly transcends anthropocentrism. The 'expanse of self-awakening' – which awakens mankind to its realization as a single,
self-aware entity in the universe – is in itself cosmological. Without
overcoming anthropocentrism – that is, without standing in a new
cosmology – mankind cannot become a human society in the sense
of one self-aware entity.

Consequently, the ethics of mankind must have two aspects: an
interhuman aspect within mankind, and an aspect which concerns
human responsibility to the non-human universe. A human community which has overcome, through Self-awakening, the existence
of the nation-state as a product of the karma of mankind, serves
mankind by transcending distinctions between races and between
people. Sovereignty which is established therein, takes self-negation
as a basic principle and encompasses all races and all peoples
in their respective particularity. For the human community as a
self-aware entity, races and peoples are no longer basic political
entities linked by power but rather are cultural and ethical existences which give life to the individual and which, through the
actions of individuals, are harmonized with mankind. Such non-
political groupings of people, without restraining the individual,

allow for free, creative activity and naturally serve human society and enrich the content of human culture. Mankind can become the bearer of history only by the realization of the individual as mediator, who is freely acting on the basis of his or her own cultural identity.

This ethic of mankind within mankind always interpenetrates with the ethics of mankind in the universe. 'The expanse of Self-awakening', which awakens mankind as a single, self-aware entity and at the same time which awakens within it the ethics of mankind, also awakens the ethics of mankind as it faces the myriad phenomena of the universe. An age wherein the power of the nation-state alienates the individual from mankind and does not truly enliven either the individual or mankind is precisely an age which also alienates mankind from the universe, or the individual from the myriad phenomena of the universe, and pushes the simple harmony established between them toward disruption. However, the sovereignty of mankind, in which the community of man has awakened to itself as mankind in 'the expanse of Self-awakening', does not consider such things as land, water, air, the sun, and all kinds of energy only as the common resources of mankind but considers them as the common blessings on behalf of the myriad phenomena of the universe. Of course all the space in the universe, beginning with the moon, is not something which should be occupied and exploited only by a specific nation. In fact, it should not be treated simply from the human point of view. Mankind is enveloped by the universe and enlivened by it. At the same time, unlike other creatures in our world man alone self-consciously comprehends the universe and is able to awaken to the generation, extinction, and change of the universe. He alone enlivens the universe in the true sense. That which constitutes the *moment* of Self-awakening of this mankind – which is comprehended by and yet comprehends the universe – is precisely each one of us. It is the 'Subjective' Self-awakening of each individual.

In the 'Subjective' Self-awakening of each one of us, not only is mankind awakened to its own true nature but indeed the myriad phenomena of the universe are awakened to their true nature. This occurs in the same place, that is, in 'the expanse of Self-awakening'. Only in this cosmological place wherein we have overcome anthropocentrism can mankind and mankind's sovereignty be established in the sense of a single, living self-aware entity.

V

In ancient times, mankind was in considerable harmony with the universe. After this primitive cosmological age, the age of the "theory of the human", wherein we awakened to the idea of human beings as distinct from nature, lasted for many centuries and gave rise in recent times to anthropocentrism. The absolute sovereign state is one result of this anthropocentrism. Only in an historical Self-awakening wherein we have overcome anthropocentrism and wherein we open up a new age of a Self-awakened cosmology are the negation and overcoming of the sovereign state possible.

In the distant past mankind existed within nature, in some sense well harmonized with nature, and was assimilated with the universe. In this phase there was a primitive cosmology but there was no 'theory of the human'. The period in which people departed from this early primitive cosmology was what Karl Jaspers has termed 'the *axis* age' (*Achsenzeit*). The second period which began at that point I shall here term 'the age of the theory of the human'. The philosophy of Socrates, which took as its motto 'Know thyself' is its archetype. It departed from both nature and the primitive cosmology, and we may say that the self-consciousness of a human as a 'human' explicitly began at that point. The tradition of Hebraism represented by Deutero-Isaiah and Jesus cannot directly be termed one of 'the theory of the human' but the post-cosmological and even anti-natural theism which we can see therein has in fact latent within it a rather strong 'theory of the human'. Both Confucius and Gautama Buddha developed their unique theories of the human. Yet, while their theories overcame the previous primitive cosmology, they also were inextricably related to a new cosmology, and particularly in the case of the Buddha, this tendency was prominent. Socrates' 'theory of the human' was not anthropocentric, but anthropocentrism was latent in its foundation. The latent anthropocentrism which we can see in Hellenism for a time received the baptism of the theism of Hebraism. This theism was eventually negated, and what emerged after being stimulated by the strong anti-natural 'human-theory' which existed within that theism is precisely modern Western anthropocentrism.

The modern Western ideologies which take this anthropocentrism as their basic principle and the various systems which are its products, such as democracy, capitalism, socialism, communism, and technocracy, control the present-day world. The absolute sovereign state which takes power politics as its basic principle is also one of its products. Today this state as the power structure which has linked itself to gigantic systems of production and to frightening technical systems with nuclear weapons at their apex has an utterly different character from all the other national forms of the past.

This anthropocentrism is now creating in all the dimensions of mankind — individual, race, class, and nation — endless conflicts which have at their base ego and power. At the same time, its anti-natural character, by destroying the natural order, is being transformed into an anti-human character which conversely threatens the very basis of mankind's existence. Anthropocentrism, at its limit, is plunging mankind itself into a trap of its own making. The opposition of sovereign super-states which do not know self-negation, the ceaseless possibilities of the total destruction of mankind by a nuclear war, the strange uneasiness of a world peace brought about only by a balance of terror — all of these are aspects of the self-entrapment produced by anthropocentrism in the political dimension.

The contemporary era is not simply an age of *mappō* (the end of the Law), but one of *hōmetsu* (the extinction of the Law). By the essential failure of anthropocentrism as it has been revealed, human beings are losing their very centre. Neither a simple cosmology, nor God, nor man can any longer become the centre to which one can entrust his or her existence. What basic law remains other than cosmos, God and man? All laws have ceased to exist. Now mankind is 'living-and-dying' in an age of lawlessness. This age of the extinction of the law, or lawlessness, always contains the danger of turning into a demonic age. Mankind today must overcome in principle anthropocentrism and must stand in the boundless 'expanse of Self-awakening' wherein God, man, and the myriad phenomena of the universe become vibrantly alive. This is a completely new cosmological standpoint. It is the standpoint of *a Self-awakened cosmology* which includes the primitive cosmology, theism, and the 'theory of the human' as well. Only in this standpoint of a Self-awakened cosmology can mankind be Self-aware of itself as a single, self-aware entity.

We must realize that today we are living and dying in an age of the extinction of the Law and the emergence of lawlessness. We must also realize that we are, therefore, exposed to the danger that it will become a demonic age. Without this historical self-realization, it will be impossible to build a world wherein sovereignty rests with mankind; likewise, it will be impossible to overcome the present-day sovereign states.

Until now, the nation-state was necessary. Now, however, the nation-state has been transformed into a demonic existence. The age of the nation-state must end. The age of mankind must begin. But, to achieve this, we must awaken to the collective responsibility for the karma rooted deeply in the basic character of mankind. And we must overcome anthropocentrism. We must enter the third historical age of mankind, namely, the age of Self awakened cosmology. We each must awaken to the root of world evil and historical evil deeply within the self and – in the identical foundation of self, the world, and history – we must awaken to the original Self which has broken through the ego. We must take the cosmological 'expanse of Self-awakening' which opens up therein as the new foundation of mankind and, transcending peoples and national boundaries, we must proceed to build a *solidarity of Self-awakening* which includes mankind in the broadest sense. We must build a cooperative society of mankind within the universe. Herein lies the practical task of all mankind today.

16 The End of World Religion

To begin with I would like to clarify the implications of my title. The word 'end' has at least two meanings: it means 'limit', 'boundary', or 'ceasing to be', and 'aim', 'objective', 'purpose', or 'reason for being'. In the first sense, it is somewhat negative, referring to a spatial, temporal, or existential limit of some kind. The second, more positive, meaning signifies a direction to move toward, a final goal to be attained, or an ultimate reason to be realized. This double implication gives a dynamic ambiguity quite appropriate to the present purpose, for I wish to discuss the limitations of 'world religions' in their present forms and the authentic form of the 'world religion' to be realized in the future.

Thus, 'The End of World Religion' means on the one hand that world religions in their present form, largely because of recent radical changes in world conditions and the human situation, are coming to an end, reaching their 'limit' in the sense they no longer genuinely deserve to be called 'world religions'. On the other hand, it signifies that, therefore, a genuine form of 'world religion' must be now sought and actualized as the end, that is, as an 'aim' to be achieved in order to cope with the present and future world situation and human predicament.

With this double connotation in mind, let me begin with an explanation of the term 'world religion'. Mensching, for instance, classifies religions into three categories: nature religion (*Naturreligion*), ethnic religion (*Volksreligion*), and world religion (*Weltreligion*). In the long ages of pre-history, human beings were in the stage of nature religion or primitive religion. Involved in the adventure of life, people felt in nature something divine which was sometimes helpful, sometimes destructive, and they worshiped natural powers with a feeling of gratitude and fear. Nature religion is a type of

261

religion which arose spontaneously among primitive people living in close contact with their natural environment, and was supported by a family, kinship group, clan, or tribe. In this type of religion there was an almost total interfusing of man, nature, and gods. 'Undifferentiation', a term to be discussed below, was its fundamental characteristic. On the other hand, ethnic religion, which generally may be said to have appeared with the dawning of human 'culture', is a type of religion in which a separation between man and nature, and between man and gods, was consciously realized and various ritual forms were developed largely to overcome that separation. Thus, ethnic religion is a relatively developed form of religion in which the person, being aware of something 'transcendent' or 'super-natural', is to some extent freed from nature. It is supported by a much larger body of people, such as a racial group or a nation. Some examples of ethnic religion may be mentioned here: the religions of ancient Egypt, Persia, Greece, Rome, India, and in its larger and still existing forms, Judaism, Hinduism, Taoism, and Shintoism. Despite the differences in *form*, however, ethnic or national religion is not essentially different from primitive or nature religion in *structure* because it also can be said to occur spontaneously within a particular living community characterized by geographical or cultural and blood relations. Furthermore, in both primitive and ethnic religions, though with some difference of degree, the principle of community is stronger than that of individual or personal consciousness.

World religion, however, is essentially different from both primitive and ethnic religions in its *structure*. Christianity, Islam, and Buddhism – these three great religions can be rightly called 'world religions'. Each of them emerged from an ethnic or national religion. But they are different in structure from their mother religions in at least the following six senses:

1.   A world religion, such as Christianity, Islam, or Buddhism, has universality. It is able to spread beyond a particular race or nation without being forever confined to that social and historical community in which it was born. In this sense, a world religion is free, not only from dependence on nature, but also from all forms of nationhood.

2.   The ethnic religions came into being more or less spontaneously in and through the tradition of community formed by a particular ethnic group, and consequently, all members of the

given group automatically and almost unconsciously belong to that religion. But each of the three world religions had a unique religious personality – Jesus, Muhammad, and Gautama – as its founder. They each proclaimed a universal salvation for mankind and a universal religious truth which they realized through a particular, decisive, and personal experience. The followers or the members of a world religion are each required to consciously and deliberately accept the truth expounded by their founder.

3. Ethnic religion develops a religious life basic and common to the particular group in which it originated. It often emphasizes the particularity of its religious life as different from that of other groups and, therefore, tends to be closed and exclusive. A world religion, on the other hand, is a special religious body whose members participate not automatically by virtue of birth, but voluntarily, by the conscious option of each individual. In stressing the universal nature of its religious truth for all mankind, it is open and all-inclusive. Eventually, proselytization becomes essential to it.

4. Ethnic religion has usually penetrated into the political, legal, economic, and moral life, and also into the social customs of the community in which it originates. It thus provides a principle of social-cultural integrity for the group. A political and military ruler is often at the same time a religious leader, and may be regarded by his or her followers as a high priest or prophet. Contrary to this, a world religion tends to reject or go beyond secular authority and this-worldliness, and thus to emphasize transcendent truth and other-worldliness in such forms as the 'Kingdom of God' or the 'Pure Land'. Separation from politics and freedom of faith are the ideals of world religion.

5. Due to its generally spontaneous and natural origin within a given community, ethnic religion is often lacking a canonical scripture, articulated dogma, and organized religious order. In contrast, world religions are based on the scriptures and systematized doctrines originating in the teaching of the founder. They also have well-organized religious bodies in which the founders are worshiped as divine beings, prophets, or ideal personalities who are imitated as models.

6. In the religious life of ethnic religions, the community has priority over its component individuals. But in world religion

the personal and internal realization of each individual member is emphasized as essential, though consciousness of community is, of course, not altogether lacking. Thus, its beliefs and values take root in the innermost core of human existence. Here, the universal nature of world religion, as inclusive of all mankind, is inseparably connected with the individualistic emphasis and internal self-realization of its members.

While the religions which typify any one of these three main types may have characteristics belonging to the other, I am using the categorization which pertains to their underlying structure. These three categories may be said to have emerged in human history in correspondence with three stages in the development of human consciousness. In nature or primitive religion man and nature were almost completely one; human being was un-self-differentiated, with little awareness of separation from nature. 'God' was at this stage more or less identical with nature. Thus, at the primitive level, 'nature' was the most basic and all-inclusive notion, and 'undifferentiation' was its fundamental characteristic.

In ethnic religion, human separation from nature and separation from God came to be consciously realized. This set humans free from nature and, to some extent, over against God. Rituals and ceremonies developed to overcome this sense of separation. In ethnic religion, however, humans realized themselves as members of some community, a family, clan, tribe or nation, with ceremonies and rituals common to that community. Not nature on the one hand or individual consciousness on the other, but human community is basic. In this connection, though, we should not overlook that such notions as will, self, and soul are important in the more developed forms of ethnic religion, as in the case of Judaism and Hinduism.

By contrast, in world religions, the person is realized as an individual existence. He or she is realized as a being who is free, not only from nature, but also from community. The separations between humans and nature and humans and God are deeply felt – yet these separations are conceived as capable of being overcome, not simply by means of those rituals common to the community, but more essentially through faith or awakening in the depths of the individual's inner spirit. Thus, not the person as a member of a community, but the person as an independent individual being is basic in world religions. Without such an individualized consciousness, neither nature, community, nor God can be truly realized.

Hence, world religion may be said to correspond to the most advanced stage of human consciousness in which nature, humans, and God are all dynamically included.

II

Christianity, Islam, and Buddhism, respectively, have spread well beyond their motherlands to cover vast areas of the earth. With Judaism as its matrix, Christianity was born in Palestine and has been propagated to all parts of the earth. Islam arose in Arabia, but has gained large numbers of followers among the peoples not only of Arab countries but also those of Africa, India and Southeast Asia. Originating in India from its mother Hinduism, Buddhism has spread into almost all of the countries of Asia, and has recently been transmitted to Hawaii, the American continent, and, to some extent, Europe. As the aim of each of the three religions is the universal salvation of mankind, they are called 'universal religions' as well as 'world religions'.

Here I should like to focus on the two world religions with which I am most familiar. Although Christianity is undoubtedly one of the great world religions, in its present form it has what must be called an 'occidental' character. As we know, the Judaic form of primitive Christianity was blended with Hellenism almost from its beginning and subsequently was Romanized, Germanized, and predominantly in Europe and America, finally 'modernized'. Throughout the course of its long history, Christianity has thus come to be embodied in the very foundation of Western culture and civilization. This embodiment is so deep and fundamental that without a sufficient understanding of Christianity no aspect of Western culture and civilization can be properly understood. At the same time, Christianity itself has thereby developed both in terms of faith and thought in response to the needs of Western people. Christianity in its present form, then, is primarily the historical result of an intertwining of Christianity, Western culture, and Western ways of thinking. On the other hand, as Western culture has also come to be embodied in Christianity, can we not say that the interfusing of Christianity and Western culture throughout their long history, an interfusing which has provided Christianity with a rich legacy as a world religion, has also limited it as an occidental form of world religion?[1]

This becomes quite clear when Christianity is introduced to non-occidental countries. It appears as foreign to the Easterner as it is familiar to the Westerner. In non-occidental countries, Christianity is often accepted or rejected not necessarily because of its essential nature as a religion, but because of its Western character. In order for Christianity to become a world religion in the genuine sense, it must break through the limits of its present occidental form.

The same may be said of Buddhism. Because of its universal nature, it deserves to be called a world religion. It has spread throughout Southeast Asia, Tibet, China, Korea, and Japan, far beyond the boundaries of its native India. In its long history, Buddhism has taken root deeply in Asian countries, and has thus come to embody the oriental cultures. Although the Buddhisms of India, Southeast Asia, China, and Japan each have their own regional characteristics, the present forms of Buddhism are all strongly coloured by Eastern cultures in general. Hence, just as in the case of Christianity, Buddhism, through its closely interrelated association with various Eastern cultures, has been provided with the qualitative richness of a world religion, and yet, in doing so has developed the limitation of becoming an oriental form of world religion. Recently, Buddhism has been introduced to the Western world and it too seems to be accepted or rejected often just because of its non-Western, oriental character.

I have said that Christianity and Buddhism have developed as world religions through their associations with the Western and Eastern cultures respectively and that as a result, they go no further in their present forms than being occidental and oriental forms of world religion. This is a historical fact and must be recognized as such. Further, there is no such thing as the 'essence' of Christianity or Buddhism *in history*. It can only be a non-historical abstraction. However transcendent it may seek or believe itself to be, a religion must of necessity take a particular historical form. It can develop itself only under certain given historical and cultural conditions. The result of this undeniable fact, for both Christianity and Buddhism, is that in their present forms, Christianity is an occidental, and Buddhism an oriental world religion. While recognizing this historical necessity, I also believe that we are coming to a point in history where we can no longer accept Christianity and Buddhism in their present historical forms as representing their *final* development. This is because the meaning of the concept of 'world', and with it the human situation and human spiritual needs as well, are now all in the process of radical change.

III

The world, we are all aware, is shrinking. With the extraordinary development of scientific technology, especially in the areas of travel and communication, geographical distances are largely overcome. No nation can now stand isolated from the rest of the world. Political, economic, and cultural interrelations between nations are drawing them increasingly closer together. We are rapidly becoming 'one world'.

That is not to say, however, that this 'oneness' is therefore harmonious. As technological advancements shrink the world, the interrelating ties between nations are drawn tighter and tighter, in a negative as well as positive sense. On the positive side, mutual understanding and cooperation among nations heretofore isolated from each other are gradually increasing. Negatively, as the differences and oppositions among nations in quest of their national interest become more conspicuous and acute, new forms of conflict arise on a greater scale than ever before. But these positive and negative aspects together signify that every nation in the world now comes to share a common destiny. This appears with growing clarity when we see that none of the important issues – the population explosion, use of natural resources, energy, food, pollution, disarmament, prevention of the proliferation of nuclear weapons, and so forth – can be solved without worldwide cooperation. How often we are told of the real possibility of the total destruction of mankind by nuclear weapons. 'To be or not to be' is now a question for the world as a whole. All mankind now shares a common fate.

Until recently the term 'world' has been generally understood as a collection or gathering of various nations. In this context, the world has been apprehended from the quantitative point of view. The League of Nations and the United Nations typify this view. A nation is the basic unit from which the world is made up. 'International' has been used in its broadest sense interchangeably with the term 'world'. An 'international exposition', for instance, is often called a 'world's fair'. The world is thus being apprehended from the side of the component nations, not from its own side.

I believe this understanding is now out of date. We must go beyond it, because our world is now becoming something more than a mere collection of various countries. We are now, in actuality, one single community sharing one and the same destiny. All mankind, as a qualitative whole, above and beyond particular nations or a particular group of nations, is now facing the common risk of uncertain survival. In such a situation, it must be repeated, the meaning and character of the 'world' is radically changing. I would like to maintain, therefore, that the term 'world' should now be grasped qualitatively rather than quantitatively – that is, not as a mere gathering of various nations but as one single human community participating in a common life and sharing the same fate. The nation is no longer the true unit for understanding the world; the world itself is the one basic unit. Accordingly, we should not seek to comprehend or apprehend the 'world' from the side of the 'nation'. We should deal rather with the nation from the standpoint of the world. In this sense, the term 'international' can no longer be synonymous with the term 'world'. The world is now 'trans-international'.

In the same way, it is no longer sufficient to talk about East and West as if the world consisted of two parts. Although the world can be so divided two-dimensionally, the East, the West and their mutual relation must be grasped three-dimensionally, as well as other cultural and economic divisions, dynamically, from the standpoint of one world.

If, at present and in the future, the term 'world' is to be grasped qualitatively as one single human community sharing the same destiny in which the East, the West and the various different nations are dynamically included – and I believe this is the reality of our situation – then we cannot simply accept as definitive the historical fact of Christianity as an occidental and Buddhism as an oriental world religion. Instead, if both Christianity and Buddhism are indeed 'world religions' in their essence, they must break through the limits of their respective occidental and oriental characters and, thereby, become *universal forms of world religion*, that is, world religions in the genuine sense. By a 'universal form of world religion', I do not necessarily mean a world religion which spreads on a worldwide scale, for that is 'worldwide' merely in the geographical and, therefore, quantitative sense. This quantitative approach has to be transcended because we are coming to a point in history when the world must be grasped from a qualitative point of view.

Instead of seeking to spread Christianity and Buddhism all over the world in the geographical sense, we must try to regrasp their universal natures as genuine world religions. It is only through the re-realization of their conceptions of universal salvation in the deepest sense that Christianity can become truly indigenous to the East and become an oriental form of Christianity, and that Buddhism can take root in the soil of the West as an occidental form of Buddhism. These will be the concrete forms taken by the two religions when they become truly universal world religions.

However, this is not to suggest that Christianity should simply put on eastern robes and become an oriental world religion or that Buddhism in the West should assume occidental dress. Just as Christianity has been both positive and necessary for Western people through its expression as an occidental world religion, should it express itself as an oriental form of Christianity, it will certainly be able to become something positive and necessary to Eastern people as well. As I mentioned before, however, the present limitations of Christianity even as an *occidental* world religion must be seriously called into question. Accordingly, an 'expansionist view' with regard to Christianity, the hope that it will merely broaden itself so as to become an oriental world religion as well, would be not only inadequate, it would also be somewhat of a mistake. Rather, for Christianity to become a universal religion in the authentic sense for all mankind, it must, first of all, go beyond its present occidental form and regrasp its spirit of universal salvation, regrasp, that is, its universal essence as a world religion which has become obscured and even somewhat limited as a consequence of its close association with Western culture. Only if its universal essence as a world religion is truly regrasped, will Christianity have a sufficient basis from which to freely express itself in the East as an oriental world religion. As an essentially universal religion, Christianity itself is *neither* an occidental *nor* an oriental world religion, and yet, in the process of history, in accordance with geographical and cultural circumstances, it can become *both* an occidental *and* an oriental world religion. This entails more than a mere change of garments. Since through its embodiment of Western culture the occidental garment Christianity now wears is so tightly interwoven with the Christian notion of salvation, even the 'body' of Christianity has come to be limited by an occidental character and must be changed to meet the spiritual needs of contemporary people, Easterners included. And precisely what has been said in the previous paragraph about Christianity can be applied, *mutatis mutandis*, to the present situation of Buddhism.

In short, both Christianity and Buddhism must break through the traditional forms of occidental and oriental world religion and become equally indigenous to both East and West, and yet must be free in essence from both occidental and oriental forms. Herein lies the real meaning, given the present historical situation, of the re-realization of the notions of universal salvation implied in these two religions. To become a 'universal' world religion does not imply a monolithic religion common to East and West, but rather calls for a dynamic structure capable of freely assuming any form, oriental or occidental, according to the area in which it develops and yet without being confined by any limitation of that area. Such a *dynamic* realization of the 'universal' world religion may become possible for Christianity and Buddhism should they genuinely regrasp their respective notions of universal salvation for all mankind.

This regrasping of their universal nature as genuine world religions has become equally necessary for Christianity in the West and Buddhism in the East. Both religions have been so deeply assimilated in the Western and Eastern minds respectively that, having lost their freshness and vitality, they appear quite obsolete and outmoded in their own societies. Here again, the need is urgent for the two religions to overcome their age-old, worn-out frameworks, to reconfirm their universal natures as religions truly applicable to all mankind, and to revitalize a genuine religious spirit on their own homegrounds.

In these two senses, that is, in order to become indigenous in the new spheres and to be revitalized in the old, both Christianity and Buddhism must now overcome the limitations of their present forms which have been historically and parochially developed. In the light of the new meaning of the term 'world', neither Christianity nor Buddhism in their present forms can be properly called a 'world religion' in the genuine sense of the term because their universal nature is still largely limited by an occidental or oriental character. Here I refer to the first implication of 'The End of World Religion', that is, the *final limit* or *cessation* of the present form of world religions such as Christianity and Buddhism.[2]

IV

Now I will take up the second implication of my title, 'The End of World Religion', the *aim* to be attained and realized by world religions.

In his Epistle to the Romans, Paul said, 'There is no distinction between Jew and Greek. The same Lord is Lord of all.' In his day, the distinction between Jew and Greek was, if anything, more fundamental than that between Easterner and Westerner in our time. This is not so difficult to imagine when we are reminded of the question of circumscision and non-circumcision in his day. Nevertheless, Paul insisted that there was no distinction between Jew and Greek. Surely this must have been due to his profound insight into the religious truth universal to human existence beyond the difference between Jewish and Greek ways of life. Following Saint Paul, we must now say 'there is no distinction between Easterner and Westerner', and see that religious truth which is common to Easterner and Westerner alike transcends oriental or occidental characteristics.[3] The need for us all to awaken to universal salvation in its most universal form is of pressing urgency, for the world is now becoming one single community with one common destiny: to perish or survive.

Christianity emerged from a Judaic background. Buddhism was born from ancient Hinduism. Although both propound universal salvation and can in that sense be called 'world religions', their basic natures are quite different. This is due at least in part to the different characters of their parent religions and in part to the different personalities of their founders.

Judaism is an ethnic religion in which the obedience or disobedience of the human will to the will of God is the crucial issue. It may be said to have gone beyond its original primitive stages, in which everything was undifferentiated, by means of an intense realization of the divine – human separation. In Judaism, God is the One, the transcendent, personal God who creates, sustains, and rules humans and the world, and above all commands people to achieve righteousness. Hence it is a highly ethical religion in which the separation or unity of humans and nature becomes a peripheral issue. Christianity, which became a world religion by breaking through the ethnic framework of Judaism, places its emphasis on Jesus Christ as the ideal of reuniting humans and God, and preaches the universal salvation of mankind through the sacrificial love of God manifested in Christ. Just as in Judaism, however, so too in Christianity human obedience or disobedience to the will of God is crucial, and although here also divine justice or righteousness is emphasized, it is seen as included in God's love. The issue of the separation or unity of humans with nature is, of course, peripheral. The problem of evil and sin is more profoundly felt than is the problem of life and death, as typified in Paul's 'the wages of sin is death'. Death is realized as the *result* of sin and not the other way around.

On the other hand, Hinduism, from which Buddhism emerged, is an ethnic religion in which some awareness of a separation between humans, nature, and God does exist. A pantheon of transcendent deities and various forms of ritual practice exist to overcome these separations. Although the problem of human will takes the form of karma, the concept of karma is cosmic as well as human. Therefore it is not primarily an ethical religion. It is a nature-or-cosmos-oriented religion in which the problem of life and death, a problem common to humans and other living beings, is more seriously coped with than the problem of good and evil. Breaking through the ethnic character inherent in Hinduism, Buddhism became a world religion by advocating a universal salvation through awakening to one's true nature, which is possible regardless of caste differences. Just as in Hinduism, however, in Buddhism the problem of life and death is taken more seriously than that of good and evil, and an absolute God who commands justice is absent.

True, Christianity and Buddhism opened up new ways of direct contact with the ultimate Reality available to all humans by breaking through the frameworks of their ethnic communities. They realized spiritual freedom from subordination to nature and community and attained individual consciousness in its deepest dimension. It must be emphasized, however, that the ways in which Christianity and Buddhism have overcome their original ethnic frameworks are not the same.

Christianity broke through the ethnic limits of its parent religion in a more personalistic, more transnatural direction, a direction in which divine will and word are basic. On the contrary, Buddhism overcame its original ethnic framework in the direction of a primordial naturalness that returns to the undifferentiation of all things, the original 'suchness' prior to will and word. Herein Buddhism radically reaffirmed the undifferentiation implied in nature religion.

The difference may be explained in the following three ways:

1. In Christianity the separation between humans and God, which was already realized in Judaism, came to be more deeply and thoroughly realized, to the extent that finally human separation from God could be overcome only through Jesus Christ, the embodiment of unconditional, self-sacrifical love. Thus, in Christianity the divine-human separation is more strongly emphasized than the primordial oneness, and the reunion of humans and God which must be attained is more essential than any type of direct awareness, here and now, of that oneness. In Buddhism it is this primordial oneness, rather than any divine–human separation that is primarily emphasized. It aims at the immediate return to original naturalness rather than toward some ideal transnatural state.

2. Accordingly, Christianity is more value-oriented, norm-oriented, future-oriented, and tends to be ethical and teleological. The holy is to be experienced in something normative, in the 'ought to be', and the absolute is regarded as something authoritative, embodying absolute righteousness. Although God's unconditional love is perhaps most basic here, the issue of obedience or disobedience to the divine ruler and judge is never neglected.

   Buddhism is nature-oriented, present-oriented rather than future-oriented, and tends to be mystical and ontological. The holy is realized in something natural, something already present here. The absolute is regarded as something intimate, a harmonious unity. The ideas of judgment and punishment, although not lacking, are much less central.

3. The divine–human relationship in Christianity may be better compared to the father–child relationship. Fatherhood represents norm, order, and justice. Sonship is ambivalent toward fatherhood. The son loves and hates the authoritative father at the same time. As the son's separation, independence, and autonomy in relation to the father is thus inevitable, an objective of reunion is sought. As Christianity is paternalistic, divine love always includes the notions of justice and righteousness. Since will is basically important, its exercise produces autonomy but also tends toward individualism.

   On the other hand, the divine-human relationship in Buddhism has a better analogy in the mother-child relation. The mother represents acceptance, unity, and harmony. The child originates within the mother. It is embraced by the mother. The more a child struggles with self-estrangement and alienation from the world after his independence, the more he longs to return to his mother's bosom. As Buddhism is maternalistic, it is receptive, incorporative, and tends toward community, but implies the risk of losing individuality.

V

Today, many people feel alienated and rootless. They have lost their home, their place of ultimate rest. The prevailing scientific, mechanistic, and objectivistic way of thinking has severed our age-old connection with our spiritual home. The principle of conflict, dominant among nations and social classes, and the individualistic tendency among today's peoples have destroyed the original unity of this home. There is alienation from nature, from family, from community, from the world, and from oneself. In reality, all forms of alienation originate in self-alienation, i.e., alienation from oneself through self-consciousness. Without self-alienation, alienation from nature, from family, from community, and from the world does not occur. This is the basic structure of alienation. The contemporary alienation or estrangement people are suffering, however, is strongly characterized by the mental climate of the contemporary society. People are separated from the abode of final rest in a way peculiar to today. 'Homelessness' is the symbol of our time, both in East and West. People come and go from East to West, from West to East, seeking new and foreign religions in the hope and expectation of thereby finding their 'home'. However, an interest in exotic, different types of religion will not suffice. The human situation we now face is too serious and critical for such remedies. As the world becomes a single human community sharing the same concern for survival, each individual in it is forced far more deeply than ever to reappropriate his or her humanity and individuality. We can be no more satisfied with mere paternalistic Christianity as an occidental form of world religion, than with mere maternalistic Buddhism as an oriental form of world religion. Both father and mother are needed to provide a real 'home' for us. Yet this should not be seen only as a mixture of Christianity and Buddhism. Christianity, we can see from its mystical tradition, is not totally lacking the maternal, receptive aspect, nor is Buddhism, judging from Nichiren, entirely alien to the paternal and justice-oriented aspect. However, neither in Christianity nor in Buddhism have these two essential aspects been thoroughly and harmoniously realized. But, to cope with the radically changing meaning of the 'world' and the resultant human predicament, Christianity and Buddhism must break through their respective occidental–paternal, oriental–maternal structures. Each must develop and deepen itself to achieve a universal form of world religion. It is for this reason that the encounter and dialogue between Christianity and Buddhism is now urgent. By deepening themselves to realize universal forms of world religion, Christianity and Buddhism can become religions in which both the paternal and maternal aspects are fully actualized in unique ways. As stated earlier, in Christianity and Buddhism, freedom of spirit and a deep individual inner consciousness have, in principle, already been realized. Thus, should they develop into universal forms of world religion, the notion of the undifferentiation of humans, nature, and God found in nature religion, and the principle of community realized in ethnic religion, can and will be *fully* developed. In this form of Christianity or Buddhism, the human, nature, and God will be clearly differentiated from one another and yet harmoniously, undifferentiatedly, interfused. Such is the *end* of world religion to be achieved for the salvation of the one world of the near future.

Some may say that both Christianity and Buddhism are now very old, perhaps too old for such a transformation. Certainly, Christianity was born twenty, and Buddhism twenty-five centuries ago. Their doctrines and church systems in their present forms are lifeless and antiquated. Personally, however, I would like to say that Christianity is *only* 2000 years old. Buddhism is *just* two thousand and five hundred years old. They are still quite young! Who can say with justification that the Logos actualized in Jesus and the Dharma realized by Gautama have already been exhaustively developed? Both are inexhaustible and full of life. If one comes to have immediate contact with the Logos and the Dharma in one's own being, how could one say that Christianity and Buddhism are too old?

The problem of 'The End of World Religion', in the double sense mentioned above, is not merely an objective and historical issue. It is our very own personal and existential problem. Whether or not one believes in the possibility of Christianity and Buddhism as future universal forms of world religion is entirely dependent upon whether or not one is in direct contact with the Logos and the Dharma.

Notes

CHAPTER 1:   ZEN IS NOT A PHILOSOPHY, BUT ...

1. Wu-têng Hui-yüan. (Ja *Gotōegen*) ed. Aishin Imaeda (Tokyo: Rinrōkaku Shoten, 1971) p. 335.
2. In Japanese there are two terms, *shukanteki* and *shutaiteki* which can be translated by only one English term, 'subjective'. *Shukanteki* is the equivalent in the epistemological sense – in terms of how to perceive, think, or know – to the English term 'subjective' as opposed to 'objective'. *Shutaiteki* refers more to a dynamic, existential self involved in responsible, self-determined action of a moral, ethical, or religious nature. It indicates the standpoint of existential commitment which is beyond the subject–object dichotomy in the epistemological sense. To indicate the distinction, 'Subjective' with a capital 'S' is used for *shutaiteki* throughout this book.
3. The negative realization of no differentiation (the second stage) is *necessary* in order for ultimate Reality to be disclosed (the third stage), but this does not imply that there must be a *time gap* between the realization of the second stage and that of the third stage. In Zen practice, the negative realization of no differentiation or no self of the 'second stage' and the positive realization of true differentiation or true Self of the 'third stage' *may occur simultaneously*. Great Death in the genuine sense out of which Great Rebirth takes place indicates nothing but the simultaneous realization of the second and third stages. However, as his discourse clearly shows, Wei-hsin experienced the first, second, and third stages successively. Such a record of a clear step-by-step process of deepening Zen realization is rare in Zen literature, so the present author analyses Wei-hsin's Zen experience along the lines of its deepening process. This analysis, however, does not exclude the possibility of the simultaneous realization of the second and third stages in Zen Awakening. In fact, as the author states in the latter part of the essay, in authentic Zen Awakening, the third and final stage includes the first and second stages and even the term 'stage' is not appropriate, for Zen Awakening is a total existential Awakening to the ultimate Reality which is beyond the negative and the positive as well as any step-by-step approach.
4. D. T. Suzuki, *An Introduction to Zen Buddhism* (London, 1949) p. 84.

CHAPTER 2:   DŌGEN ON BUDDHA-NATURE

1. Sokuō Etō (ed.), *Shōbōgenzo*, Iwanami-bunko edition (Tokyo: Iwanami Shoten, 1942) II, 'Butsudō' fascicle, p. 217.
2. 'Shamon' is the Japanese way of reading the Chinese transliteration of the

Sanskrit term, *śramaṇa*, which means monk, mendicant, or ascetic.

3. *Mappō* is the third and last period of the three periods of the Dharma after the Buddha's decease. These three are the periods of the right, the imitative, and the final (*shō-zō-matsu*) Dharma. The period of the right Dharma (*shōbō*) is the period in which Buddhist doctrine, practices, and enlightenment all exist; the second period is the period of the imitative Dharma (*zōhō*) in which doctrine and practices exist without enlightenment; the third period is that of the last or final (and degenerate) Dharma (*mappō*) in which only the doctrine remains but both practice and enlightenment have been lost. There are different views as to the duration of these periods. However, this doctrine was influential during the Heian and Kamakura periods, and at the time of Dōgen, people, including many Buddhist leaders, believed that their time was precisely the period of *mappō*. Unlike other Buddhist leaders of those days, Dōgen insisted that it was still the period of *shōbō*, not that of *mappō*.

4. The collection of Dōgen's discourses in Japanese, presently edited in 95 fascicles, which he delivered from 1231 to 1253. See *The Eastern Buddhist*, New Series (hereafter *E. B.*), vol. IV, no. I, pp. 125–6.

5. The 27th chapter, 'Lion's Roar Bodhisattva'. (Taishō, no. 375, p. 522 c).

6. Since the Chino-Japanese characters *shitsuu* do not make a distinction between singular and plural, *shitsuu* means both 'all being' in its entirety and 'all beings' in their individuality. Dōgen actually uses the term in these two meanings according to the context.

7. *Dōgenshū* (A collection of Dōgen) ed. Kōshirō Tamaki, *Nihon no shisō*, II (Tokyo: Chikuma Shobō, 1969) p. 146.

8. Strictly speaking, living beings other than human beings, such as animals, may not be said to realize their life and death even as 'facts', since they do not have self-consciousness.

9. Sanskrit '*manuṣya*,' like the English term 'man', is etymologically connected with '*man*' – to think. Hajime Nakamura, *The Ways of Thinking of Asian Peoples* (Tokyo: Japanese National Commission for UNESCO, 1960) pp. 108–10.

10. Keiji Nishitani, *Religion and Nothingness* (Berkeley: University of California Press, 1982) p. 49.

11. See Isshū Miura and Ruth Fuller Sasaki, *Zen Dust* (Kyoto: The First Zen Institute of America in Japan, 1966) pp. 253–5.

12. The Senika heresy was a heretical thought that appeared during the Buddha's lifetime, emphasizing the concept of a permanent self. It appears in the Nirvana Sutra, ch. 39. See also *E. B.*, vol. IV, no. I, pp. 145–8, and vol. VIII, no. 2, pp. 100–2.

13. *Shōbōgenzō*, I, 'Busshō' fascicle, p. 317. See *E. B.*, vol. VIII, no. 2, p. 102.

14. Ibid., p. 316, *E. B.*, ibid., pp. 99–100. When grasped neither in terms of the duality of body and soul, nor in terms of the duality of potentiality and actuality, all beings manifest themselves right here and now in their wholeness, totality, and suchness. This complete disclosure of 'all beings' takes place only in the dehomocentric boundless universe, the universe which is most fundamental for everything.

15. *Shōbōgenzō*, I, 'Busshō' fascicle, p. 315. See *E. B.*, vol. VIII, no. 2, p. 97.

16. *Immo*, the Japanese reading of the Chinese term 恁麼, a colloquial expression of the Sung dynasty often used in a Zen context. It is (1) an interrogative, meaning 'how', 'in what way', 'in what manner' and (2) a demonstrative, which signifies 'this', 'such', 'thus', 'thus and so', 'that', 'like that', etc. Here in

Hui-nêng's question, *immo* indicates the second meaning, particularly 'thus'. In *Shōbōgenzō*, Dōgen has a fascicle entitled 'Shōbōgenzō immo,' in which he discusses the Zen meaning of the term *immo* as he understands it.

17. See Chapter 1, 'Zen Is not a Philosophy, but ...' pp. 11–14.
18. *Ethics*, tr. by R. H. M. Elwes, in *Philosophy of Benedict de Spinoza* (NY: Tudor Publishing Company, n.d.) Part 1, def. 3.
19. *Speculation and Revelation in Modern Philosophy* (Philadelphia: The Westminster Press, n.d.) p. 126.
20. *Shōbōgenzō*, 1, 'Keiseisanshoku' fascicle, p. 139.
21. *Shōbōgenzō*, 1 'Busshō' fascicle, p. 317; *E. B.*, vol. VIII; no. 2, p. 102.
22. 'No Buddha-nature' refers to the ordinary idea of the term, i.e. the counterconcept of 'Buddha-nature'; 'no-Buddha-nature' indicates Dōgen's idea, i.e. the unobjectifiable Buddha-nature which is freed from 'having' or 'not having'.
23. *Shōbōgenzō*, 1 'Busshō' fascicle, p. 334; *E. B.*, vol. IX; no. 2, p. 74.
24. Ibid., pp. 321–2; *E. B.*, vol. VIII, no. 2, p. 111.
25. Ibid., pp. 334–5; *E. B.*, vol. IX, no. 2, pp. 74–5.
26. Ibid., p. 322; *E. B.*, vol. IX, no. 1, p. 87.
27. Ibid., pp. 322–3; *E. B.*, ibid., pp. 87–8.
28. Ibid., p. 322; *E. B.*, vol. VIII, no. 2, p. 111.
29. Ibid., p. 323. *E. B.*, vol. IX; no. 1, p. 88. In this paragraph Dōgen wanted to negate the idea of the endowment of the Buddha-nature *prior to* enlightenment and thus talked about its endowment *after* enlightenment. His fundamental idea, however, lies in the simultaneity of the Buddha-nature and enlightenment.
30. Ibid., p. 335; *E. B.*, vol. IX; no. 2, p. 75.
31. In the 'Genjōkōan' fascicle, Dōgen says, 'When buddhas are truly buddhas, there is no need for the perception that one is a buddha. Nevertheless, he is a confirmed buddha, performing the confirmation of buddha.' *Shōbōgenzō*, 1, p. 83; *E. B.*, vol. V; no. 2, p. 134.
32. *Shōbōgenzō* I, 'Busshō' fascicle, p. 315; *E. B.*, vol. VIII; no. 2, p. 97. Another interpretation of *shitsuu no isshitsu* which is, in the present text, translated 'All beings in their entirety', is 'A part of all beings' (is called *shujō*). Dōgen's view in Figure 2.2 follows this interpretation.
33. Ibid., p. 333; *E. B.*, vol. IX; no. 2, pp. 71–2.
34. Ibid., p. 315; *E. B.*, vol. VIII; no. 2, p. 98.
35. Paul Edwards (ed.), *The Encyclopedia of Philosophy*, (NY: The Macmillan Co. & The Free Press, 1967) vol. 3, p. 463.
36. *Sanbōin*. The other two are 'Nothing has an ego' and 'Nirvana is tranquil.'
37. *Shōbōgenzō*, 1, 'Busshō' fascicle, p. 325; *E. B.*, vol. IX, no. 1, p. 91.
38. Ibid., pp. 325–6; *E. B.*, vol. IX, no. 1, p. 93.
39. Ibid., II, 'Hosshō' fascicle, pp. 283–4.
40. *Science of Logic*, tr. by W. H. Johnston and L. G. Struthers, (London: G Allen & Unwin., 1929) vol. 1, p. 95. *Wissenschaft der Logik*, herausgegeben von Georg Lasson (Leipzig: Felix Meiner, 1923) P. B. Erster Teil, p. 67.
41. *Shōbōgenzō*, 1, 'Busshō' fascicle, p. 343; *E. B.*, vol. IX, no. 2, p. 87.
42. 'Cosmological' here does not refer to the cosmos created by or distingusihed from God, but to the cosmos in its broadest sense in which even 'God' is embraced.
43. See Chapter 1, 'Zen Is not a Philosophy, but, ...' p. 19.
44. *Shushōittō, Shōbōgenzō*, 1, 'Bendōwa' fascicle, p. 65; *E. B.*, vol. IV, no. 1, p. 144.

45. *Kenzeiki (Dainihon bukkyō zensho*, vol. 115, Tokyo, 1922); also see Heinrich Dumoulin: *History of Zen Buddhism* (NY: McGraw-Hill Book Co., 1965) p. 153.
46. *Shōbōgenzō*, I, 'Bendōwa' fascicle, pp. 67–70, See *E. B.*, vol. IV, no. I, pp. 145–8.
47. Ibid., p. 55. See *E. B.*, ibid., p. 129.
48. Ibid., pp. 65–6. See *E. B.*, ibid., p. 144.
49. Ibid., pp. 66–7. See *E. B.*, ibid., p. 145.
50. Ibid., p. 66. See *E. B.*, ibid., p. 144.
51. Ibid., p. 59. See *E. B.*, ibid., p. 136.
52. *Shōbōgenzō*, II, 'Sesshin-sesshō' fascicle, p. 208.
53. 'Undefiled' practice in Dōgen's sense does not indicate a mere moral or ethical purity realized through the observance of Buddhist precepts, but rather the practice of 'body-and-mind-cast-off', that is, the practice based on the complete negation of ego-centredness. This does not mean that undefiled practice as understood by Dōgen excludes the importance of observing precepts even though such observance is not a necessary *condition* for Awakening to one's Buddha-nature.
54. *Shōbōgenzō*, II, 'Zazengi' fascicle, p. 323; *E. B.*, vol. VI, no. 2, p. 127.
55. Ibid., I, 'Bendōwa' fascicle, p. 69; *E. B.*, vol. IV, no. I, p. 147.
56. *Gakudō-yōjinshū* in *Dōgen Zenji Goroku*, ed. Dōshū Ōkubo, Iwanami bunko edn (Tokyo: Iwanami Shoten, 1941) p. 42.
57. Ibid., p. 26.
58. *Shōbōgenzō*, II, 'Hotsubodaishin' fascicle, p. 407.
59. Hakujū Ui (ed.) *Hōkyōki*, Iwanami bunkō edn (Tokyo: Iwanami Shoten, 1940) p. 44.
60. *Shōbōgenzō*, I, 'Busshō' fascicle, p. 318; *E. B.*, vol. VIII, no. 2, p. 102. This is not an exact quotation from the Nirvana Sutra. It is partly based on Po-chang's (Hyakujō) words in *Rentō-eyō*, vol. 7.
61. Ibid.
62. Ibid.
63. Ibid., 'Kūge' fascicle, p. 171.
64. Ibid., 'Uji' fascicle, p. 164; *E. B.*, vol. XII, no. I, p. 126.
65. Ibid., p. 159; *E. B.*, ibid., p. 116.
66. See *E. B.*, ibid., p. 120.
67. *Shōbōgenzō*, I, 'Uji' fascicle, p. 161; *E. B.*, ibid., p. 120.
68. Ibid., I, 'Genjōkōan' fascicle, pp. 84–5. See *E. B.*, vol. V, no. 2, p. 136.
69. Ibid., I, 'Busshō' fascicle, p. 318; *E. B.*, vol. VIII, no. 2, p. 103.
70. Ibid., p. 319; *E. B.*, ibid., p. 104.
71. Ch'ing-yüan and others are eminent Zen masters of Táng China. They are not cited here in chronological order.
72. *Shōbōgenzō*, I, 'Uji' fascicle, p. 161; *E. B.*, vol. XII, no. I, pp. 120–1.
73. Although, in his later book, *Zur Sache des Denkens* (Tübingen: Max Neimeyer, 1969), Heidegger discusses 'Zeit und Sein' (Time and Being), emphasizing 'Ereignis' as a 'gift' of 'it' (*Es gibt*) in which time and being are inseparable, strictly speaking, Heidegger's position and Dōgen's are not the same.
74. *Shōbōgenzō*, I, p. 217.
75. Martin Heidegger: *Was ist Metaphysik?* (Vittorio Klosterman, Frankfurt A. M., 1949) p. 31.
76. *Shōbōgenzō*, I, 'Busshō' fascicle, p. 341; *E. B.*, vol. IX, no. 2, p. 84.

CHAPTER 3: TRUE PERSON AND COMPASSION –
D. T. SUZUKI'S APPRECIATION OF LIN-CHI AND
CHAO-CHOU

1. For translations of the *Lin-chi Lu*, see Ruth F. Sasaki, trans., *The Record of Lin-chi* (Kyoto, 1975); Paul Demiéville, trans., *Les Entretiens de Lin-tsi* (Fayard, 1972); and Irmgard Schloegl, *Zen Teaching of Rinzai* (Berkeley, 1976).
2. For translation of the *Chao-chou Lu*, see Yoel Hoffmann, trans., *Radical Zen – The Sayings of Jōshu* (Brookline, 1978).
3. Tōrei: *Gokesanshō-yōromon* (Taishō no. 2576, p. 607a).
4. *Essays in Zen Buddhism*, III (London, 1934) pp. 30–3 (hereafter *Essays*).
5. Published by Chūōkōron-sha; Tokyo: 1949; hereafter *RKS*, republished by Shunjū-sha, (Tokyo, 1961). It is included in *Suzuki Daisetz Zenshu*, 'The Collected Works of D. T. Suzuki', vol. III (Tokyo: Iwanami, 1968).
6. However, English translations of some important passages of the *Lin-Chi Lu* appear in the following writings of D. T. Suzuki: *Essays*, I (London, 1927) pp. 332–3; *Essays*, II (London, 1933) pp. 33–5; *Essays*, III, pp. 30–3; and *Zen Buddhism and Psychoanalysis* (New York, 1950) pp. 33–43 (hereafter *ZBP*).
7. *Jōshū Zenji Goroku* edited in collaboration with Ryōmin Akizuki (Kamakura: Matsugaoka Bunko, 1962; Tokyo: Shunjū-sha, 1963).
8. *ZBP*, p. 32. *The Record of Lin-chi*, trans. Ruth F. Sasaki (Kyoto, 1975) p. 3.
9. Ibid., p. 32.
10. *RKS*, p. 27.
11. Ibid., p. 112.
12. Ibid., p. 112.
13. Ibid., p. 113. By way of introduction, Suzuki writes, 'With all his rejection of letters and words, Lin-chi himself, having delivered sermons using thousands of words, must be said to have had some thoughts. One may say that the shout (*katsu!*) and the stick (*bō*) rush out from beyond thought. With this alone, however, the problem of the human being is not settled. It is because there was the thought to be transcended that one could transcend even the thought. If there is nothing from the beginning, there can be no problem of transcending. So thought must become an issue.' (Ibid. p. 4)
14. Ibid., p. 17.
15. *ZBP*, p. 33.
16. *RKS*, p. 221.
17. *ZBP*, p. 32.
18. *RKS*, p. 236.
19. *Wu-mên-kuan. Gateless Gate*, Case 46.
20. *RKS*, pp. 239, 252.
21. *ZBP*, p. 41.
22. '*Reiseitekijikaku*' may be translated literally as 'spiritual self-realization' or 'awakening of spirituality'. See D. T. Suzuki, *Japanese Spirituality*, trans. by Norman Waddell (Tokyo: Japan Society for the Promotion of Science, 1972).
23. *ZBP*, pp. 16–17, 19, 51; *Zen and Japanese Culture* (New York, 1959) pp. 165n, 192–3, 199, 226, 242–3, 250 (hereafter *ZJC*).
24. *ZBP*, pp. 57–8; *Studies in Zen* (New York, 1955), pp. 80f, 147, 159f.
25. *ZJC*, pp. 360–1.

26. *Shinran-kyogaku*, no. 6 (Kyoto: Bun'eido, 1965) p. 105. The same kind of question is found in Suzuki's review of Father H. Dumoulin's book, *A History of Zen Buddhism* (*E. B.*, vol. 1, no. 1, September 1965, p. 125).

27. D. T. Suzuki, *Manual of Zen Buddhism* (London, 1956) p. 98.

28. 'Supra-individual' indicates being free from all limitations including form and colour, time and space, 'I' and 'you', one and many, and so on, while 'individual' is limited by these conditions.

29. *RKS*, pp. 13, 30.

30. Ibid., p. 117.

31. *ZBP*, pp. 33–4.

32. Ibid., pp. 38–9.

33. *The Record of Lin-chi*, trans. Ruth F. Sasaki, p. 12.

34. *ZBP*, p. 29.

35. Ibid.

36. *An Introduction to Zen Buddhism* (London, 1948) p. 81.

37. 'Jōshū Zen no Ichitokusei' (A Characteristic of Chao-chou's Zen), *Gendai-bukkyō-kōza* (Series on Modern Buddhism), vol. 1 (Kadokawa Shoten; Tokyo, 1965) p. 308 (hereafter *JZI*).

38. *The Essence of Buddhism* (Kyoto, 1948) p. 91.

39. *ZBP*, p. 69.

40. *JZI*, p. 308.

41. *ZBP*, p. 69.

42. *JZI*, p. 308.

43. Ibid., p. 309.

44. *ZBP*, p. 69.

45. Ibid., p. 68.

46. The 'Fourth step' is *ken chu shi*, the fourth of the 'five steps', known as *go-i* in Zen training. *Ken chu shi* is the step in which the Zen man, completely going beyond the noetic understanding of Zen truth, 'strives to realize his insight to the utmost of his abilities' (*ZBP*, p. 60) by stepping into the actual world of duality. For a discussion of the 'five steps', see *ZBP*, pp. 59–76.

47. *ZBP*, p. 68.

CHAPTER 4:   ZEN AND WESTERN THOUGHT

1. For the Japanese characters here and throughout, see the glossary.

2. Nāgārjuna was a great Buddhist thinker who lived in southern India around the second or third century A.D. He established the Mādhyamika School and in China and Japan has traditionally been regarded as the founder of Mahayana Buddhism.

3. *U* (being) and *mu* (nothingness) are, along with *ji* and *ri*, the key terms employed throughout this discussion. As stated in the text, *u* and *mu* (derived from *ji*) and *ri*, all in an absolute sense, are here understood as the three basic categories for human thought and existence. These terms are used in this article (originally written in Japanese) because of their rich and subtle nuances. (For instance, *mu*, which stands for the English term 'non-being', has an important connotation which is different from 'non-being'. This connotation will be discussed later in this essay.) Differing from most European languages, nouns in

Chinese and Japanese generally make no distinction between singular and plural. Hence the term *u* can mean *beings, being, or Being itself.* On the other hand, the term *mu*, due to its nature, cannot have a distinction of singular and plural. However, corresponding to the relative and absolute meanings of the term *u*, the meaning of the term *mu* varies accordingly.

Since the term *u* is used in this essay in contrast to *mu* and *ri*, the author, in most cases, uses the term without differentiating between beings, being, and Being itself. However, when it is necessary to show such differences, they have been indicated by the use of modifiers and the device of capitalization. Differences in usage of *ji* and *ri* are expressed through the same procedure.

In Japanese, there is no distinction between small and capital letters. Accordingly, in order to show their usage in the absolute sense as opposed to the relative sense, an adjectival term such as 'absolute' must be added in each occasion. However, the terms *can* be used within the Japanese language, as they stand, in both a relative and an absolute sense. When these terms are used within the context of English, this advantage turns into a disadvantage.

Although English has an advantage in making a clear distinction between the relative and the absolute sense of such terms by using a lower case or an upper case letter, there is no way for such Japanese terms as *ji, ri, u* and *mu*, when used within the context of English, to cover both the relative and absolute senses at once. Insofar as they appear in the lower case, they naturally indicate their usage in the relative sense.

In the following discussion the author tries to be consistent in using these terms in the lower case whenever the relative usage is meant and in the upper case whenever the absolute usage is meant, i.e. in the sense indicating one of the above three fundamental categories for human thought and existence. However, since there is no proper way for them to cover both the relative and absolute senses at once in the English context, the author is sometimes forced to use *ji, ri, u,* and *mu* in the lower case not only to indicate their relative sense but also to cover both the relative and absolute senses at once, though this way of writing the terms may be confusing.

4. As for Heidegger, who emphasizes nothingness, see p. 47, 67, 119, 134.

5. In the T'ien-t'ai Sect, the view of emptiness of Hinayana Buddhism is called the analytic view of emptiness, and the view of emptiness in Mahayana Buddhism is called the view of substantial emptiness.

6. Ibid.

7. Hajime Nakamura, *The Ways of Thinking of Eastern Peoples,* (Tokyo: Japanese National Commission for UNESCO, (1960) p. 24.

8. There may still be various objections to defining Aquinas' theological standpoint as one of 'Being' or *U*. Recently a small number of Western theologians and philosophers, who are familiar with the situation prevailing in the philosophical world of modern Japan, have severely criticized as inappropriate the viewpoint which has frequently come to be taken in Japan that Christianity is a religion of 'Being' or *U* in contrast to Buddhism being a religion of 'Nothingness' or *Mu*. It is necessary for us to listen humbly to their criticism. I personally think that it is better to avoid, insofar as it is possible, this way of categorizing Buddhism and Christianity. But ultimately this way of categorization may be inevitable, for the criticisms raised from the Christian side concern the propriety of setting up the Christian standpoint as 'Being' *within* the sphere

of Western standards, while still failing to consider the 'Nothingness' or 'Emptiness' of Buddhism in its own essential meaning. However, that which previously came to be articulated in Japan in these terms took Buddhist 'Nothingness' or 'Emptiness' as its criterion. When we take Buddhist 'Emptiness' as a criterion, reasons can still be found for being able to establish as 'Being' even those positions which are not necessarily taken as Being within the sphere of Western criteria. This is also the reason that in this essay I have presumed to use the very problematic concept of 'Being' in the case of Thomas Aquinas as well.

Further, it should be understood that, in this essay, in reference to Christianity, *ri* is used to express the personalistic character of Christianity, while *u* or 'being' is used to express its ontological character.

9. E. Gilson, *God and Philosophy* (New Haven: Yale University Press, 1941) pp. 63–4.

10. This does not mean that 'nothingness' was never focused upon in Christian thought. It can be found in passages such as 'emptiness of emptiness, all is emptiness' (Eccles. 1:2); or when it is said that the creation of God is 'creation out of nothing'; or when Christ is said 'to have emptied himself, taking on the form of a servant' (Phil., 2:7), etc. But it is clear that 'nothingness' here was not realized as a basic principle.

11. See Chapter 2, 'Dōgen on Buddha-Nature', p. 55 and Chapter 10, 'Buddhist Nirvana', p. 212.

12. 'Mind' in the phrase 'directly points to man's Mind' is radically different from mind in its ordinary sense. It indicates the Buddha-nature or Dharma-nature which is essential in man and which is beyond mind and consciousness in their psychological and philosophical senses.

13. Shin'ichi Hisamatsu, 'Zen: Its Meaning for Modern Civilization'. *E. B.*, vol. 1, no. 1, p. 24.

14. In various developed forms of Mahayana Buddhism, there are cases in addition to Zen in which the mediation through the Mind of Gautama the Buddha is not necessary. Therein, 'Mind' realized by Gautama the Buddha was profoundly realized anew and interpreted as various *ideal Buddhas* (*ributsu*, for instance, Vairocana Buddha and Amida Buddha) and new schools or sects were established with these ideal Buddhas as their foundations. Hence the Mind of Gautama the Buddha was no longer the key factor. Even in such cases, however, since 'Mind' – which was interpreted as the various ideal Buddhas – was transmitted through 'word' and 'scripture', and since these ideal Buddhas played an essential mediating role, they must be said to be different from Zen in principle. This is the reason why in Zen these are all called Buddhism 'within the teaching'.

15. The statement 'by abandoning the four terms and wiping out the hundred negations say what the Buddha-dharma is' demands that the student express the truth of Buddha without any conceptualization or categorization. See *Zen Dust* by Isshu Miura and Ruth Fuller Sasaki (New York: Harcourt, Brace & World, 1966) p. 269.

16. A monk asked Ummon, 'What is the Buddha?' 'It is a shit-wiping stick', replied Ummon. (*Wu-mên-kuan. Gateless Gate*, Case 21.)

17. A monk asked Master Hōgen, 'I, Etchō, ask you, master; What is Buddha?' 'You are Etchō.' replied Hōgen. (*Pi-yen-chi, Blue Cliff Collection*, Case 7.)

18. Paul Tillich, *The Courage to Be* (New Haven: Yale Univ. Press, 1957) p. 40.
19. See Chapter 5, 'Non-Being and *Mu*'.
20. The eightfold negation consists of the four pairs: neither birth nor extinction, neither cessation nor permanence, neither identity nor difference, neither coming nor going. There is no primacy of one concept over the other in these four pairs. In Nāgārjuna, the real nature of existence (*tathatā*) manifests itself when fixed concepts such as birth and extinction are removed. Hence the eight-fold negation is synonymous with the Middle Path.
21. The original term for 'non-action' is *wu-wei* in Chinese and *mu-i* in Japanese: that for 'no-business' is *wu-shih* in Chinese and *buji* in Japanese. Both *wu-wei* and *wu-shih* are Zen terms (although *wu-wei* is also found in Taoism) which probably cannot be adequately rendered into any European language because there is nothing in the Western way of thinking corresponding to them.

    Zen emphasizes that it is illusory to search for Reality (the Dharma or Buddha-nature) *externally* because for Zen Reality is *here* and *now*. *Wu-wei* and *wu-shih* indicate one should totally cease *searching for* Reality by realizing this illusion. (Since searching internally still implies 'externally', the very act of searching, whether externally or internally, must be given up.) Both *wu-wei* and *wu-shih*, however, can be properly attained only after the total, existential realization of the illusory nature of the very act of searching. It is essential not to withdraw from, but to overcome, 'searching'. This immediately means that *wu-wei* and *wu-shih* are not negative but positive, in the sense that both indicate the realization that Reality (the Dharma) *is* here and now, where one finds oneself. Through this realization one is liberated from the dualistic (e.g. the real and the unreal) and illusory view of life.

    Accordingly *wu-wei* (non-action) and *wu-shih* (no-business) constitute that existential basis, that dynamic ground, which is ontologically prior to the duality of value and dis-value, and out of which creative actions both for oneself and others freely spring. And yet these actions are for the one who performs them 'non-actions', and in them he has 'no-business'.
22. When Hui-nêng, the Sixth Patriarch, was asked by the monk Ming (Myō) what Zen is, he said: 'At the moment of not thinking of good, not thinking of evil, what is your Original Face?' Upon hearing these words, Ming is said to have attained Awakening. (*The Platform Sutra*. Taishō, no. 2008, p. 349 b. See also D. T. Suzuki: *Essays*, First Series, London: Rider, p. 208).
23. This is the first of 'The Four Great Vows' which are fundamental to Buddhist life. They are as follows:

> However innumerable beings are, I vow to save them;
> However inexhaustible the passions are, I vow to extinguish them;
> However immeasurable the Dharmas are, I vow to master them;
> However incomparable the Buddha-truth is, I vow to attain it.

(See D. T. Suzuki: *Manual of Zen Buddhism*, London: Rider, 1957, p. 14.)
24. In connection with the above discussion, problems between Zen and Christianity should preferably not be omitted. However, since they are big problems deserving of treatment beyond the scope of the present paper, the author will take them up elsewhere. See Chapter 8, 'Tillich from a Buddhist Point of View', and Chapter 9, 'Self-Awakening and Faith: Zen and Christianity'.

CHAPTER 5: NON-BEING AND *MU* – THE METAPHYSICAL NATURE OF NEGATIVITY IN THE EAST AND THE WEST

1. Paul Tillich, *Systematic Theology*, vol. 1, (The Univ. of Chicago Press, 1951), p. 189.
2. Paul Tillich, *The Courage to Be*, (New Haven: Yale Univ. Press, 1957), p. 34.
3. Ibid., p. 40.
4. Tillich, *Systematic Theology*, vol. 1, p. 188.
5. Ibid., p. 235–6.
6. Lionel Giles, *The Sayings of Lao Tzǔ*, (London, 1905) p. 20.
7. Ch. 40, from the translation appearing in Fung Yu-lan's *A History of Chinese Philosophy*, vol. 1, p. 178.
8. *Chuang Tzǔ*, translated by Herbert A. Giles, (London, Quaritch, 1926) p. 23.
9. Ch. 37 in Fung Yu-lan's *A History of Chinese Philosophy*, vol. 1, p. 178.
10. As to Sanskrit terms, *asat* or *abhāva*, as equivalents to *me on* or non-being, see Chapter 4, 'Zen and Western Thought', p. 94–5.
11. The static realization of Emptiness (the attachment to Emptiness) and the dynamic realization of Emptiness may be said to correspond to the second and third stages as illustrated in Chapter 1, 'Zen is not a Philosophy, but....'
12. Hegel may be mentioned here to be different from Nietzsche and Heidegger. As for the author's view of Hegel in contrast to the Buddhist idea of Buddha-nature or *Śūnyatā*, see Chapter 2, 'Dōgen on Buddha-Nature', pp. 52–5.

CHAPTER 6: ZEN AND NIETZSCHE

1. In Nietzsche's writings there is no literal formulation for this sentence. But it seems justifiable to interpolate it from his writings, particularly *Der Antichrist*, sections 18, 36, 55, and *Der Wille zur Macht*, sect. 141 etc.
2. *Der Wille zur Macht*, (hereafter *W. Z. M.*) Kröner edition, sect. 4.
3. *Der Antichrist*, Kröner edn, sect. 7.
4. Ibid.
5. *W. Z. M.*, sect. 380.
6. When Nietzsche speaks of the 'arrival of nihilism', it is of course *nihilism in the Nietzschean sense*, which should not be confused with *nihilism prior to Nietzsche*. Nihilism prior to Nietzsche is an awareness of nihilum of human life and of this world, that is, nihilum existing all along. This form of nihilism had been effectively overcome by faith in 'God' and a 'true world' behind this world. Nihilum had once been filled by God in human history. Nietzsche, however, insists that *now* this God is dead and proclaims the arrival of nihilism. Accordingly, nihilism in the Nietzschean sense is not a nihilism prior to faith in God, but nihilism after and beyond faith in God. It does not proclaim that 'God does not exist', but that 'God is now dead although he was alive.' In Nietzschean nihilism, the nihilum once filled by God is again and much more deeply realized as nihilum. Clearly awakening to the falsity of God fabricated in the depth of nihilum, Nietzsche advances 'active nihilism,' which is a living of nihilum without God.

7. *Der Antichrist*, sect. 9.
8. Ibid., sect. 15.
9. The triple world is the Buddhist conception of the world of transmigration which consists of the three realms of sensuous desire, form, and formlessness.
10. *The Awakening of Faith*, tr. by Yoshito S. Hakeda, (New York, Columbia University Press, 1967) p. 48.
11. Ibid.
12. Ibid.
13. *W. Z. M.*, sect. 616.
14. *Wu-mên-kuan. Gateless Gate*, Case 19.
15. *Ch'uan-hsin fa-yao; Ja.*, *Denshin hōyō* (Taishō, no. 2012, p. 380 b).
16. Ibid.
17. Heidegger: *Holzwege*, (Frankfurt a. M. 1950) p. 199.
18. *W. Z. M.*, sect. 158.
19. *Antichrist*, sect. 39.
20. *W. Z. M.*, sect. 160.
21. *Antichrist*, sect. 41.
22. *W. Z. M.*, sect. 169.
23. *Antichrist*, sect. 45.
24. *Ecce Homo*, Kröner edn. p. 406.
25. *W. Z. M.*, sect. 251.
26. *Zarathustra*, Kröner edn, p. 26.
27. *Antichrist*, sects 10, 11.
28. *Götzendämmerung*, Kröner edn, p. 99.
29. Ibid., p. 130.
30. *W. Z. M.*, sect. 424.
31. Ibid., sect. 888.
32. 'No-matter' stands for *buji* (Ch. *wu-shih*), which has no equivalent idea in the West. For Zen, Reality is here and now, so it is illusory to search for Reality beyond here and now. Hence, 'no-matter' is necessary to awaken to Reality. However, 'no-matter' is existentially realized not by withdrawing from but rather by overcoming 'searching'. It is 'no-matter' not before but beyond 'searching'. It is the dynamic basis out of which one freely works for both oneself and others. Cf. Chapter 4, 'Zen and Western Thought', p. 115–16.
33. *The Record of Lin-chi*, trans. Ruth F. Sasaki, p. 10.
34. Ibid., p. 29.
35. *Zarathustra*, p. 78. 'The preachers of slow death' are Christian clergymen who teach the necessity of enduring suffering.
36. *Antichrist*, sect. 35.
37. *The Record of Lin-chi*, trans. Ruth F. Sasaki, p. 10.

CHAPTER 7:   MAHAYANA BUDDHISM AND WHITEHEAD

1. *Process and Reality*, corrected edn (New York: The Free Press, 1978) p. 50.
2. Ibid., p. 18.
3. Ibid., p. 88.
4. Ibid., p. 88.

5. Ibid., p. 343.
6. Ibid., p. 88.
7. D. W. Sherburne, *A Key to Whitehead's Process and Reality* (Bloomington, Ind.: Indiana University Press, 1971) p. 207.
8. *Process and Reality*, p. 345.
9. Ibid., p. 345.
10. W. Christian, *An Interpretation of Whitehead's Metaphysics* (New Haven, Conn.: Yale University Press, 1959) pp. 380–1.
11. Kenneth W. Morgan, ed., *The Path of the Buddha* (New York: The Ronald Press Company, 1956) p. 47.
12. *Process and Reality*, p. 349.
13. Ibid., p. 348.
14. Ibid., p. 343.
15. Ibid., p. 348.
16. Ibid., p. 29.

CHAPTER 8: TILLICH FROM A BUDDHIST POINT OF VIEW

1. Paul Tillich, *Christianity and the Encounter of the World Religions* (New York and London: Columbia University Press, 1963).
2. See Masao Abe, 'Buddhism and Christianity as a Problem of Today', *Japanese Religions*, vol. 3, no. 2, pp. 13–15.
3. It should be noted that Tillich distinguishes between 'quasi-religion' and 'pseudo-religion'. 'Quasi', according to Tillich, indicates a genuine similarity, not intended, but based on points of identity, while 'pseudo' indicates an intended but deceptive similarity. (p. 5)
4. See Chapter 13, 'Religion Challenged by Modern Thought', pp. 231–40.
5. See Chapter 2, 'Dōgen on Buddha-Nature', pp. 34–6.
6. Paul Tillich, *Systematic Theology* vol. 1 (Chicago, Illinois: The University of Chicago Press, 1951) pp. 236–7.
7. The English equivalents of absolute *Mu*, non-being or nothingness, do not sufficiently convey the original meaning whose logical structure is: absolute negation (the negation of negation) is absolute affirmation. See Chapter 5, 'Non-being and *Mu* – the Metaphysical Nature of Negativity in the East and the West', especially pp. 127–32.
8. Paul Tillich, *Systematic Theology*, vol. 1, p. 237.
9. Ibid., p. 176.
10. The Buddhist position is that true individualization necessitates identity and nonsubstantiality. See Chapter 1, 'Zen is not a Philosophy, but ...' p. 18.
11. Paul Tillich, *Systematic Theology*, vol. 1, p. 245.

CHAPTER 9: SELF-AWAKENING AND FAITH: ZEN AND CHRISTANITY

. This is a record of the present author's lecture and discussion at a Seminar on Zen Buddhism for Christian missionaries, arranged September 1974 by the NCC Study Center in Kyoto.

2. 'Dialogues, East and West: Conversations between Dr Paul Tillich and Dr Shin'ichi Hisamatsu', E. B., vol. v, no. 2, 1972, p. 115.

CHAPTER 10: BUDDHIST NIRVANA: ITS SIGNIFICANCE IN CONTEMPORARY THOUGHT AND LIFE

1. *The Book of the Kindred Sayings*, Part v, tr. by C. A. F. Rhys Davids and F. L. Woodward, London: The Pali Text Society (1930) p. 356.
2. *Pi-yen chi* (The Blue Cliff Collection), Case 45. See also D. T. Suzuki: *Introduction to Zen Buddhism* (Rider & Co.) p. 72.
3. Masao Abe, 'Christianity and Buddhism Centering Around Science and Nihilism', *Japanese Religions*, vol. 5, no. 3, pp. 36–62. Also see Chapter 6, 'Zen and Nietzsche'.
4. *The Larger Sukhavātī-vyūha* (Taishō, no. 360).
5. Masao Abe, 'Man and Nature in Christianity and Buddhism', *Japanese Religions*, vol. 7, no. 1, pp. 1–10.
6. See Chapter 2 'Dōgen on Buddha-nature', pp. 54–5.
7. Ibid.

CHAPTER 11: THE IDEA OF PURITY IN MAHAYANA BUDDHISM

1. *Mahāyāna-saṃgraha* (Ch. *Shē ta ch'êng lun*, Ja. *Shōdaijōron*), a Buddhist treatise compiled by Asaṅga (about 310–90), Taishō, no. 1594. French translation by E. Lamotte, *La Somme du Grand Véhicule d'Asanga* (Louvain: Bureaux du Musion, 1932).
2. Dōgen, 'Shōbōgenzō Buddha-nature' fascicle, tr. by Norman Waddell and Masao Abe, *E. B.*, vol. IX, no. 1, p. 88.
3. Dōgen, 'Bendōwa' fascicle, tr. by Norman Waddelll and Masao Abe, E. B., vol. IV, no. 1, p. 129.
4. Ibid., p. 144.

CHAPTER 13: RELIGION CHALLENGED BY MODERN THOUGHT

1. Hideki Yukawa (1907–81) was a Nobel Prize Winner for Physics in 1949 for his theory of meson and was a Professor Emeritus at Kyoto University until his death.

CHAPTER 14: RELIGION AND SCIENCE IN THE GLOBAL AGE

1. *The Encyclopedia of Philosophy*, ed. by Paul Edwards, vol. 7, p. 159.
2. In this paper I am not arguing that science as such brings forth atheism and nihilism. I am rather arguing that the *modern scientific world view* which is impersonal and mechanistic has brought forth atheism and nihilism. Natural science is not incompatible with religion, but scientific ideologies or scientism which absolutizes scientific truth as the *only* truth is incompatible with religion. When discussing scientific world views in this paper, I am mainly concerned with scientific ideologies or the scientific way of thinking in relation to religion.
3. *The Complete Works of Friedrick Nietzsche*, ed. by Dr. Oscar Levy, vol. XII, p. 73.
4. Masao Abe, 'Christianity and Buddhism: Centering Around Science and Nihilism', *Japanese Religions*, vol. 5, no. 3, pp. 49–50.
5. Keiji Nishitani, *Religian and Nothingness* (Berkeley: University of California Press, 1982) p. 77.
6. Alfred North Whitehead, *Process and Reality*, p. 32.

In writing this Chapter, the author owes much to Keiji Nishitani's *Religion and Nothingness*, published by University of California Press, 1982, especially Ch. 4, pp. 77–118.

CHAPTER 16: THE END OF WORLD RELIGION

1. Kazuo Muto, 'Kirisutokyo to Mu no Shisō', (Christianity and the Thought of Nothingness), *Zen no Honshitsu to Ningen no Shinri* (The Essence of Zen and Human Truth), ed. by Shin'ichi Hisamatsu and Keiji Nishitani (Tokyo, Sōbunsha, 1969) pp. 423–4.
2. See Masao Abe 'Buddhism and Christianity as a Problem of Today', *Japanese Religions*, vol. 3, no. 2 (Summer 1963) pp. 11–22, and vol. 3, no. 3 (Autumn 1963) pp. 10–31; see also 'Man and Nature in Christianity and Buddhism', *Japanese Religions*, vol. 7, no. 1 (July, 1971) pp. 1–10.
3. Seishi Ishii, 'Shūkyōteki Sekai toshiteno Ai no Ba nitsuite' (On the Place of Love as the Religious World), *Postmodernist*, no. 2 (Tokyo, Ibunsha, 1973) p. 65.

Glossary of Sino-Japanese Characters

Chinese names and terms are followed by the notation (Ch). All others are Japanese.

Baso Dōitsu 馬祖道一
'Bendōwa' 辨道話
bō 棒
buji 無事
busshō 佛性
busshō no gi o shiran to omowaba, masani jisetzu no innen o kanzubeshi; jisetsu moshi itareba, busshō genzen su
欲知佛性義　當觀時節因緣　時節若至　佛性現前
'Butsudō' 佛道
Ch'ang-sha Ch'ing-ts'ên (Ch) 長沙景岑
Chao-chou Lu (Ch) 趙州錄
Chao-chou Ts'ung-shên (Ch) 趙州從諗
Ch'eng-tao ke (Ch) 證道歌
chien-hsing (Ch) 見性
chih (Ch) 知
Ching-tê ch'uan-têng lu (Ch) 景德伝燈錄
Ch'ing-yüan Wei-hsin (Ch) 靑原惟信
Chōsha Keishin 長沙景岑
Chü-chih (Ch) 俱胝
Daiju Ekai 大珠慧海
Denshin hōyo 傳心法要
Dōgen 道元
Dōgen Zenji Goroku 道元禪師語錄
dōji jōdō 同時成道
engi 緣起
Enō 慧能
en-u 緣有
Fu-jung Tao-k'ai (Ch) 芙蓉道楷

290

fushiryō 不思量
Fuyō Dōkai 芙蓉道楷
Gakudō-yōjinshū 學道用心集
'Genjōkōan' 現成公案
goi 五位
Gokesanshō-yōromon 五家參詳要路門
Gotōegen 五燈会元
Gunin 弘忍
Gutei 倶胝
Gyōshō 行昌
henkaifusōzō 偏界不曾藏
hishiryō 非思量
Hōkyōki 寶慶記
hōmetsu 法滅
hongaku 本覺
honshō shōjō 本性淸淨
hon-u 本有
'Hosshō' 法性
Ho-tsê Shên-hui (Ch) 荷澤神会
'Hotsubodaishin' 發菩提心
hsin (Ch) 心
Hsin-hsin-ming (Ch) 信心銘
Hsing-ch'ang (Ch) 行昌
Huang-po Hsi-yün (Ch) 黃蘗希運
Hui-k'o (Ch) 慧可
Hui-nêng (Ch) 慧能
Hung-jên (Ch) 弘忍
Hyakujō Ekai 百丈懷海
immo ni 恁麼に
Isan Reiyū 潙山靈祐
Issai no shujō wa kotogotoku busshō o yūsu: Nyorai wa jōjū ni shite henyaku arukoto nashi
一切衆生悉有仏性　如來常住無有變易
jên (Ch) 人
ji 事
Jiku Shōsho 竺尚書
jinen 自然
jinen-hōni 自然法爾
jisetsu nyakushi 時節若至
Jōshū Jūshin 趙州從諗
Jōshū Zenji Goroku 趙州禪師語錄

'Jōshū-zen no Ichitokusei' 趙州禪の一特性
Ju-ching (Ch) 如淨
Kataku Jinne 荷澤神會
katsu 喝
'Keiseisanshoku' 溪聲山色
ken chu shi 兼中至
kenshō 見性
Kenzeiki 建撕記
keshin metchi 灰身滅智
kimetsu 起滅
koreshimobutsu-immorai 是什麼物恁麼來
kū 空
Kuei-shan Ling-yu (Ch) 溈山靈祐
'Kūge' 空華
kyōryaku 経歴
Lin-chi I-hsüan (Ch) 臨済義玄
Lin-chi Lu (Ch) 臨済録
mappō 末法
Ma-tsu Tao-i (Ch) 馬祖道一
mondo 問答
mō-u 妄有
mu 無
mubusshō 無仏性
mu-i 無爲
mujō 無常
mujōbusshō 無常仏性
Mumonkan 無門関
mushojū 無所住
muye, 無依
myo-u 妙有
nin 人
Nyojō 如淨
Nan-ch'üan P'u-yüan 南泉普願
Nangaku Ejō 南嶽懷讓
Nansen Fugan 南泉普願
Nan-yüeh Huai-jang (Ch) 南嶽懷讓
nin 人
Ōbaku Kian 黃蘗希運
Pi-yen-chi (Ch) 碧巖集
Po-chang Huai-hai (Ch) 百丈 懷海
Reinan 嶺南

Reinanjin mubusshō 嶺南人無仏性
reiseitekijikaku 靈性的自覺
Rentō-eyō 聯燈會要
ri 理
rikushōjō 離垢清淨
Rinzai Gigen 臨濟義玄
Rinzai no Kihonshisō: Rinzairoku ni okeru "nin" shisō no kenkyū
臨濟の基本思想——臨濟錄における"人"思想の研究
Rinzairoku 臨濟錄
risei 理性
rishō 理性
sanbōin 三法印
'Sansuikyō' 山水経
Seigen Ishin 青原惟信
Sekitō Kisen 石頭希遷
'Sesshin-sesshō' 説心説性
shakkūkan 折空観
shamon 沙門
Shên-kuang (Ch) 神光
shikaku 始覺
shikantaza 只管打坐
shin 心
shinjindatsuraku 身心脱落
Shinrankyogaku 親鸞教學
Shih-t'ou Hsi-ch'ien 石頭希遷
shiryō 思量
shitsuu busshō 悉有仏性
shitsuu no isshitsu 悉有の一悉
shi-u 始有
shōbō 正法   首山
Shōbōgenzō 正法眼藏
Shōdaijōron 摂大乘論
shōji 生死
shōmetsusei 生滅性
Shou-shan Shêng-nien (Ch) 省念
shō-zō-matsu 正像末
shujō 衆生
shukanteki 主観的
shushōittō 修證一等
shutaiteki 主体的
Shuzan Shōnen 首山省念

Sōtō Zen 曹洞禪
Ta-chu Hui-hai (Ch) 大珠慧海
taikūkan 体空観
Tao-tê ching (Ch) 道德経
Tê-shan Hsüan-chien (Ch) 德山宣鑑
T'ien-t'ai (Ch) 天台
tōkan jisetsu innen 当観時節因縁
Tokusan Senkan 德山宣鑑
Tōzan Ryōkai 洞山良价
Tung-shan Liang-chich (Ch) 洞山良价
u 有
uji 有時
u-mu 有無
wu-wei (Ch) 無爲
Wu-mên-kuan (Ch) 無門關
Wu-shih (Ch) 無事
Wu-têng Hui-yüan (Ch) 五燈会元
Yakusan Igen 藥山惟儼
Yüeh-shan Wei-yen (Ch) 藥山惟儼
Yoka Daishi 永嘉大師
yū 用
yung (Ch) 用
Yung-chia Ta-shin (Ch) 永嘉大師
zazen 坐禪
'Zazengi' 坐禪儀
zōhō 像法

Index